Advance praise for
Sacred Space

"Get out your highlighter. This is a book you'll underline in a hundred places. It is filled with practical, proven techniques for managing energy. Drawing upon the wisdoms of the cultures, Denise Linn writes with knowledge and a beautiful, clear style. I recommend this book for anyone whose intention is to bring heaven and earth together in every way possible, starting with the personal environment."

—Gloria Karpinsky
Author of *Where Two Worlds Touch*

"This fascinating book will open your eyes to powerful energy fields that can be used to create harmony and love in your home, your head, and your heart."

—Susan Jeffers, Ph.D.
Author of *Feel the Fear and Do It Anyway*

S·A·C·R·E·D

S·P·A·C·E

*Clearing and Enhancing the
Energy of Your Home*

DENISE LINN

BALLANTINE BOOKS • NEW YORK

This book has been written with safety in mind, but when following the advice set out in it, the reader should proceed with due care and caution. Lighted candles and other naked flames are frequently suggested as ways to enhance the energy of your home. They should never be left unattended in a room, as they are a fire hazard. All guidelines and warnings should be read carefully, and the publisher cannot accept responsibility for injuries or damage however they might arise.

Originally published in somewhat different form in Great Britain in 1995 by
Rider, an imprint of Ebury Press, Random House, UK Ltd, London.

Library of Congress Catalog Card Number: 95-94469

ISBN: 0-345-39769-X

Cover design by Kathleen Lynch
Cover illustration by Daniel O'Leary
Text design by Ann Gold

Manufactured in the United States of America
First American Edition: January 1996
10 9 8 7 6 5 4 3

This book is dedicated to our daughter,

Meadow Marie, who always

has a Sacred Space in our hearts

CONTENTS

ACKNOWLEDGMENTS

Thanks to:

David Linn, my husband and life companion for support and love;

Claire Brown for your excellent editing skills and friendship;

Brand Fortner Ph.D., my brother, for scientific editorial assistance;

Sandra Holtzinger for helping me understand the importance of home;

Marika Burton for your beauty and magic;

Vicky Patterson, Astrid Neeme, Credo Mutwa, Karen Kingston for contributions to this book;

Kathy Lynch, Rebecca Nelson, Patti Nugent, Barb Kelly, Karl Bettinger and Paulina Howfield for the depth of your love.

And thanks to Lynne Franks, soul sister and friend.

1

HOME AS BEING

*O*ur homes are mirrors of ourselves. They reflect our interests, our beliefs, our hesitations, our spirit and our passion. They tell a story about how we feel about ourselves and the world around us. A home is more than a place to lay your head and seek comfort from the elements. It is a place where you can interface with the universe. It is a crossing point in time and space that can attract energy or repel energy.

Your home can be a place of renewal and hope. It can be a sanctuary within which you can retreat and recharge during the changing times, an oasis of peace amidst turmoil. Homes can be places of healing and regeneration. Not only can your home help to strengthen and heal you, but your home can be a template of harmony within which you and all who enter can be invited to step up to a higher level of spiritual frequency.

Your home can be the overlap between the inner universe and the outer universe, the crossing point between inner and outer realities. It can be a focus point for magic and power and spirit. Your home can be a power point, a vortex of energy on the planet. Like an echo heard throughout infinity, your home can be a transmitter of luminous energy. The energy radiating from your home can be like a small stone dropped into a still pool of the universe, whose ripples will be felt at the farthest shore of the cosmos.

As the twentieth century comes to a close, our homes are going to be increasingly important. It is now essential that our homes become sacred places as we solidify our place in the universe. It is valuable to infuse our living spaces with a sense of cosmic order—to bring integrity into our homes so that they are in balance with our basic beinginess and the flow of creation. Our homes can offer sanctuary and renewed hope during times ahead which may be potentially difficult, yet absolutely exhilarating. They can provide us with a sacred space where we can remember who we are and remember why we are here on the planet at this time.

In the evolution of our earth, as we approach the end of the millennium, there has never been a more powerful time to be alive. Now is a time filled with potential for change, for realization of our dreams, for evolution on both a personal and a global basis. All around us we see a world increasingly polluted and fraught with conflict as ancient prophecies come to fruition. And yet, despite these grim manifestations of possible doom, there is an underlying sense of hope.

We know in our hearts that an opportunity, golden and glistening as a new morning, sits waiting just beyond the horizon. The question is, how can we take the opportunity available at this time and use it to transform our lives, our relationships and our world? One of the keys to answer this question lies in the environment around you, and more specifically your home. There are ways that you can transform this energy. By harmonizing and clarifying the energy in your home, you can open channels within your living space, so that your home is a collection point for energy. Your home in turn will radiate this energy in the form of love and light to the rest of the world and the universe beyond.

Your home can be a transmitting station for the Light!

This book is about energy. It is a book about understanding the energy in your home and how it interacts with the energy of the universe. My intention in creating this book is to show you ways in which you can cleanse and accentuate the energy in your home so that not only does it provide a sanctuary for you, your family and friends, but it can also be a vortex of radiating energy that is beneficial for many others. In this book you will learn many different techniques, some which have been used by shamans and healers for centuries, to cleanse the energies in your home. You also learn how to enhance and intensify the energy in your home so that your home becomes a ray of hope and light in the shifting times of change.

House as "Being"

To understand how to cleanse and clear the energies in your home it is essential to understand how our living spaces fit into the context of life around us. To do this it is valuable to understand three basic tenets that underlie all the space-clearing techniques you will be learning:

1. Everything is composed of constantly changing energy.
2. You are not separate from the world around you.
3. Everything has consciousness.

Understanding these tenets leads to the awareness that: your home is composed of energy; it is not separate from you; it is an evolving being. This book is about understanding that your home is an evolving energy that has consciousness. It has a "Beingness" with which you can communicate; a "Being" that can provide protection and healing for you and your family as you understand and honor its livingness. Learning to interface with your living spaces can contribute to creating a life that is balanced and in harmony with the energy of all that surrounds you.

EVERYTHING IS ENERGY

Ancient Native Americans understood that all forms of life, from the clouds, to the trees, to the buffalo that roamed the Great Plains, were all transient swirling patterns of energy. This is an understanding that goes back to the most primordial times in cultures spanning the world. It is one of the most basic underlying perceptions of life held by native cultures. Our present-day concept that the universe is fixed and staid is dramatically at odds with this fundamental insight.

All life is energy. We are immersed in an ocean of energy. The energy that is around us flows and moves, in constant, ever-changing currents through time and space. Physicists acknowledge that the atoms and molecules in all things are in constant motion. Beneath the surface of fixed objects, existing in a linear river of time, is the reality that energy swirls into form, dissolves and coalesces once again. The world is a dance of the two opposing yet harmonious forces in the universe: yin and yang, mystery and form. The world around us and within us is an interplay of these patterns of energy in ever-fluid relationship. Energy ebbs and flows around us, not constrained by the limitation of the past and future. We are in an infinite, yet patterned, timeless drama of light and dark. Underlying this motion is a cosmic order. There is an innate harmony inherent in all life as waves of energy and pulsating electrons spiral "form" in and out of existence.

WE ARE NOT SEPARATE
FROM THE UNIVERSE AROUND US

There is nothing "out there" that isn't you. Because of the linear way in which we perceive reality I don't think that we can ever understand this intellectually, communicate about it verbally or even write about it in a comprehensive way. However, I do believe that deep inside each of us *we all do know this*. I believe that inside each of us is a longing, a yearning, and a remembering of an exquisite place of oneness and unity beyond time and space.

Many of the difficulties people are experiencing at this time in the evolution of our world stem from one erroneous belief—the idea that we are separate beings, unconnected to our planet, to its animals and the trees, separate from each other, and sometimes even divorced from ourselves. The Western belief is that we are separate from our living spaces and our environment. The idea that we can exist independently of our environment is an illusion. And it is an illusion with potentially grave consequences for our health and happiness. It is the belief in this illusion which makes possible the epidemic of global pollution, racial hatred, wars, greed, and so many other ills which fill our newspapers and trouble our sleep.

As we move toward the new millennium, huge changes in technology, natural resources and the force fields surrounding the planet are taking place. In our modern, Western culture, it is often difficult emotionally to feel our connection to things further than our private domain. Yet it is essential now that we not only expand our "identification of self" to our personal environments but that we extend our "sense of self" beyond the boundaries of time and form to encompass not just our home but our community and our planet. Extending your "sense of self" to your home is a good first step, and an essential one.

Our planet is changing so quickly that it is affecting deeply the way we relate to each other and to our environment. Though advances in technology have added much to our lives, they have also separated us from the environment around us. In our dash for technology we have "forgotten" the primordial wisdom that all creatures and all things on our planet are connected. We have "forgotten" that we are connected within a living pulsating universe—a universe that sings with life, that pulses with intensity of spirit. We have forgotten that everyone and everything has a living energy.

Our ancient ancestors all over the world did not share this belief of separation. Their world-view centered around the fact that none of us exists independently of our fellow creatures, of the sun, the moon, the soil, the flowers, the oceans, and all the other wonderful myriad beings and things which make up reality as we know it. Everything is relative to every other being; nothing exists in isolation. An example of the Native American comprehensive view of "relationship" is expressed in the sacred Ceremony of the Sweat Lodge. When entering into the sweat lodge one declares "to all my relations." This isn't just an acknowledgment of the others attending the lodge or members of immediate family: it is an affirmation of the interrelatedness of all of life and the intimate connection with all of creation.

In modern Western culture the usual way of interacting with the world around us is to feel that we are separate and autonomous. We usually identify with our body and feel separate from all the other parts of ourselves. Most of us identify ourselves with our physical bodies. We draw a kind of boundary line that stops with our skin. But this is not the only way we define ourselves. Many of us occasionally identify with things further beyond our physical selves. Sometimes we identify with our children or even our possessions (a man will run into a burning building to rescue valuables at great danger to his physical body because in that moment he is identifying himself more with the valuables than with his body). We may identify also with the clothes we have on. For many people the way they dress is an expression of who they believe themselves to be. It is also clear from the way that some people react while driving in heavy traffic that they identify with their cars.

Yet, when you take a moment to reflect on it, you will probably remember a number of times when you suddenly felt at one with the world around you. You may have had the sensation of being drawn into the beauty of a sunset illuminating the evening sky. Or you may have felt a joyous and cleansing sense of your own relationship to the universe while watching the pounding of waves on the shore. These experiences remind us of the truth we all knew before this life—that we are essentially one with all things. We are no less part of the mountains, the sea, the clouds or the stars than we are of our own bodies. We are all manifestations of pure energy, forever fluctuating in its manifestations, and forever connected. Everything that is and ever will be is within you. The universe is your extended body.

I believe that it is essential to make the journey back to this connected view of reality, a view which is as innately natural to us as our connection to our mothers when we were in the womb.

EVERYTHING HAS CONSCIOUSNESS

Not only is the universe around you a vast flowing energy field to which you are intimately connected but *everything in the universe has consciousness*. Even the most hardened skeptics would agree that animals are conscious beings. And modern science has proven that plants have intent and can respond to the energy field of humans. However, no less conscious are the stones and mountains and rivers. Native people understood this well and would ask for the blessings of the Spirit of the Sea before embarking on a fishing trip. Plants were thanked when they were picked. Before a hunt the hunters asked for forgiveness from the animals. After the hunt the animals were thanked for the "giveaway" of their life for the benefit of the tribe. The Earth beneath their feet was not inanimate and inert: the Earth was Mother. Thanks were given to her and forgiveness was asked before digging into her flesh. It was in this way that native people recognized and honored the consciousness of everything in the world around them.

Ancient people understood that we are all connected and that everything is alive. A smooth, river-tumbled stone is no less alive than a great Orca whale. A tall proud cedar tree is no less alive than a cougar padding through a verdant meadow. My Cherokee Indian ancestors called the trees their brothers because they recognized the livingness in the trees. *Everything is alive.*

From these three tenets it follows naturally that:

1. Your home is comprised of endlessly transforming energy fields.
2. You are not separate from your home.
3. Your home is alive, and has consciousness.

YOUR HOME IS COMPRISED OF A MULTITUDE OF OVERLAPPING ENERGY FIELDS

Your home is not just a composite of materials thrown together for shelter and comfort. Every cubic centimeter, whether solid or seemingly empty space, is filled with infinite vibrating energy fields. There are vast undulating patterns of energy fields overlapping within it and around it. There are a multitude of realms within your home. In addition to the purely physical realm of your home's structure and the physical objects within it, there are emotional energies and a multitude of spiritual and etheric energies constantly moving and swirling within your home.

The physical environment surrounding your home—its positioning relative to the sun and the wind, surrounding vegetation, land masses and waterways—as well as the way your home's structure interacts with the environment, affects the energy fields in your home. The materials with which your home and the physical things inside it are made, and the chemicals within these materials, also affect the energy fields. For example, the energy of pine wood is more fluid and radiant than the denser, heavier, grounded energy of oak. The *location* of a raw material will also affect its energy. For example, the energy of a Californian oak will be different from the energy of an oak from England. And an oak from a natural forest will have a different energy from an oak that has been grown on a tree farm. How the materials are made and whether they are handmade or machine-made affect energy fields. In addition, the colors of walls and furnishings, the kinds of lights, the air quality, the smells, the size of the rooms, and how far away your home is from the earth below, are just some of the physical things that affect the energy flows.

The thoughts and feelings of you and your family and house guests are constantly influencing the emotional energy in your living spaces. Emotions have their own energy structure which lingers long after the emotions have been felt. Perhaps you have walked into a room after an argument and felt a thickness in the air. This is a remaining energy field from the intense emotions felt during the argument. Psychometry is based on the idea that a person's feelings, thoughts and personality imprint on their physical objects and surroundings. All the feelings and thoughts of the current inhabitants *as well as previous inhabitants* influence the emotional energy in your home. The thought forms, personalities and activities of those who lived on the land *even before the house was built* also affect the emotional energy of the house. Each physical object inside the home has the emanations of the people who previously owned it as well as the energy of the object's creator. And buildings that are erected over old grave sites are affected by the emotional energy surrounding the sites. The structure of the dwelling can also affect the emotional energy. For example, high ceilings can feel uplifting and lower ceilings can feel either emotionally confining or cozy. Every part of your home exudes and/or elicits an emotional energy field.

Your house has an aura just as you have an aura. The aura of your house is influenced by the physical form and the physical objects of your home; the emotional thought-forms lingering within it; but it is also influenced by the permeating spiritual energy fields around your home. Spiritual energy fields are generated by the trees, the earth and the landscape which are infused with surrounding angelic and devic forces. Primal earth energy, called ley lines, also affects your house's spiritual aura. (Ley lines are created by a naturally formed electrical current that courses through the crust of the earth along channels or lines.) However, the most important thing influencing the spiritual energy in your home is the love that is given and received within its walls.

YOU ARE NOT SEPARATE FROM YOUR HOME

You are not separate from the home that you live in any more than you are separate from the air you breathe. Your home is not just an extension of your thoughts and feelings but in a larger sense your home is you. You are no less your home than you are your body. Both are outer manifestations of your inner energy fields.

In the deepest sense your home reflects and mirrors your consciousness. Just as the body is symbolic of our inner states, so your home reflects your inner state. Even the most traditional doctors are beginning to acknowledge that there is a mind/body connection and that the body can reflect consciousness. If a person gets a sore throat and loses their voice, this has often been shown to mean that there is something that they want to say but can't. Emotional difficulties manifest in the body. A house mirrors your inner states no less than does your body. For example, plumbing in a home can represent emotions. Clogged plumbing can mean clogged emotions. Overflowing plumbing can mean overflowing emotions. You can shift personal consciousness by shifting energy in your home. The windows are your eyes to the world around you. Just the simple act of cleaning your windows, *with the Intent of being able to see your way in life more clearly*, will have an effect on the clarity in your life.

YOUR HOME HAS CONSCIOUSNESS

Not only does every part of our world have consciousness, but your home has consciousness. Homes as well as people are nourished by how we hold them in our heart. They have a living spirit that is sustained through the reverence and love that we hold for them. Without that care they become inanimate and lifeless: the spirit recedes and they become merely physical structures that can neither sustain nor nurture us. Our homes have become lifeless structures, rather than vibrant, alive, pulsating power points which we can enter for rejuvenation and renewal. Your home is an evolving creative being. It can be introverted or it can be outgoing. It has cycles just as you and all of nature has cycles.

You can communicate with your home. Your home can be your ally or it can be an adversary. Your home cares about you and would like to befriend you. Your home doesn't just reflect you and your feelings and interests, but in a much deeper way your home interfaces with you and through that interconnection you both can grow. Your home evolves as you evolve. The regard in which you hold your home can rouse an ancient and replenishing spirit from the deep to fill your home; this power can heal you in the very center of your soul and heart.

Understanding these tenets creates a groundwork from which you can cleanse and enhance the energies in your home.

2
MY JOURNEY

*T*he journey that led me to discover and explore energy began in a very dramatic way when I was seventeen years old. I lived with my family in a very small farming community. One warm summer afternoon I was out riding on my motorbike. I felt carefree and happy as I rode down lovely country roads. The corn seemed to be thrusting up toward the heavens on either side of the road. Overhead, the sky was a brilliant summer blue.

Suddenly the peace of the day shattered. A large American car violently rammed into my motorbike. I struggled to keep upright. The car rammed into me again and I fell on to the side of the road.

I struggled to stand up. My shock turned to terror as I lifted my head to face my unknown assailant. With cold determination, he aimed a gun at me. The two black holes of the gun seemed enormous, out of proportion. I couldn't comprehend that he was pointing a gun at me. My thoughts were racing: "I didn't do anything to him! Why did he run into me? Why is he aiming a gun at me?! Why?!!!" He looked at me without any emotion and squeezed the trigger. The deafening blast changed my life forever.

I was left on the side of the road where a passing farmer found me and called the ambulance. It's peculiar the things you remember in traumatic situations. As the ambulance was hurtling to the hospital, though the pain was excruciating, I remember looking out of the ambulance window and thinking how very beautiful the sky was and how lovely the trees were at this time of year.

Life is so very precious.

At the hospital everything seemed amplified. The lights appeared glaring and bright. Searing pain. Shrill harsh voices. Slowly, the lights began to dim. Pain subsided. Voices faded into stillness. I found myself in a soft womblike darkness. I felt as if I were being drawn deep down within a velvet black cocoon.

Instantly the black bubble seemed to burst. The most brilliant luminous golden light enveloped me. It was so vibrant that the brightest sun would pale in comparison. Everywhere around me, into infinity, was light. Infused in the light with crystalline delicacy was pure sweet music. This liquid light symphony was ebbing and flowing throughout the universe in perfect harmony. The fluid harmonics pervaded my being until I merged with the light and sound. Light and sound were not separate from each other. I was light-sound. And this surrounding, all pervasive universe of warmth and light and music seemed completely natural *and completely familiar.*

Everything seemed more real than anything else I had ever experienced! It was as if my teenage life up to that time had only been a dream. Just as when you awake in the morning and your dream begins to fade in the "reality" of the day, my entire life up to that time seemed to dissolve into a fine mist as I stepped into this new "hyperreal" reality. My previous life seemed nothing more than an illusion to me.

All time seemed to flow in a continuous, everlasting "Now." There was no past and no future. Everything was contained within an infinite present. I remember trying to think of the past and I couldn't, because it was inconceivable. It literally didn't exist. It was as impossible for me to imagine linear reality when I was "there" as it is for me to fully understand non-linear reality when I am "here."

Completely infused within this world of light/sound/infinite-now was "Love." This was so very different from the way we usually think of love. Our culture's conception of love involves loving someone or something as an entity separate from ourselves. The love I experienced was infinite and limitless. There wasn't anything that wasn't Love. The love I experienced was not separate from anyone or anything. It was as natural as breathing. Everything simply *was* Love, a part of it, without any separation. It was a love beyond form, without boundaries.

And *I wasn't alone.* You were there with me. Everyone was there. There wasn't anyone who wasn't there. We were all One. We weren't separate. There was no beginning, no end, just infinite eternal light. No longer confined to my body, I experienced being one with all things and all beings. I was everyone that I had ever loved and everyone that I had ever hurt. I was everyone that I had known and I was everyone that I would never know. I was the hungry beggar on a side-street in Delhi. I was the thief in New York City. I was the baby held in her mother's arms in Kenya. I was the spiritual adept in a mountain temple in Japan. I was everyone and everyone was me.

Although this experience remains in my memory like a kind of jewel to which I can reach out with aching fondness, it no longer makes any sense to my conscious mind. One's ordinary mind is not big enough to grasp the totality of what I felt and knew within every cell of my being at that time. It was completely outside of what is normally conceivable. But at the time it seemed completely natural. It was the most natural and real experience that I have ever had.

The only way that this can even begin to make sense to my conscious mind now is when I imagine our life here on earth as a hologram or a reflection of the spiritual dimension that I encountered when I was shot. Here is the imagery that I use. Imagine that Spirit can be likened to a giant luminous mirror-ball in the heavens. Shafts of light radiate in all directions from the mirror-ball's individual mirrors, creating reflections throughout time and space. Now imagine that each person on earth identifies with an individual reflection to the extent that they feel that they *are* that reflection. They look around and see other reflections, but of course all the reflections seem separated by time and space. However, if those individuals were to expand their perception they would eventually recognize that all reflections emanate from the same source. We *are* truly One. We are not separate. We are the reflection and we are the Source of our reflection. We are One.

Even though I felt a deep fusion with infinity, curiously I still seemed to have the ability to perceive from a fixed point of consciousness. From my center-point of awareness I saw a golden river of light in front of me. I knew that if I could reach the other shore of the river I would not return to my seventeen-year-old body. I would no longer have to bear the pain of being separate from others. I wouldn't have to be trapped in a body that was very damaged and in excruciating pain. I stepped into the river and felt fluid light surround me.

Shimmering luminous light flowed gently on either side of me. Yet before I could reach the other side of the river I heard a voice reverberate inside my mind, "You may not stay here. There is something you need to do." I screamed, "No-o-o-o-o!!!" and resisted with all my might. I felt as if I had been lassoed and was being dragged back inside my body.

When I woke I was in a hospital bed fighting for my life. The body that I was forced back into was seriously wounded. The gunman's bullet had bounced off my spine and lodged in my lung, tearing away my spleen and an adrenal gland. My stomach, one lung and my small intestines were damaged as well. Eventually a kidney was removed and a six-inch plastic tube was inserted to replace the aorta of my heart.

However, even though the gunman's assault had been terrifying, something mysterious and magical had also occurred when I was shot, something which changed the course of my life forever.

My perception of life and the world around me had changed completely and forever. Though I had many wounds to heal—not only the physical wounds caused by the bullet, but also deep emotional wounds from a childhood gone wrong—I "knew" that nothing that had happened to me in my past was an accident. I "knew" that my life was guided and that there was a higher purpose to my existence. I was not brought back from the symphonic world of light and unity which I had briefly experienced in order to invent a cure for cancer or to present an earth-shattering new philosophy. My mission was simply this: to embrace and love all of life, to experience the deep connections between all things.

In those few moments I spent within the realm of death, my perception of life was completely and irrevocably shifted. After I returned everything seemed the same, and yet everything was totally different. Before being shot I thought "I" was my body. I thought "I" died when my body died. Growing up in a family of scientists, I had been taught that the only true reality was the one that you could test and measure in physical terms. After my near-death experience I no longer thought that my life began at birth and ended at death. I no longer believed that I was separate from other beings. Time no longer seemed rigid and finite. I perceived the universe around me as malleable and changeable rather than linear and fixed. Everything on the planet was alive. All life was precious.

I began to perceive radiant glowing light around supposedly inanimate objects. I could hear the songs of the grasses and the deep sonorous chants of the trees. Every object on the planet was not just physical matter but was also infused with vibrant light and harmonious sound frequencies. Every sunrise was a miracle. Every flower was an exquisite creation, a remarkable blending of light and love. Every moment was filled with color, sound, form and life-force energy. I could perceive the deep sighing of Mother Earth beneath me. I could feel the earth's gentle cadence of life pulsing through my feet. I was aware that the air around me swirled with soaring eddies of energy. Infused in everything was Great Spirit, infinite, yet personal and caring.

As a result of my near-death experience I now believe that we are each manifestations of pure energy, infinite and eternal, and that we are all intimately connected. I believe that everything around us is part of this eternal energy and that we are constantly responding to the energy fields around us, even if we are not consciously aware of them. I believe that we all have the innate ability to create and manifest the universe around us. I also believe that we can affect the energy fields of our home so that our home becomes a positive-energy template for our life.

After being shot my life became a quest to understand more deeply the experiences that I had on the "other side." I also wanted to learn more about healing. My wounds were so severe that my doctors had told my parents that I wouldn't live very long, and if I did live I would be incapacitated for my entire life. However, my touch with the Infinite ignited a healing force inside me which burned through the doubt and pain and limitations surrounding me, and I healed very quickly.

I became interested in understanding about healing and in learning alternative healing systems. I was fortunate to find some special teachers along the way. My first teacher twenty-five years ago was a wonderful Hawaiian kahuna (shaman) named Morna Simeona. She taught me to recognize the energy and the consciousness in all things. She talked to the trees and to the menehunes (Hawaiian elves) in the most matter-of-fact way. The inner realms were as real to her as the outer realms are to us.

During this time, I also organized some of the first courses for Westerners with a remarkable woman of Japanese origin, named Hawayo Takata, who trained me to understand how we can channel energy through our body to heal others through a system called Reiki. This learning was complemented by my training with a shiatsu master, who taught me about the meridian energy system (the ancient Asian system of energy coordinates on the body, which underlies the therapies of acupuncture and acupressure massage). My teacher Dancing Feather, a medicine man of the Taos Pueblo tribe, taught me the power of simplicity and humility as fundamental forces for healing and change in all life.

I've also been very fortunate to have had the opportunity to learn from the New Zealand Maoris, the Aborigines of Australia and the Zulus in Bophuthatswana in Africa. In addition, I am deeply indebted for all I have learned from my own Native American tradition and enrolled membership in the Cherokee tribe. Most of the healing work that I have done over the last twenty-four years has been based on the three premises that all of these tribal people reinforced for me: everything is composed of constantly changing energy; you are not separate from the world around you; everything has consciousness.

My interest in healing homes grew out of my work as a healer and teacher and my understanding of these three principles. I specifically became aware of the power of space-clearing as a result of the hundreds of healing seminars that I taught over the years. I began to notice that the results of the seminars often had as much to do with the energy and layout of the room as with my own skills. The better the energy in the room, the less I had to do. I could do the same seminar in two different rooms and the results in one room would always produce remarkable results and the other room would always produce a less satisfying experience. It seemed that the variance in results could not be explained from a merely psychological perspective. For example, the fact that one room had a view out the window and another room didn't, would lead one to assume that the room with the view would be the favored room psychologically and hence would produce better results. But that wasn't always the case. There seemed to be something inherent in the actual building itself that contributed to exceptional healing results.

I began to notice this apparent phenomenon not only from venue to venue but also within a seminar room itself. There were often places in the room where healing results were always more evident than in other places. I could do ten seminars in the same room with completely different people and completely different subjects. Yet there would be one area of the room where people were bubbling with enthusiasm about the results they were getting, another place in the room where people would be having emotional releases from incidents from their childhood, and in a different corner people would appear withdrawn and quiet.

When I noticed these phenomena happening again and again within one venue, even though I was giving different seminars to different groups of people, I began to suspect that the physical dynamics of the room naturally drew the people who were shy to one area, emotional people to another area and outgoing people to yet another area. So I tried an experiment. I would take someone from the "withdrawn" area of the room and have them sit in the "bubbly" part of the room. In a short while they would be acting just as enthusiastic as everyone else in that area of the room.

I noticed the same thing occurring in the healing work of my private practice. There seemed to be something inherent in the room in which I was working that would either contribute to or diminish my work. In fact, when the energy of the room was just right I really didn't need to anything. *People began to heal just by being in the room!*

Soon I noticed the same phenomenon manifesting itself in my garden. There was one place in my garden where everything grew magnificently and yet just a few feet away with the same soil, same amount of sun, wind, water and fertilizer, the plants meandered and waned. The realization began to dawn on me that there are energy fields in places and living spaces that can affect the way we feel and the way we heal. And I realized that we can affect and change those energy fields in such a way that promotes healing and balance.

When I enter a seminar room there are a limited number of variables to work with to adjust the energy of the room. One thing that I usually can affect is the seating arrangement. I have driven a few hotel managers to distraction by coming into a hotel room before a seminar, and beginning to clear the energy in the room using ancient techniques such as waving a feather in the air and chanting Native American chants. Then I push and shove the neatly laid-out chairs into new formations. I move the chairs around, trying one formation and then another until I find a particular formation that contributes to energy flowing more easily in the room. In fact, sometimes I have even moved the stage to a different part of the room or changed the location of the sound system. Though this is a hotel manager's nightmare, the healing results during the seminar are more dramatic and powerful.

Another thing I discovered in my private practice was the value of including a client's home in their healing process. For example, a young man came to me who had been suffering from severe depression for many months. He was in the care of doctors and even on medication, but he still was feeling very depressed. I work with my clients very individually. Sometimes I do past-life therapy with them, sometimes I suggest a change in their diet, sometimes I do shiatsu or hands-on healing. However, with him I had the intuition to work with the energy of his home. I said, "Tell me about your drawers?"

"What?!"

"Tell me about your drawers."

"My drawers? Well, they are really messy."

"When was the last time you cleaned them?"

"I can't remember," he replied.

"I'd like you to go home and clean your drawers. Start with the ones in your bedroom. Do you have any plans for the day?"

Completely bewildered, he answered, "No." He had come to me for depression and I was talking about housekeeping. It didn't make any sense to him.

I asked him if he was willing to drive directly home and methodically clean through his drawers getting rid of anything that he didn't use or didn't love. He was confused but he agreed. I told him I would call him in four hours' time to see how he was doing. Still very befuddled, he drove home. When I called four hours later he was excited and astonished.

"I can't believe this! I feel so good. I have tried so many kinds of therapy and I haven't felt this good. How can it be that just cleaning my drawers and getting rid of things can make such a difference?"

I explained to him that our homes are symbolic representations of ourselves, and in fact in a deeper sense are extensions of ourselves. I talked about our homes being templates for us. Change the template and it can affect our energy. I explained that cleaning his drawers was changing his template. As he was getting rid of things that he didn't need in his drawers he was participating in a symbolic act of releasing everything he didn't need in his life. There is great power in symbolic acts. Releasing garbage from his drawers affected a corresponding release of emotional garbage from his life. Eventually I was able to go to his home and clear and purify his home. However, I feel that the real healing began when he participated in a symbolic act of release by clearing his drawers. In a few short weeks he was happy, got a job and was no longer suffering from depression.

Again and again in my healing practice I have recognized the influence that one's home has on personal energy fields. I saw that substantial changes could be implemented in one's health, relationships, abundance and creativity just by shifting the energy in the home.

My training to do space clearing in homes took various forms. My first teacher, the Hawaiian kahuna, taught me the importance of clearing the energy in someone's home. She taught me how to exorcise homes and how to exorcise earthbound spirits (ghosts.) My shiatsu teacher gave me insight into the acupressure points in the body, and through that training I gained insight into the acupressure points in the home and environment. My two years spent in a Zen Buddhist monastery taught me the power of placement and simplicity in a home. My time in native cultures gave me house-cleansing techniques that had been passed down from generation to generation. This book is a distillation of my training combined with my personal insight into how you can transform your home into a living sanctuary.

In all the techniques that are included in this book it is valuable to remember that:

- Every technique that you employ is influencing the myriad energy fields in your home.
- When you clear your home you are also clearing your life, for your home is a reflection of you—changing your home's energy changes your energy.
- Your home has consciousness and everything you do to affect its energy positively is improving your relationship with a living consciousness.

3

THE FOUR STEPS
TO HOUSE CLEARING

Please read this chapter before using any of the techniques given in subsequent chapters.

Your home's energy field can become a beacon of light within the vast, pulsating panorama of energy and spiritual vitality which is the cosmos. It can constantly receive energy from the myriad forces which surround it and, in turn, it can send out its own unique energy, its own pure and individual spark of meaning and strength. After you have cleared and harmonized your home, it can function both as a collecting point and a transmitting point for energy. Your home can become an island of peace in time and space that will attract the love and clarity of the universe, and in turn will radiate these qualities out into the world. In order to achieve this effect, it is necessary first to master the Four Basic Steps of house clearing. In this chapter I will give you an overview of these steps, which are essential in any house clearing:

1. Preparation
2. Purification
3. Invocation
4. Preservation

These four steps form a foundation which you can build upon with the specific techniques that you will learn in later chapters. You can use these four steps as a kind of basic framework, within which you can improvise with various techniques to suit the specific needs of your situation. These are the steps you will need to go through first in clearing your own home.

Preparation

Preparation for house clearing can take many forms. However, it is important that some kind of personal preparation occurs before the clearing. There are two things which are essential to include in your preparation. First, you need to be very clear about what your intention is for the clearing that you do, and second, you need to prepare by doing personal spiritual and physical exercises.

BECOMING CLEAR ABOUT YOUR INTENTION

Where Intention goes, energy flows.

Your Intention is very important in any clearing that you do. This isn't only your conscious Intention, it is also your subconscious or inner Intention. Your inner Intention will determine the outcome of your house clearing and it is important to consider what your Intention is when you are clearing a space. If the foundation of the Intent is a positive, strong energy, the clearing that you do will flow easily and beautifully. Thinking about your Intention is also a good way to begin to expand your awareness of the interior spaces of your home and to begin to interact with them. Ask yourself the following questions.

What is my overall Intention for my house clearing?
If your overall conscious *and subconscious* Intention is to instill an uplifting energy into a home for the betterment of the occupants and the betterment of humankind . . . so it will be. If your overall Intention is to create a safe and magical haven for the rearing of children

. . . so it will be. Your Intention can be likened to a journey. Your overall Intention is your destination and your specific Intentions can be likened to the signposts along the way. Take time to ask yourself what is your overall goal for the house and the people who dwell within it walls? To what purpose are you undertaking the energy clearing of the home?

Your overall Intention can be likened to the creation of a building. When a house is built, the frame work goes up first. The rest of the building is created around that basic structure. Your Intention is the structure for your house clearing. Once you have the energy structure in place, then everything else you do will coalesce around this energy form.

Find the overall Intention that feels right for the space that you are clearing. Your Intention may be to contribute to the expansion of beauty and serenity in the home. Or your Intention may be to make a contribution to the vibrant health and well-being of the home's occupants. Do you want to create an environment in which you can undertake the creative work you have dreamed of doing all your life? Or perhaps you wish to create a warm social center where friends and family can meet and share their hopes, laughter and tears together. Another overall Intention could be the creation of a haven of prosperity and abundance.

Take the time to clarify, define clearly, write down and agree upon your Intent. Your definition of Intent may take time and patience, but it is an *essential* first step. This work is similar to preparing the soil before you seed the ground. Your investment of time and energy will return to you many times over. Once you are clear about your overall Intention, you do not need to keep thinking about it.

Your Intention will be instilled into the home at the time of the clearing, even if you are not constantly thinking about your Intent.

The reason that you do not need to think constantly about your Intention is because it radiates out of your personal energy field as you are clearing the house. Your Intent becomes instilled in your energy field and then all of the techniques that you use will work in alignment with your radiating Intent.

What you are *consciously* aware of as you clear a home is only a small percentage of what is actually occurring. Intuitively you might put a bright crystal in a window even as an afterthought, yet what

you may think of as only an afterthought may shift and positively influence probabilities that will spark a series of events in motion and
have far-reaching effects. When your Intent is clear and focused, then
everything you do in the house clearing becomes an act infused with
power. The more clearly you can articulate your Intention at the beginning of the process, the greater the effects which follow.

*What specific results do I want for myself and the other occupants of the
home?*
After you have clarified exactly what your overall Intention is, decide
what immediate and specific results you want. For example, if your
overall Intention is to generate a loving, creative energy in the home, a
specific Intention might be to shift energy in the home so that you can
write poetry easily and creatively. This specific goal could be further
broken down into small objectives. For example, you might decide that
you need to create a beautiful work space separate from the normal living spaces of the rest of your home in which to do your writing. You
would then need to decide what characteristics of such a room (or a
part of a room) would be most conducive to your overall goals.

If your overall Intention is to create a social center where friends
and family could meet and share together, then you might want to
consider what specific elements your heart tells you would help bring
this overall Intention into being. Do you see the social center of your
home in the kitchen, with a large oak table in the center of a light-
filled room? Are people gathered there laughing and chatting while
you prepare nourishing, delicious meals? Or do you see you and your
friends gathered together in the evening in a warmly lit room, perhaps with a fire crackling in a grate? Are the gatherings for pure enjoyment or are they centered around a common focus such as a
support group for environmental issues?

You might want to think of your overall Intention as being like an
aerial picture taken from a plane. Your specific Intentions would then be
coming to earth and bringing into focus the street you live on, your
house, the rooms inside, the furniture, the books on the table, the flowers in a vase—all the details which will bring your overall goals to life.

To decide on specific Intentions you might consider talking to all
members of the household and asking them what are their exact
goals and visions for the period of time they will be living in the

home. What are their dreams, how do they see it? It might be valuable to have a house meeting to discuss the purpose of the house clearing. Talk specifically about what each member would like to feel while in the home. It often helps to write down the overall Intention and the specific Intentions as a group. Not only will this bring you closer together as a group, but the energy of everyone who participates will contribute to the power of the clearing, and everyone will reap greater benefits as a group from the new energy which will flow through the house.

What long-term results do I expect to achieve?
As you are clarifying Intention, be sure to include the long-term results that are part of your vision. Let me share some examples:

1. OVERALL INTENTION   A home conducive to art and creativity.
   SPECIFIC INTENTIONS   Empty out seldom-used spare bedroom, install appropriate lighting for a studio, make time in schedule every week for painting.
   LONG-TERM RESULTS   The creation and sale of the paintings, the exploration of my creative potential.

2. OVERALL INTENTION   A home that contributes to the spiritual development of all occupants.
   SPECIFIC INTENTIONS   Creation of a beautiful meditation-room area and an altar in the home, objects and colors in the home that elicit a spiritual feeling, daily private meditation times in normal routine.
   LONG-TERM RESULTS   All members of household have increased sense of connection to their spiritual source. All members feel more physically and spiritually vital and energetic.

3. OVERALL INTENTION   A home that is abundant and prosperous.
   SPECIFIC INTENTIONS   A financial increase at work, objects within the home that feel abundant (you can list specifically what they might be), fulfillment of personal dreams (i.e., a luxury liner cruise).
   LONG-TERM RESULTS   A continuing and growing feeling of expansiveness and always knowing that you have enough for all your needs to be met.

Your list of specifics may be very long or relatively short. Try to get a very clear picture of the long-term results you envision. They can be a beautiful picture you keep in your mind, which can infuse even your smallest actions with a wonderful sense of purpose and deep meaning. By doing this you create a template for the future. You instill a template that energy adheres to in the months following your house clearing.

SPIRITUAL AND PHYSICAL PREPARATION

The day before you perform a Space-Clearing Ceremony decide what method(s) you are going to use. Make sure that you have all the tools that you will need. Different practitioners will have different guidelines for preparation. These are my personal guidelines:

The day before

One of the fastest ways to cleanse the energies in a home is simply by cleaning it. Almost everyone can notice the difference in the feeling of a home before and after it has been cleaned. Not only does the general straightening of the clutter make a psychological difference in feeling but whenever your home is cleaned there are subtle shifts in the energy fields that people will feel. I don't necessarily believe in having a compulsively neat house. I feel that it is important to feel comfortable and creative and relaxed in your own home. If you don't feel like doing the dishes after a meal and feel like letting them sit until the next day, so be it. If you feel like throwing your clothes over your shoulder as you undress, let 'em fly. My home often looks like a major disaster area. However, before a house clearing, it is valuable to clean your home. The deeper the cleaning, the better. Wash the windows. Vacuum under the bed. Really give your entire home a deep and thorough cleaning. This will greatly facilitate the clearing and will give your home a stronger energy field.

The night before

Do not eat the night before, or eat only very lightly so you are not going to bed on a full stomach.

Prepare all the tools that you will need for the clearing the next day. Purify them either by moving them through smoke (see Chapter 6) or, if the weather is nice and clear, you can leave them out in the sun for a few hours the day before. For example, if you are using a rattle in your ceremony, hold the rattle over smoking sage or some incense, and allow the smoke to cleanse your rattle symbolically in preparation for the ceremony. Also, be sure to purify the clothes that you will wear during the ceremony. You can do this by making sure that they are clean and either letting them air in the sun (weather permitting) or moving smoke over them.

Before going to bed, ask Spirit to work with you in your dreams to prepare you for the cleansing. (When I speak of Spirit, I mean whatever your sense of a higher goodness is, whether it be a sense of a personal god or goddess, or that special feeling you have when you walk through a grove of stately trees, or your belief that within every human being there is the potential for goodness.) Connect with your idea of Spirit, and ask it to infuse every cell of your body while you are sleeping, making you powerful and ready to act as a channel for energy as you clear your house the next day.

Upon rising

For optimum results rise before the sun is up or in the early morning. The energy of the earth is fresher and most potent at this time.

Meditate, asking for guidance and assistance from personal guides and guardians, and Spirit. At this time project your energy forward into the day and visualize or imagine yourself going from room to room, cleansing and clearing each room. Then imagine that the ceremony is complete and your entire home is radiating with bright sparkling energy.

Take a salt bath. This is for the purpose of ablution before your ceremony. Add one pound of salt to your water and soak for at least twenty minutes (see pages 96–97). It is all right to rinse off after your bath. If you don't have a bathtub, then gently rub salt all over your body while you are in the shower, let the salt sit for a few minutes and then rinse it off. If using the shower method be sure that you have rubbed the salt onto the bottom of your feet.

Put on the clothes that you have laid out especially for the ceremony. Do not wear any jewelry. I feel it is preferable to work without shoes on, as the soles of your feet can more easily become sensitive to the energies in the house; however, this is optional.

Gather together all the items that you are going to use for the clearing. You are now ready to begin.

Purification

Energy in a room can be compared to water in a mountain stream. Imagine that there is a bend in the stream and that in this bend leaves and sticks and debris have collected over time, partially clogging the little stream of clear cold water. You can reach down and clear it out yet after a while, as more leaves wash downstream, the leaves will begin to collect again. Room purification is similar to removing the debris from the little stream, in that you can energize the places in the room where energy tends to go dormant or stagnant. However, you will notice that after a while the energy will become sluggish in those corners again, so that it is necessary to perform this ritual on a regular basis.

Before you can begin to instill new energy fields in a home it is important to cleanse the overall energy first. Invoking energy into a home before it is cleared can be likened to picking a beautiful bouquet of flowers but then putting them in a vase filled with old wilted flowers. The reason why rooms need to be cleansed is because the energy becomes stagnant and this stagnant energy affects the health and well-being of the occupants of the home. Energy particularly becomes stagnant in the corners of a room because energy travels in circular, spiral movements which precludes corners. It also becomes stagnant because of illness or negative emotions that have been experienced in the room. Stagnation occurs too because of the emanations of the objects in the room or due to the placement of the objects in the room.

There are many ways that you can cleanse the stagnant energies in a home. In subsequent chapters I will share numerous techniques and methods that you can use for your clearing. In deciding which of these to employ in your purification process, I suggest that you approach the room in the same way a sculptor would approach a block of marble before starting a new sculptor. She first takes a large sledgehammer and fells great blows to the raw stone, leaving the crude form exposed. Then her tools become more and more refined, until finally she uses only the finest grade sandpaper to polish the finished work to a lustrous sheen.

Before beginning, stand back and let the room speak to you. Clearly envision the finished project, just as the sculptor envisions the intricate form caught within the uncut stone. With this vision clearly within your mind, start with your most powerful tool to begin breaking up and moving the energy around the room. As you proceed, you will want to use more and more refined room-clearing tools. For example, if you are clearing energy using bells, begin with your biggest, loudest bell. When you have completed circling a room using that bell, then proceed to a higher, more refined sound, perhaps a smaller bell. Allow the bells to become more and more refined. Perhaps your last choice of instrument might be a tuning fork which creates a very refined energy.

Begin by standing at the front door to your home, holding in your mind your intention for the clearing. When you enter the home, I suggest you do the following:

Open to energy flowing through your body
Stretch each and every part of your body. Energy travels through your body through the meridian system but also along the surface of the bones. As your bio-electrical energy travels throughout your body and through the joints, it is important to have your joints open and free. Make sure that every joint gets stretched.

The exercises that dancers or martial artists use to warm up are useful for this. For example, begin by reaching slowly up toward the ceiling with your fingers, first with one hand and then the other. Make your motions slow and fluid. After you have done this for several repetitions, you might want to slowly stretch your arms over to one side, and then over to the other side. Keep your knees slightly bent while doing this, repeat several times, and then slowly reach toward your toes. This is only one suggestion. Any physical warm-up which feels good to you is appropriate. Do not do anything which causes you pain. The point is to get energy flowing through you—to unlock any blocked areas—so that joy and radiance enter you and exude from all of your cells, head to toe.

Also drink a large glass of "energized" pure water before you begin (see Chapter 5). Drinking a glass of water facilitates the flow of bio-electrical energy through your body. There are several ways that you can energize the water. Either hold your hand over a glass of water and project (imagine) rainbow light flowing from your hand into the water, or place the glass of water in sunlight or moonlight for two hours.

Expand your aura to fill the room

Step into the middle of the room that you are going to clear. Mentally announce yourself and radiate your overall Intention into the room. Begin to take very deep, full breaths. Each time you exhale expand your aura to fill the room. Expand your sense of Self so that *you* become the room. Let every breath encompass the room to the point where you feel as though you are breathing the room.

Offer prayers

Still your mind and offer prayers of thanksgiving for the help that you will receive as you clear the room. The best prayers are spontaneous ones offered from your heart rather than formalized or memorized ones. In your prayers ask for assistance and guidance from Spirit for the Space-Clearing Ceremony that you are about to perform.

Sensitize your hands

Roll up your sleeves and sensitize your hands. Make sure that your hands are very clean. One effective method for sensitizing your hands is to hold them just a few inches apart with the palms facing each other, then slowly begin moving them together and apart. It should feel as if there is a magnet in each hand and that these two magnets are pushing and pulling your hands apart and together. At the same time as you are doing this, imagine that there is a ball of light in between your palms. Imagine the ball of light getting brighter and brighter with every movement of your hands. Continue to breathe deeply and fully as you do this.

Circle the room

Starting with the easternmost corner of the room, begin to circle the room. Use your left hand to feel and perceive places where the energy feels "sticky" or erratic. Use your right hand to do the clearing with either a bell or rattle, water sprayer or salt, etc.

Let your heart guide you in deciding the location of stagnant energy fields. Open your mind wide to let this information come in. Do not worry if at first you have trouble perceiving the stagnant areas. Be patient and trust that a higher part of you *does* know exactly what is needed even if you are not consciously aware of where the stagnant energies are. With practice you will become more adept at quickly perceiving which areas are stuck. It is a matter of developing your intuition while letting go of doubt and a too-intellectual approach.

You may find that there will be times when you will want to use your right hand to perceive energy while your left hand holds your clearing tool. This is perfectly all right. It is important to do what feels best to you. There may also be times when you will need to use both of your hands for clearing. You will know when to do this by listening to the room. By opening your mind to all of the energy in the room, you will eventually come to hear what it is asking you for, and will be able to adapt your approach to the individual needs of any room or situation. It is necessary to adjust your ceremony to the tools you have at hand and the circumstances a particular room presents you with.

Keep circling the room as the energy becomes lighter and more refined. There are four ways to tell when the room has been cleared of stagnant energy:

1. Colors will look brighter, just as when the sun shines after a heavy rain. (A room with stagnant energy looks physically dull and lifeless.)
2. Sounds will be crisper and clearer. (In a stagnant room sounds seem muffled.)
3. You will feel you can breathe more deeply. (You will often feel shortness of breath or as if there is a lack of oxygen in a room with stagnant energy.)
4. You will feel lighter and freer. (A stagnant room will make you feel heavy—it can even feel as if you are trying to walk through molasses.)

Invocation

After you have cleared stagnant energies in a home you will want to fill the home with radiant light and crystal-clear energy. This is called *invoking, consecrating, dedicating* or *sanctifying* energy. All of these words describe what occurs when you "call" energy into a home and I use these words interchangeably. The *American Heritage Dictionary*'s definitions of these words are useful because they describe some of the special qualities and power inherent in the meaning of this process:

INVOKE   To call upon a higher power for assistance, support or inspiration.

CONSECRATE   To declare or set apart as sacred, to dedicate solemnly to a service or a goal, to make venerable or hallow.

DEDICATE   To set apart for a deity or religious purposes, to set apart for a special use.

SANCTIFY   To set apart for sacred use, to make holy, to make productive of holiness or spiritual blessing.

It is essential that you "call" or invoke energy into the home after it has been cleared. Not doing so would be like cleaning a flower vase but never putting fresh flowers into it. You can "call" energy in with some of the same tools that you used for clearing. However, when you use those same tools, your intention is changed. You have the Intention of "calling" energy instead of clearing energy. For example, you can use a bell to break up stagnant energy when you first enter a home, but later you can use the same bell to invoke energy and invoke Spirit. A drum can be a powerful device to dispel stagnant energy but it can also be used later to invoke a healing energy into the home.

When you sanctify your home you are asking for Spirit to fill your home. You are calling upon guardians in the realm of Spirit to come forth bringing an energy of healing and love.

BE SPECIFIC

When calling forth Spirit into your home be specific about the direction in which you desire the energy to flow. Perhaps you want to dedicate the energy of the home to healing, or perhaps you want to dedicate the energy of the home to fun and joy. Once the home is cleared, it is like an unpainted canvas: you can fill it with whatever you desire. I suggest that you dedicate the entire home to one purpose (overall Intention) and then you can go room to room invoking different dedications for each specific Intention. For example, you might dedicate an entire home to the "emotional well-being of the family," then dedicate the energy of the room of a teenager, who is deeply involved in school studies, to "clarity of thought and purpose." The dedication of the child's room would come under the umbrella of the overall dedication for the entire home, but would be specifically tuned to his own needs. The three steps in invocation are similar to purification.

Open to energy flowing through your body

After doing the house clearing, you need to shift gears so that you can sanctify the house. To do this begin to gently "shake" your body all over, only as far as your physical condition allows. Let everything in your body become very loose. Take a few deep breaths and just shake. The shaking might feel as if it starts as fine vibration deep inside your body and then begins to expand to fill your entire body. There should come a point in your shaking where you are not deciding how to shake, you are just allowing yourself to be shaken. Completely let go of your mind when this happens. As you shake, withdraw your energy from the past and the future. Time is an invention, an illusion. Shake thoughts of the past away. Shake concerns for the future away. Let everything go and enter into the exquisite Now. When this occurs there is a remarkable explosion of creativity and energy that will fill you. Allow the shaking to subside and be still for a few moments to be open to energy flowing through your body.

Expand your aura to fill the entire home

Let the energy that is all of you and your awareness fill your house. (This sum total of all the energy which makes you a unique individual is what we sometimes call a person's aura.) Hold the Intention of what energy you desire to invoke for the home. Let your Intention surge out of you in waves of energy. Begin to take very deep, full breaths, and each time you exhale, keep expanding your aura to fill each room. Expand your sense of Self so that you become the entire home. Let every breath encompass the home to the point where you feel like you are breathing the home.

Offer prayers
Still your mind and ask for beneficent guides and guardians to fill the home. Once again, the best prayers come from your heart rather than formalized or memorized ones. However, by way of example, I've included a very basic prayer for consecrating your home. To sanctify the entire house, stand in the room that feels most central to the home.

> *May the Creator that dwells in all things come forward and fill this home.*
> *I ask that this house be a sanctuary for all who shall enter.*
> *I ask that good thoughts and good actions emanate from this home.*
> *May this home bring comfort and healing for all who live here.*
> *May this home be a healing center of light and love.*
> *I ask this in the name of the most holy Creator.*

When you have completed your prayer you can "seal" it by using whatever tool you have chosen. If you use a bell, at the end of each line of the prayer ring the bell, and then solemnly at the end of the prayer ring the bell again. Another example would be sprinkling water into the four directions at the end of the prayer. Please remember it is not the specific instrument that you use, but rather it is what is in your heart and mind that is important during any ceremony.

After you have completed the consecration of the entire home, then move from room to room invoking energy into each room (remember to include your specific Intentions). Stand in the center of each room while you consecrate it. If it is a large home you don't need to spend a lot of time in each room, but it is important that each room is acknowledged. When you are cleansing a home, even the closets, nooks and corners need to be included, but when you are invoking energy for a room it is not necessary to go into every closet. Your intention can quickly flow through the unimpeded energy paths of a cleared room. Simply open all of the doors in each of the rooms before you begin.

When you have completed sanctifying the entire home be sure to give a prayer of thanksgiving for the assistance that was received.

Preservation

Once you have cleared a home of stagnant energies and have invoked energy into your home, then it is valuable to preserve the energy that you have called in. I use what I call Home Protectors and Home Energizers to maintain and sustain the energy fields that have been invoked. In Chapter 14, there are numerous examples of things that you can do to preserve the energy that you "set" in the home. For example, at the conclusion of the Invoking Ceremony you can take a quartz crystal that has been cleansed (see pages 101–7) and dedicate the crystal to balance and peace within the home. You can place the crystal in a centrally located room in the home, so that it can continue to radiate a balanced, peaceful energy.

Another example of preservation of the energy is to write down clearly on a piece of paper what the overall Intention for the entire home is. Then you might obtain a houseplant for the sole purpose of helping to preserve the energy that you have created. Fold the paper with your written intention and place it in the soil near the roots of the plant. Every time you water the plant, reaffirm your intention for your home and know that the life spirit of the plant will contribute to the energy in your home.

The above four steps form a framework for all the other techniques in this book. As you follow them, your home will shine with lovely radiant energy.

It is important to mention that these techniques are for clearing your own home and they can produce excellent results. However, please do not use this book as a manual for professionally clearing the homes of others before you receive additional intensive training. (I train house-clearing specialists, which I call Interior Realigners, who practice the craft of Etheric Design.) Professionals not only access energy to cleanse and clear homes, but they are also skilled in addressing underlying psychological concerns of house occupants, which is absolutely essential in any professional house clearing. (I have included information about this additional training in the Appendix.)

4

PURIFYING FIRE

The still blackness of the forest night is punctuated by a crackling fire. A great circle of smooth round stones surrounds the fire. An old medicine man steps forward out of the sheltered darkness of the trees, entering the sacred circle. Raising his hands overhead to the evening sky, he begins slowly shaking his rattle. Round and round the fire the old man walks, his gnarled fingers wrapped around the deer-ankle stem of the rattle. The rhythmic sound of his rattle, swelling and falling into the shadows of the night, sends out a "call" that echoes through time and space. He calls upon the Spirit of the Fire. He calls his Ancestors. He calls his Spirit Allies. He calls Great Spirit.

Abruptly the medicine man stops . . . and gently looks overhead. A shooting star lights its way across the heavens. With a soft sigh he smiles. His sacred circle is full. He is full. He sits long into the night watching the last smoldering embers of the fire as he waits for the rising sun.

From prehistoric time humans have been fascinated by the power of fire. Ever since the first caveman discovered how to ignite flames to dispel darkness and disperse coldness, fire has been considered sacred. Fire was thought to be a gift from the gods and it was used to gain entry into the unseen realm of spirit. Native tribal members danced around leaping flames to call forth spirits. Monks in high mountain lamaseries chanted prayers to the gods while gazing into a single flame. Ancient visionaries looked into the movement of fire to foretell the future and review the past.

Fire stands with water, air, and earth as one of the primary elements of existence. Fire enthralls us with its primal presence. Fire is pure energy, and has long been associated with Spirit, with the spark of life and the power of renewal. It can maintain life and it can destroy it. It can purify and transform . . . and it can annihilate. It is the mediator between the visible and the invisible, light and dark, energy and form.

Fire has been used for ceremony since the dawn of time and as religions developed many associated fire with divinity. In Greek mythology, fire was reserved for the gods alone until Prometheus stole the sacred flame and gave it to human beings. In many cultures a sacred fire was kept burning in the center of the village. This was true among the ancient Egyptians, Persians, Greeks, Incas and Romans. The Cherokee Indians had the Most Sacred Fire burning continually within a huge seven-sided building and rekindled it once a year during the Corn Festival. It was thought to hold the spirit of the tribe together. The Sacred Fire provided them with a sense of connection to their ancestors, to the stars, to the great beyond. Many religions associate fire with light and spirit. In later times Christianity, Judaism and Hinduism used fire in holy ceremonies.

The use of fire in the home for spiritual cleansing and dedication is one of the oldest, surest and most immediate of space-clearing techniques, for fire can be a catalyst between the known and the unknown. It transcends yet embraces form. It is the absolute purifier and transformer as it consumes its fuel. One of our greatest symbols for transformation is the phoenix rising anew from the ashes. The phoenix does not merely rise as a newer edition of its previous form, but flies forth exalted and glorified, a hallowed spirit. Alchemists held that fire was "the agent of transmutation," believing that all things come from, and return to, fire.

The understanding of fire as a catalyst for change has emerged from many cultures. In ancient China, when a house caught fire the villagers didn't rush to the rescue since they believed that the fire was purging the home of unbalanced energies and therefore it was a good thing to let it burn for a while. (However, personally I'm glad we have firemen and fire engines.)

Fire is excellent to use in house clearing as it can serve as a catalyst in the four essential parts of the process. When using fire to clear a room or a home it is valuable to first use fire for personal Preparation. Fire then can be used for clearing the lingering or stagnant energies within the room in a Fire Purification. After the room has been cleared, fire can be used in Invocation to fill the room with new life-enhancing energy. Calling the sun's light into your home can help in the Preservation of the energy field that you have invoked into your home.

Fire Preparation

Here are several techniques which can bring forth the Spirit of Fire in your personal Preparation before using fires to clear the energies in a room. The more you can connect with and "call" the Spirit of Fire into yourself, the more the life-giving properties of fire will fill your home.

To connect with the Spirit of Fire:

1. Sit still and quiet your mind.
2. Light a candle and gaze steadily into the flame.
3. Feel the warmth of the candle. Imagine that the warmth of the flame is filling you.
4. Expand your awareness and imagine that you become the sun. Feel the warmth of the sun fill you and radiate from you.
5. Visualize the "Spirit of Fire" filling you. Like the great phoenix in flight, let the power and beauty of fire fill you. There is enormous beauty in fire. Fire can be a single candle flame in a monastery, or the purple and orange conflagration of a sky at sunset. It is the icy fire of a shooting star in the heavens, but it is also the gentle warmth of the sun in a summer meadow. Feel and find the part of you that dwells in the understanding of fire. For some, connecting with the energy

of fire is a physical sensation. They might feel a surge of warmth travel through the body. For others, connecting with the Fire Spirit is mental imagery of fire. Below is a meditation to assist you in connecting with the element of fire. Connect with the fire that dwells in your mind and soul, and your clearing ceremonies will be powerful and brilliant.

6. Give thanks for the Spirit of the Fire entering you and your home.

Blue Flame meditation

This is a meditation that you can use to further access the Fire Spirit inside you. You can record it for yourself on a tape, or take yourself through it mentally prior to your House-Clearing Ceremony. It is an excellent way to open yourself to the energy of fire. When you turn your attention inward, as during meditation, you discover the vast world of "inner space" which is as real as the external world. This meditation will help you achieve a deep level of relaxation and will also alter your consciousness so that you increase your ability to perceive and be aware of the energies in the room or house.

To begin this inner journey, put your body in a comfortable position, making sure that your spine is straight and your body is free of constraints. Let your eyelids grow heavy . . . easily and naturally growing heavier and heavier. Your entire body is feeling more and more relaxed with each breath . . . from the top of your head all the way to the very tips of your toes . . . deeper and deeper, more and more relaxed . . . with each breath, with each passing moment feeling more and more relaxed. Now, begin by watching your breath . . . just watch your breath ebb and flow . . . ebb, flow, each breath allowing you to feel more and more relaxed and your body to move into a state of complete muscular equilibrium and poise.

Muscles come in pairs, one muscle pulls to the right and its partner pulls to the left, one will pull up and one will pull down. With each breath your muscles are moving in perfect equilibrium, so that your body has a delicious sense of weightlessness. Body and mind in perfect harmony.

Take a few more deep slow breaths. With every breath that you take feel yourself becoming more and more relaxed. Let all thoughts, cares and concerns drift away like clouds drifting overhead on a warm summer afternoon. Now, as you are completely relaxed, imagine that you are inside a very beautiful temple. In the center of this temple is a tall blue flame that reaches higher than your head. You find yourself walking toward this blue flame. As you hold your hands out toward this flame you notice that there is a light cool breeze coming from the flame. This is the Sacred Blue Flame. It refreshes, re-energizes, and purifies. Now imagine that you are stepping into this cool blue flame. As you stand in the center of the flame you are aware of impurities dissolving within you. You are aware of a clarification and balancing occurring within you.

Now be still and listen to your inner voice, your inner knowing and visions. Feel the deep silence and the deep peace that resides within you. During this time you are open to guidance.

As you stand in the Blue Flame allow these words to sink deep within you. You can reach any height, for you know that you are unlimited. The light shines bright within you this day. You are in harmony with all things seen and unseen, and others are in harmony with you. You are open and you express your feelings easily. You are relaxed in every life situation. You are free to receive love and love is all around you. You are in excellent health and every cell of your body radiates health. Each and every experience is necessary for you to grow and expand and you cherish every experience.

You are free to receive love. You are responsible for your life, completely and totally. You breathe deeply and are relaxed and poised. You are in control of your life. You are open to new ideas and you accept the wealth that life has to offer. Ideas come to you easily; you act and you do it now. All your actions are appropriate. You are calm and relaxed.

Love is all around you and you are loved. You are in harmony with spirit and know that you are infinite, immortal, eternal and universal. This is your day. Go out into your day with joy and peace, knowing that there is a divine plan for you and you are perfectly aligned with that plan. You see clearly into the inner realms and you allow a powerful healing life-force energy to surge through you.

Now step out of the Blue Flame and know that you are ready to begin your room clearing. When you open your eyes you feel focused and alert, yet very relaxed.

Candle meditation

This is another meditation that can be done just prior to Room Clearing. Light a candle. Now sit in front of the candle and focus your attention on the blue part of the flame. Breathe in and out focusing on the blue light. Doing this will allow you to focus your own inner energies. Feel energy filling your body with warmth and clarity and relaxation. This meditation prepares you by allowing you to become more in tune with your intuition.

Complete this meditation by putting your hands at least a foot over the top of the candle and gently "wash" your hands in the warmth of the flame. Make sure that your sleeves are rolled up so as not to be a fire hazard. This symbolic cleansing of the hands is especially important when doing any of the techniques which involve your hands.

"Calling down the sun"

Some people consider that fire "called down from the sun" is the most potent fire to use in house clearing. To "call fire" from the sun simply take a magnifying glass outdoors (it needs to be a clear day to do this) and hold it over paper until a very small fire is created. This fire can then be carefully transferred to your candle or to a fireplace.

Fire Purification

My first teacher, Morna Simeona, a Hawaiian healing kahuna (shaman), taught me a powerful fire-purifying technique that instantly clears the energy in a room. I met Morna in an unusual way. I was twenty years old and living in Hawaii. I woke one morning thinking how nice it would be to get a massage. I had never had a professional massage but I had heard about its benefit. I opened the Yellow Pages in the Honolulu phone book, only to see page after page of massage therapists. I was uncertain whom to call.

The Royal Hawaiian Hotel, a stately old hotel in Waikiki, listed a massage center so I called and booked a massage for later that day. Arriving at the massage center, I sat nonchalantly in the waiting room thumbing through a magazine. Suddenly I "felt" someone enter the room. As I looked up I saw a beautiful middle-aged Hawaiian woman with soft, kind eyes looking at me. I began to weep. My weeping turned to sobs. I was utterly confused. Here I was sitting in a hotel massage waiting room sobbing uncontrollably for seemingly no reason. When I could speak I said, "What's wrong with me? Why am I crying?"

Gently and lovingly she said, "It's just a release. Don't be concerned. Come with me. I'm your massage therapist." In that instant I knew that I had met someone very special. As I followed her down the corridor everything that, a moment before, had seemed inanimate, seemed to come alive. I glanced at a small vase of flowers. Each flower sparkled with life and seemed to be almost humming. The corridor walls seemed to be breathing—pulsing in and out. Everything looked "normal" yet seemed completely different. It was as if suddenly the world around me had become alive. I was shocked and yet it all seemed natural and right. In the massage room Morna instructed me to lie on the massage table. As she put her hands on me I felt an electric pulse surge through my body. I instantly fell into a deep sleep. When I awoke from my massage I felt refreshed and cleansed. I also awoke knowing that I wanted to learn from this remarkable woman.

Morna came from a long line of healing kahunas. Her mother, her grandmother and her great-grandmother had all been kahunas. Eventually, Morna was declared a Living National Treasure of the United States.

At first Morna was very hesitant to train me, but when she found out that I was of American Indian heritage she agreed. (Though my heritage was important to Morna, I personally don't believe that you need to have native blood to understand the ancient wisdom of earth-based cultures. I believe the ability to understand comes from your heart rather than your blood.) From my training with her I learned Hawaiian healing techniques and massage. I also learned about herbal medicine. Morna, who was often called upon to exorcise spirits from individuals and from houses, also taught me how to cleanse energy from houses and rooms. Though usually her techniques were directly descended from ancient rituals, she also included present-day ingredients in these ceremonies. Her Fire-Clearing Ceremony continues to be one of the most powerful clearing techniques that I have found.

I use this technique if there has been an argument or intense emotions in a room (leaving a dense, heavy feeling) and I want to clear it quickly. It is also excellent to use in a room after someone has been ill. You'll notice an immediate improvement in the feeling there.

Another time I use this procedure is when, moving into a new house, I want to clear stagnant energy. It is also an excellent technique for therapists and healers who want to clear any psychic residue after a day of clients.

For fire purification, you will need the following items:

DEEP PYREX BOWL   Metal is not as good because the metal interacts with salt. Pyrex is necessary because glass or ceramic will usually crack due to the fire's heat. The bowl must be deep enough to contain the fire (*at least* four to six inches, preferably deeper).

SEVERAL FIRE BRICKS   The fire bricks keep the Pyrex bowl up off the surface of the floor so the heat doesn't scorch the carpet or floor.

ONE TEASPOON OF ALCOHOL   (do not under any circumstances exceed this amount of alcohol because of fire hazard). Morna usually used rubbing alcohol but any alcohol will work.

TWO TEASPOONS OF EPSOM SALTS OR SEA SALT

FIRE BLANKET   (a blanket designed especially for putting out fires; contact your local fire department if you are unable to find one in your area). This is essential.

Before starting the procedure, please read the warning on page 45. Then, place the fire bricks in the center of the room to be cleared, in an area that is completely clear of fire hazards. Place the Pyrex bowl securely on top of the bricks. After being very clear about your intention for the ceremony and dedicating the fire, place the Epsom salts in the bottom of the dish and then pour the teaspoon of alcohol into the bowl. Before the alcohol evaporates, light the mixture with a long-stemmed match.

Sit or stand near the fire. Focus on the flames, keeping in mind the fire's purpose. Allow the fire to burn until it is completely out. The

Pyrex bowl will be hot so you must let it cool for five minutes before you touch it.

You will instantly perceive a difference. After the purifying fire, a room that previously seemed hazy and dull will seem crisper, sharper and cleaner, and the colors will seem brighter. People who come into the room may say it feels easier to breathe.

Warning: When creating this kind of fire, make sure you don't have any alcohol on your hands when using the match so that you don't set your hands alight. Also, keep your face and clothing well away and make sure there is nothing inflammable nearby. Never add additional alcohol to the mixture after it has been lit as there is the potential for the flame to travel up to your alcohol container. I also suggest that, as a safety precaution, you have a fire blanket or metal lid (not a water fire extinguisher) available with which to smother flames should an accident occur. Never leave the fire unattended and keep small children and pets out of the room. If these measures are not followed and someone does sustain a burn, then first-aid advice is to plunge the burn into cold water. However, you should have no problems if you take these few simple precautions, and perhaps test the procedure in a fire-safe area outside before using it for space clearing inside.

Even when I am not specifically using fire in my clearing techniques, I almost always keep a candle burning in the room that I am clearing, as it helps to neutralize any stagnant energy that is released during the purification process. As with every candle, make sure it is never left unattended and is in a safe place. The installation of smoke detectors in a home is wise additional protection, especially when using candles and other naked flames. However, these detectors should be checked regularly.

Fire Invocation

Fire is a living being. It is no less alive than the very earth that we walk on and the air that we breathe. Fire Spirits are filled with warmth, passion and zest. They can be your daily companions and can contribute to your home being filled with light and life.

The very act of lighting a candle can cause a change in your state of awareness. It can uplift the energy in a room and can connect you to the living spirit of fire.

You can use fire for dedicating and invoking fresh clear energy into a room once the room has been cleared. The most common means of using fire for invoking energy into a room is through the use of candles.

There are numerous types of candles that you can use for invoking new energy. Most candles are made from beeswax, paraffin or stearine; some drip and some are drip-free. Though a candle of any material can be used, I prefer, whenever possible, to use candles that have been handmade and hand-dipped, since in these candles a human being has participated in their creation. This spirit of creation is released once again as the candle is burned. All the different styles of candles—tapers, straight candles, glass-encased candles and votives—can be used according to your needs. Any use of fire or candle should be embarked upon with extreme care. Make sure that no candle is left unattended and that there is never anything combustible in the general vicinity (this includes curtains).

There are two aspects that are important when using candles. The first is to focus your Intention. This means that before you light the candle you are very clear why you are lighting that candle. You focus your attention on the results that you wish for in a particular area. The second aspect, called "intensity of purpose," is to concentrate intensely or project your purpose while lighting the candle.

The Western cultural tradition of making a wish (focusing attention) while concentrating (intensity of purpose) on blowing out candles on a birthday cake is very similar to the mechanics used in this technique for house clearing.

FOCUSING INTENTION

Once the room is cleared you are ready to dedicate the energy of the room with your candle. Hold the unlit candle in your hands. Take just a moment to center yourself and imagine yourself surrounded in radiant peace. Then focus your intention on the results that you desire for the room. You might desire that the room be filled with light and warmth. Or you might focus your intention on protection and safety.

Then, bless your candle by holding it next to the center of your chest, your heart chakra (energy center associated with love). Or you might hold it above your head asking for the blessings of Spirit, or whatever higher power you believe in. There is no right way to bless your candle. As always follow the path that feels best to you and follow the wisdom of your heart.

INTENSITY OF PURPOSE

Place the unlit candle in a safe place in the room. Take three deep, full breaths and begin to feel a quietness expand inside you. Allow a "feeling" of the results that you intend for the room to fill you and then begin to visualize the room filled with that feeling. When this feeling/visualization has reached a clear intensity, then light the wick of the candle, feeling the intensity of your purpose. In that moment the candle's flame acts as a magnifier and projects your thoughts and feelings into the room.

Now simply gaze into the flame and allow your Intention to fill the room. You could even say aloud or silently several times a word that expresses your wishes for the room. For example, "Peace. Peace. Peace." With the candle being a focus point, know that energy generated by your Intention and intensity is filling the room.

Now just let go and relax. This is when true magic occurs. In some traditions a candle is never blown out. You either squeeze it out or use a candle snuffer. This is done out of respect for the Fire Spirits.

CANDLES AND COLORS

Combining the power of fire with the energy of color can be particularly potent, as there is no doubt that color affects us all. When you choose candles for clearing the energy in your home, I suggest you pay attention to the colors you are choosing, and use the color that is best for whatever purpose you wish to achieve. For instance, if you are working on achieving a sense of peacefulness and balance in your home, you might choose something from the blue family. If, on the other hand, you are visualizing lively energy permeating your space, you might want to use yellows or reds.

Dedications for specific desires have traditional color associations. If you are seeking love or wish to conceive a child, you might want to burn a pink candle in your bedroom. If you are trying to increase abundance, a green candle is helpful. A yellow candle might enhance feelings of joy and conviviality. The following information about color may assist you in choosing the color of your candle.

RED candles can be used in a room if you want to stimulate physical activity. For example, if you have a room or a place in your home where you have exercise equipment and you want to increase your physical strength, you may want to burn a red candle in that area. Or, alternatively, if sensuality has waned in your relationship, you may want to burn a red candle in your bedroom and dedicate it to passion.

The following prayer can be said while lighting a red candle:

> *I dedicate this candle to courage, strength and passion. May the blazing life force of a red setting sun fill this room now! May all who enter this place be filled with strength, determination and zeal.*

ORANGE candles can be used in a room where family and friends will be gathering. For example, you might want to burn an orange candle just before a party to stimulate camaraderie and enthusiasm in the room. You could dedicate this candle to joy and happiness for the evening ahead.

The following prayer can be said while lighting an orange candle:

> *I dedicate this candle to boundless joy and optimism. May the beauty of an orange poppy opening to the morning sun fill all who enter here with warmth of companionship and freedom of self expression.*

YELLOW candles can be used in a room where you or your children study, or where you want to stimulate philosophical conversation or increased concentration.

The following prayer can be said while lighting a yellow candle:

> *I dedicate this yellow candle to the clarity of sunlight. May this room be filled with joy and clear focus. Bring wisdom, joyous communication and good luck to all who shall enter here.*

GREEN candles are beneficial in any area where the family spends time. They are also helpful when used in the room of someone who is ill. Green candles stimulate feelings of balance, harmony, peace, hope, growth and healing.

The following prayer can be said while lighting a green candle:

I dedicate this green candle to healing, rebirth and abundance. May the color of spring leaves unfurling fill this room with healing, balance, renewal and vigor.

BLUE candles are excellent for bedrooms or for rooms where meditation is done.

The following prayer can be said while lighting a blue candle:

I dedicate this candle to serenity and inner truth. May all who enter this room be touched by the gentle blue of the wide open sky, and may this room be filled with Spirit and peace.

PURPLE candles, like blue ones, are soothing. In addition, this color is often associated with psychic awareness and intuition. I recommend lavender and violet candles for meditation rooms or for your home altar.

The following prayer can be said while lighting a purple candle:

I dedicate this candle to inner visions and inner truth. May the deep purple of the evening sky bring a deepening of intuition and peace to all who enter this room.

WHITE encompasses all colors. White candles can be used in any room at any time.

The following prayer can be said while lighting a white candle:

I dedicate this candle to spiritual awakening and attunement. May the purity of the white snow in wintertime fill all who enter here with divine realization.

As color is very personal it is important that *you* pick whichever color candles feels good to you, rather than always following a prescribed formula. I have included the above information only to get you started. (There is detailed information on color in Chapter 12.) There may also be colors that I haven't mentioned that feel right to you for a particular room. For example, I sometimes use pink candles in my living room because I associate the color pink with love and it gives a warm feeling in this much-used room. In my meditation room I often burn turquoise-colored candles because I associate turquoise with my Native American roots. In addition, I personally find the turquoise color combination of blue and green very soothing.

SEVEN-DAY CANDLES

Burning a seven- or fourteen-day candle is an easy way to maintain the balance of energy in your home after you have performed space-clearing rituals of any kind. Candles of this sort can be purchased from religious stores. They come in tall, heat-proof colored glass containers and are designed to be left burning continuously for the specified number of days. It is important to put them in a safe place, nonetheless, to minimize any danger of fire. Though most seven-day candles are designed to extinguish if accidentally knocked over, please keep well away from small children and pets.

I usually like to keep at least one seven-day candle burning continuously in my home, for it greatly increases the living spirit in the home. It gives off a warm and welcoming feeling to anyone walking into a home or room where such a candle has been maintaining a silent vigil. Many people like to use the seven-day candle on their home altar. (There is information about creating a home altar on page 173.)

OIL LAMPS AND LANTERNS

Though I prefer to use candles rather than oil or paraffin lamps, they too can be used to good advantage. Oil lamps sometimes come with colored oil so you can combine fire with color. I particularly like the oil lamps that are made of thin clear glass with a glass wick where the steady flame seems to float gently above the container. I have seen excellent use made of these lamps in meditation rooms. There is something very serene and almost ethereal about that particular light.

Paraffin lamps have the disadvantage of having a strong odor, but they can also fulfil the function of helping to establish an energy within a room.

FIREPLACE FIRES

A fireplace is a natural spiritual center in a home. Since earliest times, humans have gathered together around fires. The fire was where food was cooked. It created a circle of light and warmth and a sense of community. We all have an innate primal memory of sitting around the fire in the dark. The power of that memory is activated by even the smallest symbolic use of fire in the fireplace. A fire can bring warmth, strength and a feeling of peace to the person and place where it is made.

When you make a fire in your fireplace, you might want to say a blessing for each log that you put into the fireplace. In some Native American tribes, when they make a fire in preparation for a Sweat-Lodge Ceremony, each log that is placed in the fire is blessed individually. This is thought to increase the spiritual potency of the fire.

For example, when you place the first log into the fireplace you might say, "I dedicate this log to peace in this home." You don't need to spend much time on each blessing for it to contribute to the energy that is generated by the fire.

When you sit in front of a fire, spend a moment looking into the flames in silence. Be open to visions of the future, to messages from Spirit. Be still. Listen. Learn. Let the fire speak to your heart, your body and your soul.

Fire-Dedication Ceremonies

If you are fortunate to have a fireplace you may want to use it to do a Fire-Dedication Ceremony. Write on a piece of paper what you want for your home and put it into the fire. Know that the fire is sending your prayer to the causal planes to allow it to move into manifestation. Perhaps you want to have more warmth and love in your home. Write "I dedicate this fire to love, warmth and friendship in this home." You can also draw a picture of what you desire and place that on the fire. You do not have to be artistic. Hold the paper in your hand and charge it with positive energy while holding it. Place it in the fire. Watch it burn, knowing that as it converts to heat, ashes and smoke your wish is rising to the unseen realms so the Creator can help move your dream into a reality. Save a small portion of the ashes and, when they are cold, lightly scatter them around your home. This helps to preserve the energy of fire in your home.

A woman came to me whose ex-husband was being quite abusive to her. Every day the postman brought threatening letters from him and several times he had broken into the house and been physically abusive. She was fearful for her safety and the safety of her children. In spite of court orders requiring him to stay away, his harassment of her was escalating. She was desperate and didn't know what to do. She called me and asked if there was something that could be done that would make her home a safer place for her and her children. I suggested that she take additional legal advice, and in addition I went to her house to see if we could create a more protective energy there. After clearing the energies in her home, we ended by using a Fire Ceremony with quite remarkable results.

I first created a "fire-circle of protection" in a central room in her home. To do this, I placed ten small candles in glass containers on the floor in the shape of a large circle about six feet in diameter. I then instructed her to sit inside this circle and I entered into the circle with her. In the center of the circle I placed a large unlit candle inside a glass container. As we sat in the circle I asked her to concentrate on what she desired. I gave her instructions to be positive rather than negative. For example, instead of saying, "I never want to see my ex-husband again," she should think, "My children and I are safe and live in peace." I asked her to "focus her intention" on the results that she wanted in her home. Then I instructed her to allow the feeling to build until she was filled with intensity of purpose, and at that moment she was to light the candle and place her Intention fire. She did this and we silently watched the large candle flame for a few minutes. It was a moment of power and stillness. We then snuffed the candle out and in turn snuffed out all the remaining ten candles.

The next day the woman called me, very excited. The postman had come and didn't bring an abusive letter. The next day and the next day, no more letters arrived. And, in fact, in the three and a half years since we did the First Ceremony she has not seen or heard from her former nemesis. This was quite remarkable in that she hadn't told anyone about the ceremony in which she had participated. It worked instantly.

Fire Preservation

To energize your home with the element of fire and to preserve the sacred space that you have created through the use of fire, here are several suggestions:

- Hang cut-lead crystals in a window to bring the fire energy of the sun into your home.
- Hang mirrors in strategic places so that sunshine can be reflected into your home.
- Call the Spirit of Fire into your home.

CALLING THE SPIRIT OF FIRE INTO YOUR HOME

To draw the Spirit of Fire into your home, follow these steps:

HONOR THE "FIRE" THAT COMES INTO YOUR HOME: Bless the wires that bring the fire energy of electricity into your home. To bless the wires, place your hands on your main fuse box, or if it is unreachable, direct your attention toward it and say:

Thank you, Fire Spirit.
May the Fire that flows through you bring blessings to this family.

If you are in an apartment and cannot get to the main electrical source for your home, say the above blessing on individual electrical connection points in your home.

INVOKE THE SUBTLE ETHERIC ENERGIES OF FIRE: Light a glass-enclosed, seven-day candle and dedicate it to the Spirit of Fire. The candle then will become a constant entrance point for the Spirit of Fire to enter your home, bringing warmth and life and transforming strength.

CALL FORTH THE MAGIC OF THE SPIRIT OF FIRE TO FILL YOUR HOME: Open a window or a door on a sunny day and direct your attention toward the Sun. Ask that the Spirit of Fire enter your home. Ask that Fire Spirit fill your home, bringing its healing, transforming, strengthening energy.

5

HOLY WATER

Imagine yourself walking through a misty forest with tall, stately evergreen trees. The air is fresh and moist. The ground under your feet is thick with soft, spongy moss. The poignant smell of pine needles clears your head, and you can see very clearly. You are walking by a stream which widens out into a pool. A cascade of water is falling into this pool from the rocks forming a cliff high above you. As you breathe in the mist from this waterfall, you feel excited and every inch alive. You feel like you can do anything!

One of the most powerful tools for cleansing the spirit of a house, a room or any personal space is water. Water has innate purifying properties. It has been used in spiritual ceremonies and has been linked to the mysteries of human existence since ancient times. The use of water can cleanse and purify a house of negative, stagnant energy and restore to it a feeling of clarity and peace. Just having water in the home can invite a wonderful spiritual energy into it.

There are many legends from all over the world that are based on the belief that water bestows life, youth, wisdom and immortality. To the ancient Egyptians it was the source which gave birth to the gods. Hindus believe that waters are the beginning and end of all things on earth. To the Mesopotamians, water represented the unfathomable source of human wisdom. Many cultures developed water cults believing that the sounds and movements of water exemplified the soul of a living spirit.

In the Christian tradition, water is central to the ritual of baptism. Jesus was submerged in water by John the Baptist to mark the beginning of his adult spiritual work. He came out of the water "born anew," and this tradition has been continued by Christians to symbolize beginning their spiritual quests ever since.

In native cultures, water is frequently used in healing ceremonies. Cherokees would lay an injured person in water, letting the movement of the stream or river gently wash over the body. It was thought that the water soothed the spirit of the person who was injured and washed the injury away from the body.

Water is excellent for clearing a room of negative emotions, as water has been long associated with emotions. In dream work, water is often a metaphor for emotions. For example, a dream of frozen water is often linked to a person's feeling blocked or frozen emotionally, blocked by emotions which he or she is unable to express adequately. A dream of stagnant water almost always symbolizes a period of stagnation and nonproductivity in a person's life, whereas a dream of flowing water usually accompanies free-flowing emotions, a sense of release and meaningful movement through life.

I became aware of the importance of water in our bodies and in our homes through my healing work. I noticed that healing results were much more profound when my patients had had some water to drink prior to undergoing therapy. (I often recommend that clients drink at least one glass of water before a healing session.) The water in their body acted as a conductor to the energies which were channelled into them.

I also noticed in my seminars that results were often more dramatic when the participants were adequately hydrated. Again it seemed to me that the water in their bodies acted as a conductor of healing energy in much the same way that water acts as a conductor of electrical energy.

In addition, I noticed when I was clearing a house that I was able to perceive energy more clearly and was more effective when I was adequately hydrated. Not surprisingly, I also noticed that when I misted a 'room with water either during a healing session or during a seminar, emotional and physical results were amplified. My experiences gave credence to the idea that water in our homes could act as a conductor for transmission of energies. Your use of water in your home can help establish your home as a spiritual sanctuary and can greatly assist your home becoming a transmitting station for the Light.

Water can be used in all four of the energy-clearing steps. Water is an important part of any personal Preparation, for it is one of nature's great cleansers. It is excellent for Purification, especially purification of emotions. Water has been used for Invocation of spiritual energy in baptism and even further back in time. And water is one of the great ways to create a Preservation of Energy in the home.

Water Preparation

Water can be included as a powerful ingredient in any preparation for energy clearing. Physically cleansing yourself with water before your clearing ceremony, using water for cleansing your home and having "charged" water within your home calls forth the living Spirit of Water. This is important and valuable, for we are in constant interrelationship with the Spirit of Water through the waters of life that course through our veins. Water makes up the greater part of our physical bodies. You can go for long periods of time without eating, but if you stop drinking water, your body will not survive.

Every beat of your heart connects you to the universal Spirit of Water, which links you to the waters of our entire planet. The water that you drink and the water that flows through your body is the same water that was, at one time in the evolution of the planet, frozen high on the snowcapped mountains. The waters within you were once cascading down mountain streams to the sea below. The water inside you has been high in a cloud mass above the earth, has fallen as soft gentle rain, and has seen the bottom of the deep sea. The water that runs through your body has ebbed through the bodies of your ancestors and will flow through the bodies of your descendants.

The power of the Spirit of Water is intuition and emotion and spirituality. It is renewal and rebirth. It is soothing cool showers on a sultry afternoon. Water heals, cleanses and rejuvenates. From a gentle mist to a summer's rain to a raging thunderstorm, water cleanses all that it encompasses. Water Spirit resides in a still mountain pond; it is the oasis pool in the desert where wild animals are drawn to life-giving waters; it is in the majestic sea where dolphins leap and whales swim deep.

The Spirit of Water is childhood and innocence. It calls forth the healing of emotions and the healing of the past. It brings life, nurturing and healing. Calling forth the Water Spirit into your home will help you explore the depths of your soul.

To connect with the Spirit of Water:

1. Sit still and quiet your mind.
2. Begin by feeling the water within you and around you. Imagine that you are aware of the waters flowing through your body. Notice the moisture in your skin, your mouth and your eyes. Feel how the moisture in the air touches your face, surrounds your hands and envelops your entire body.
3. Drink a glass of water and imagine that you are aware of how your body absorbs the water and how the water sustains and hydrates your body.
4. Expand your awareness until you can sense that the water you are drinking and the water within you is part of the water flowing in streams and rivers.
5. Now expand your awareness even more so that you feel a oneness with all lakes and the vast expanse of all seas.
6. Continue until you imagine that you have become the "Spirit of Water." Imagine that you are now the tiny dewdrops that come in the night to quench the thirst of the leaves; you are a dolphin splashing and dancing in the crystal blue sea.
7. The more you connect with and "call" the Spirit of Water into yourself the more the Spirit of Water will fill your home.
8. Give thanks for the Spirit of Water entering your home.

"Charging" Water

Any water that is used for house clearing should be "charged" in preparation for the ceremony. Charging water is like charging your car's batteries. You are infusing the water with energy. Water that has come from a spring or from the sea does not need to be charged, as it has already been energized by the sun and earth and air. However, most water that is available to us to use for energy clearing has either been sitting in a plastic container in a grocery store or has come from a tap and has been chlorinated and fluoridated and filtered and has lost its vibrancy and spirit.

SOLAR-CHARGED WATER

Take the water that you plan to use for your ceremony and place it in a bowl. A ceramic or glass bowl is better than metal, unless you have some specific purpose in mind for the metal's energy to infuse into the water—for example, using a copper bowl to infuse the water with the energy of copper. Leave your bowl in the sunlight where it can soak up the healing properties of solar energy. The bowl needs to be left outside rather than next to a sunny closed window. Usually about three hours is sufficient for the water to become solar charged. Solar water has an outgoing exuberant yang energy and is great to use in dark rooms or rooms that feel as if they have a dark or heavy energy. It's also good to use in a room where someone has been ill.

LUNAR-CHARGED WATER

You can create Moon Water by leaving water outdoors in a place where it will be infiltrated by moonbeams. Moon Water has a wonderful feminine healing aspect and can contribute to softening energy in a room. This is particularly good in a room where intense emotions such as anger or sadness have been felt. Moon Water is also excellent to use in bedrooms for it helps contribute to an atmosphere that is good for sleep and conducive to dreams.

RAINBOW WATER

It is not always easy to find three hours of sunlight or moonlight if the weather is overcast. And sometimes the winter temperatures will freeze any water that you leave outside. Here is a technique to "charge water" on overcast days or winter days. I learned this Rainbow water method from my Hawaiian kahuna teacher. To the Hawaiians rainbows were thought to be gifts from the gods and water was holy. It was used for blessing and healing ceremonies. You can use this ancient Hawaiian shamanic technique for purifying and energizing water.

Take your hand and place it palm down over the container of water that you are going to use for your ceremony. Do not touch the water, but slowly move your hand in a circular, clockwise motion over the water. While you do this, imagine a cascade of rainbows coming out of your hand radiating the water with serenity and joy.

My teacher would begin her room clearing by first drinking a small amount of the Rainbow water before she cleared any room. She would then use the remaining Rainbow water in clearing the room. She said that by drinking the water she was being infused with the same Rainbow Light Energy that was cleansing the room, and that this made her a better instrument for the ceremony.

CRYSTAL-CHARGED WATER

Another way to energize water is to place a cleansed, clear quartz crystal in a clear glass container of water for twenty-four hours. (For information on cleansing crystals, see Chapter 7.) This method works especially well if you can place the container in a window where light can penetrate the crystal—the light helps activate the crystal. This water is excellent to use in a healing room in the home. This Crystal Water is also good for watering and misting your indoor plants.

Water-Purification Ceremonies

Water cleansing can be done during your move into a new home, for spring cleansing purification rituals or just whenever the energy in your home is out of kilter. You can tell when home energy is out of kilter because everything is a bit off. For example, if the toaster breaks, lights burn out, people are cranky and tired, and no one is really listening to anyone else, this is a good time for water cleansing.

SPRING-WATER PURIFICATION METHOD

In certain native traditions, the shaman dips the ends of branches or sprigs of plants into energized water and then flicks them around the room as part of a purification ritual. To cleanse a room using water in this way, begin by blessing a small bowl of spring water or "charged" water. To bless ceremonial water, take your bowl of water to the center of the room that you are going to clear and hold your hands over it. Ask for blessings for the water and for your room clearing. You might say:

May this water be filled with Spirit and may this room be cleansed and cleared by the Power of Water. As water renews and heals, may this room be renewed and healed. So Be It.

Pick up your bowl of water and walk to the easternmost corner of the room. Take a sprig of a herb or plant, or a small branch from a tree and dip it into the water to soak for a moment. Then flick the sprig into each corner and into the adjacent areas, and say (either out loud or silently):

Water, Water . . . Wash this Room Clean and Bright
Water, Water . . . Cleanse this Space with Love and Light!

Continue walking around the room in a clockwise direction. Continue flicking water as you walk around the room. If you come to a place in the room that feels exceedingly stagnant or sticky then dip your sprig into the water and flick the water seven times into the air. If the energy still does not feel clear, then flick the water another seven times. Many native cultures practice the ritual of flicking water seven times during ceremonies; some use sprigs and some use their fingertips.

When you are dipping a branch or sprig into the water, the energy of the branch combines with the water so you have double potency for your Energy-Clearing Ceremony. Here are some suggestions for the different kinds of sprigs that you can use.

PINE   Dip a pine sprig when you are clearing very heavy energy. Just as pine oil is added to household cleaners because of its disinfectant qualities, pine is extraordinarily purifying. Flicking water with a pine sprig is an excellent technique to use in a room after illness. It is also good for times when the energy feels dead and lifeless, or if it feels as though you are trying to walk through molasses. For extra effectiveness add a drop of pine essential oil to your charged water.

CEDAR   I was taught by someone within my own tribe, the Cherokee, that to flick water with cedar was a sacred act of cleansing, for "both water and cedar are sacred to the people." Cedar has some of the same properties as pine, but it is softer and more spiritual in its nature. Use cedar when you want to do a cleansing of spiritual energies.

LEMON VERBENA   A sprig of fresh lemon verbena is excellent for getting stagnant energies to shift or for use in a room after an argument. (If you don't have access to fresh lemon verbena you can take dried lemon verbena and soak it in the water.) This is also good in a room where you just can't think straight or there seems to be a stop-flow of energy. Lemon verbena is invigorating and stimulating.

GREEN GROWING SPRIG   For general clearing, any green growing sprig is good (please remember to thank the plant for its "giveaway"). If you are doing a spring clearing, then any spring sprig or branch is good. A branch with small leaves and stiff branches seems to be the most effective for flicking the water into the room.

FLOWERS   If you want to gently lighten the room's energy, or if you are clearing a space for a meditation room, then using a flower is best for flicking the water into the room. A flower brings a gentle lightening of the room's energy. Every flower has its own energy. For example, you can use a rose for love and a daisy for joy.

WATER PURIFICATION BOWL

You can use this method in conjunction with any other clearing method you are using. It can be used for every kind of room clearing. Before you begin a Space Clearing Ceremony take a bowl of "charged" water and place it in the center of the room that you are clearing. Hold the Intention in your mind that this water will absorb stagnant energy that is released during the ceremony. If you have very dense energy to clear in a room, add sea salt to the "charged" water. When the ceremony is complete, carefully take the water and pour it down a drain. Run clear cold water afterwards for thirty seconds. Sometimes after a very intense clearing the water will actually look murky and dull. Clean the water container out with cold water and allow it to air-dry or, if possible, to dry in the sun.

ROOM MISTING FOR PURIFICATION

Emotional energy tends to stagnate in a room long after the events that gave birth to the emotions have passed. After an argument, the air in a room might seem thick and almost charged. This is, in fact, precisely the case. There is an electric "charge" left hanging in the air as a residue from all the negative emotions. The fastest way to neutralize this residual energy is to mist the room. Spraying your home with water to create sacred space is one of the simplest and most effective techniques for shifting your home's energy and cleansing residual emotions.

Misting not only neutralizes emotional charge in a room almost instantly, it also creates a special negative-ion-rich environment. (Information about negative ions is included in Chapter 6.) A negative-ion-rich environment is the same environment that you will find next to a waterfall or by the sea or in a pine forest. When you are in a negative-ion environment you feel uplifted and alert and revitalized. In a positive-ion environment you will be sluggish and lethargic.

Evergreen forest air is permeated with a negative-ionic charge because negative ions gather at the tips of pine needles. Negative ions are also generated by the spray of a waterfall or the crashing of waves on the shore. One of the reasons that you feel so good when you are in a pine forest or at the seashore is because you are enveloped in negative ions. Misting is a way of bringing this same rich atmosphere of negative-ionic energy into your home.

When misting use an atomizer: the finer the spray, the better, but any spray bottle will do. It is best to fill the bottle with spring water. However, if you do not have access to anything other than tap water, then you can "charge" the tap water using the previously suggested methods. You should instantly feel the difference in the room after you have misted.

The key is to spray lightly all over your room. Don't soak everything. Just send light little puffs of moisture into the air everywhere. Your plants will also benefit from the regular use of a fine mister.

If you have a therapy treatment room in your home, mist after each client to purify the room. It will completely clear the room so that there are no emotional energy residuals left over from one client to the next. Before I started misting the room between clients, a second client would often encounter some of the same issues as a first client. I feel that this occurred because the second client would walk into the residual energy field left by the first client and unconsciously pick up on the emotions left hanging in the room. It is also important to wash your hands between clients (even if you haven't touched them) and to mist yourself so that the room is cleared and you are cleared between clients.

Invocation

FLOWER REMEDIES FOR THE HOME

A method that many people have found to be quite effective for positively affecting the subtle energies in a house and for invoking life-force energy into a home is to use flower remedies in a spray mister. In the early 1930s a renowned British physician, Dr. Edward Bach, noted that many illnesses seemed to be directly related to the patient's emotional state. He felt that traditional medicine wasn't addressing these underlying causes of illness, so he made it his personal quest to treat the patient and not the disease. Over several years he formulated thirty-eight flower-based formulas that he felt treated the underlying cause of many diseases. His remedies were made of dilute forms of flower and plant extracts and were said to contain the healing energies of the plants. I have found that mixing Bach flower remedies (or California Flower Essences or Australian Bush Flower Essences) in a mister and occasionally misting a room (or a whole house) can have a very beneficial effect on the subtle energies of your home. Though space doesn't permit listing the qualities of all remedies, I suggest having on hand Rescue Remedy (a flower remedy) for adjusting the etheric energies of a room after a disturbance, argument or difficulty has taken place. Here are a few of the available flower remedies and their qualities:

Cherry Plum:	calm, quiet courage
Wild Rose:	vitality, lively interest in all things
Water Violet:	gentleness, tranquility, poise, grace
Centaury:	quietness, wisdom
Vine:	wisdom, leadership, help for others
Star of Bethlehem:	clears tensions and residue of tension
Gorse:	positive faith in overcoming difficulties
Rescue Remedy:	balances energy after argument or illness

I suggest you use your intuition for deciding what remedy is the best for a room. To do this, turn all the labels around so you can't see what is in each bottle and then lightly run your fingers over the bottles. There often will be one or more remedies that will seem to "tug" at your fingers. Take a few drops of the remedy and mix with clear spring water or distilled water and then mist the room.

HOMEOPATHY FOR THE HOME

For over two hundred years, individuals seeking an alternative to conventional medicine have turned to homeopathic remedies. The homeopathic philosophy is that minute doses of the substance that causes a disease can help to heal someone who is ill with that disease. The key tenet of homeopathy is the law of potentness which declares that a curative agent's potency increases as it is diluted. Homeopathy is based on the hypothesis, ancient as Hippocrates, that "like cures like." Some remedies are so diluted that it is almost impossible to find any trace of the original substance. Samuel Hahnemann developed the modern homeopathic philosophy in the early nineteenth century. Today its proponents include such well-known persons as Queen Elizabeth II and Mother Teresa. Numerous double-blind studies and studies on animals have given credence to the viability of homeopathy.

To use homeopathy in your home, add a few homeopathic drops (use homeopathic alcohol tinctures rather than the powdered remedies) to a plant mister and spray throughout your house. A must for anyone using homeopathic remedies is to use the homeopathic remedy Arnica for any room within which there has been a disturbance or a sudden shock or upset. As with the flower remedies, you can consciously decide which remedy is good for a room, or you can run your fingers over the bottles to see which one is best for the room. Don't be concerned about using exactly the "right remedy"—you can't hurt the energies of a room with homeopathy or flower remedies no matter what solution you use. Both homeopathic cures and flower remedies fine-tune the subtle energies in a room and are excellent to use in a meditation room.

AROMATHERAPY FOR THE HOME

To invoke energy that is conducive to positive emotions into your home you might like to try combining aromatherapy with misting. Add just a drop of essential oil to your misting water. Don't use more than this, or you could clog up your sprayer. (The benefits and significance of aromatherapy are discussed in Chapter 6.)

I keep misters at different locations in the house. I have an atomizer filled with spring water and lemon grass essential oil in the kitchen. When the dishes are done and the floor is swept, as a finishing touch I spray the kitchen with my revitalizing lemon grass water. The whole kitchen sparkles after that.

I also keep a sprayer of water and lavender essential oil in the living room. Several times during the day, in passing, I mist the living room. This way when we retire to the living room in the evening it has an energy that has been renewed during the day.

In the bedroom I keep a spray bottle with water and geranium essential oil and I spray the room after I've made the bed. If I enter the bedroom during the day, I'll mist it again. It works well to leave the water sprayer out so it is easy to give a room a quick spray upon passing. The solution of water and oil stays fresh for a long time so you don't usually need to replenish the containers except when they are empty.

Any time you feel in need of personal refreshment, you can also mist yourself. Keep a small atomizer bottle in your purse. Fill it with energized water and a drop of your favorite aromatherapy oil for use when you are away from home. Misting is good for your skin, and can give you a quick pickup during the day, since it revitalizes your energy field and also cleanses your aura.

Preservation

HUMIDIFIER

Using a humidifier is an easy way to supply fresh moisture to your house as well as preserving the element of water in your home. In cold countries many homes are actually drier than the Sahara during the winter, due to the effects of indoor heating. A cool-water humidifier can counteract the harmful effects of this aridity. I like the sonic humidifiers because they are quieter than other models. I suggest that you use charged water in your humidifier. Not only will it produce helpful negative ions, keep your skin softer, and help you sleep better, but it will also help with your dreams. Many people have reported that their dreams became richer in color and texture as well as more prophetic after they began using a humidifier in their bedroom. I believe that not only is water a carrier for emotions, but it is also a carrier for psychic impulses. Also, many people notice a difference in their psychic or visionary dreams when there is a humidifier in the room because of the negative ions that it produces.

(If you live in a climate where it is always exceedingly moist, like Hong Kong, you may want to obtain a dehumidifier for a room in your home if you find that you are often very emotional and have difficulty finding your emotional balance. Having a room in your home where you can go to "dry out" can bring some relief from an excess of emotions.)

HOME WATERFALL

Having a home waterfall not only increases the moisture in the air, creating a negative-ionic atmosphere, a little waterfall can also provide a background of healing sound for you in your space. Any room with a waterfall instantly feels alive and vibrant. Many plant nurseries and gift stores carry home waterfalls. These range from a small trickle of water over pebbles to larger ornate Greek-type statues pouring water into a pond below. Some of these can be quite expensive. However, if you want to make your own home waterfall it can be easy. Find a large deep bowl. Obtain a small electric, water-submersible pump. (Many garden centers sell these fairly inexpensively.) Place the small pump in the middle of the bowl, take some river rocks and place them around the pump so that they cover the pump and are above the water's surface. Place the hose connected to the pump up through the rocks. Turn it on and voilà!—an instant home waterfall.

You can bring the spirit of water into your garden by creating an outdoor waterfall or pool. Though this project may sound quite daunting, it really isn't that difficult. Place a pre-formed pool (bought at a nursery) into a hole you have dug in the ground. Add rocks and an underwater pump for a waterfall effect. Another way to create a waterfall is to use a liner (usually less expensive than a pre-formed pool). Dig a hole in the earth, line it with the liner and fill with water and your submersible pump. The pumps are operated electrically so you must use a qualified electrician either to bury the outdoor electrical cord in PVC pipe to the electrical source or to place the pipe so that people won't trip over it. Many plant nurseries can give you explicit instructions on how to create your own waterfall. A garden waterfall attracts birds, fairies, elementals, water sprites and spiritual energies into your garden.

POOLS

Even without a waterfall a simple pool of water makes an attractive sight and brings a soothing energy to your entire garden. These don't need to be big (I have one that is only eighteen inches wide) and, again, are very easy to install. Dig a small hole and place your liner or pre-formed pool in it. Surround it with river rocks. Add a few floating plants, replenish the water every time that you water the garden, and you have a special sacred garden pool. Alternatively, you could fill a large waterproof barrel or jar with water and water plants. This portable pool can be used indoors or outdoors to draw the Spirit of Water into your garden or home.

Another kind of pool is a bird bath, placed in the garden or inside your home, filled with water or floating flower blossoms.

BOWLS OF WATER

Placing bowls of water throughout your home can promote a healing energy. A single beautiful flat bowl of water with one flower floating in it can serve as a focus for centering and balancing energy. Or you can place tumbled quartz crystals in a bowl of water. The water increases the transmitting ability of the crystals. Pretty bottles containing water and colorful rocks might be placed on window ledges. They can channel the light from outside into your home. You can also place bottles of colored water (food color or watercolors work well) on windowsills. This will bring the vibration of color into your home. (For information about the use of color see Chapter 12.) Remember to change the water in the bottles and bowls frequently to keep them clear.

AQUARIUMS

An aquarium with fish can add a sense of harmony and beauty to a home, while at the same time increasing the negative-ion content of the air. If you don't enjoy fish, consider filling an aquarium with only water plants and rocks for an underwater Zen garden. The plants will also release fresh oxygen into the air. As mentioned above, it is essential to keep all containers of water fresh and clean in order to maximize the healing effects of the water. Studies done on the effect of aquariums on patients in doctors' waiting rooms have shown that aquariums have a universal calming and soothing effect. Any living creature will add energy to a home, and the serene tranquil effect of fish is so soothing that the stress of the outside will seem less significant when you enter there.

To draw further the Spirit of Water into your home you might consider taking the following, additional steps:

CLEAN THE WATER THAT IS COMING INTO YOUR HOME Use a water-purification system to purify your tap water. I personally prefer a system operating on the principles of reverse osmosis to filter our water. However, there are many other good systems on the market.

INVOKE THE MORE SUBTLE ETHERIC ENERGIES OF WATER Bless the pipes that bring water into your home so that water enters your home the "blessing way." To bless the pipes place your hands on them and say:

Thank you. May the water that flows through you bring blessings to this family.

If you are in an apartment and cannot get to the main pipes, then say the above blessing on the taps in your home.

CALL FORTH THE MAGIC OF THE SPIRIT OF WATER TO FILL YOUR HOME
Open a window or a door and ask that the Spirit of the Water enter your home. Even if it is not a rainy day there is almost always some moisture in the air.

6

THE ALCHEMY OF AIR

I sit absolutely still. The morning air is sharp and clear. The pungent smell of pine from the surrounding trees assails my nostrils. The first rays of morning sun explode in shards of light over the Cascade mountain range in the distance. As my breath becomes still and my mind quiets, I feel the coming presence of Spirit. In that exact same moment the wind chimes above my head begin to lightly tinkle with crystalline purity.

The air is always completely still in the morning when I sit to meditate on a garden bench outside our mountain cabin. Always, in the precise moment that I feel the rush of Spirit, the chimes begin to lightly shimmer with exquisite sound. In the stillness, I know that I am not alone. Great Spirit has soared down to touch me on the wings of the Spirit of the Air.

The life force in the air around us, seemingly subtle and unseen, is composed of the most rarefied energy fields. Air spirits swirl and dance with the most pristine etheric energies, filled with gossamer wings of sylphs and the sweet breath of angles. In this chapter you will learn how to "call" the Spirits of the Air into your life, as well as more practical techniques for cleaning the air in your home, so that it is more conducive to radiant health and joy.

Preparation

We are in constant communion with the air through our breath. To prepare for room clearing, using the element of air, it is valuable to first connect with the Spirit of the Air through conscious breathing. Using this technique, we can discover the universal Spirit of Air that links us to our entire planet. It is a common element which we share with all other living creatures and plants on earth. The air that you just inhaled was inhaled by your most distant ancestors and will be inhaled by your descendants. Without the sheltering blanket of air surrounding our beautiful planet, life as we have always known it would simply not be possible. We begin life outside the womb with a sharp and startling gasp that brings our first breath of air into our lungs, and we go on breathing until we are ready to leave our bodies on this plane.

The power of the Spirit of Air is change and transformation. It is the breath of life, inspiration and aspiration. It is the soothing cooling breeze on a sultry afternoon. Whereas water heals, cleanses and rejuvenates, air transforms. From a whispered breeze to a gentle whirlwind to a raging hurricane, air changes all that it encompasses. From great fields of grasses rippling like the sea, to shimmering aspen leaves with branches playfully dancing in the wind, to delicate seed pods lofted into the air by a sudden gust, air brings new perception and change.

Air is the realm of the eagle and the owl. It is freedom, perception, communication. In the element of Air, you see situations from a higher perspective. Calling forth the Air Spirit into your abode will help you find your wings so that you may fly high.

To connect with the Spirit of Air:

1. Sit still and quiet your mind.
2. Begin by feeling the air around you. Notice where it touches your face, surrounds your hands and envelops your entire body. If you are outside, or near an open window, feel the movement of air over your skin, in your hair. Is the touch so light it is imperceptible? Or is it stronger, colder, invigorating?
3. Be aware of the air that enters your lungs when you inhale. Become aware of inhaling the air that is immediately around you.
4. Expand your awareness so that you imagine you are inhal-

ing the vast expansive sky. With each breath expand your awareness until you imagine that you are inhaling and exhaling the heavens, the blue sky above you, the softness of clouds, the thrilling intensity of wind.

5. Continue until you feel that you have become the "air." You might even imagine that you are an eagle soaring in great powerful circles over mountains and valleys.

6. This Cosmic Breath will allow you to connect with and "call" the Spirit of the Air into your home.

7. Give thanks for the Spirit of the Air entering your home.

Purification

SPIRIT SMOKE

Smoke connects us to the Spirit of the Air and, throughout the ages, smoke has been used as a part of religious purification rituals in many cultures around the world. Ascending smoke forms a channel connecting us to Great Spirit. Our prayers rise on smoke to God, and the answers to these prayers travel back to us by the same path.

Outside a Buddhist temple there is usually an urn holding burning sticks of incense. Worshippers will stop for a moment to breathe in the smoke, or draw it to their body with cupped hands to purify themselves before entering the temple.

SMUDGING

A Native American traditional way of using smoke to purify a space is through the practice of smudging. Smudging is a ritual burning of herbs, using the smoke produced to alter energy for one's self or another, or to cleanse the energy of a specific space. Many herbs can be used for the smudging ritual cleansing. The most common ones include sage and sweetgrass, or cedar. But you can also use other herbs more easily obtained in your area.

Sage is used as a part of many Native American ceremonies because of its purification powers. In the Sun Dance Ceremony, the dancers wear wreathes of sage on their heads, and chew the leaves to alleviate their thirst. Sage is associated with purity, with things of the spirit and of the heavens.

Sweetgrass is another herb used almost universally among North American tribal peoples. Its fresh, clean smell, which is something like new-mown hay, is said to drive away negative thoughts and ill spirits. It is used in the sweat lodge, in healing ceremonies and in many kinds of purification and dedication ceremonies.

I come from the Cherokee tradition where cedar is often used during ceremonies. Cedar is also especially effective in dispelling negative energy. The evergreen needles of the cedar, rather than the bark, are used for smudging. When working with an herb that comes in a loose form, such as evergreen needles or tobacco, it is necessary to vary your smudging technique somewhat from that used with herbs which can be bound together into bundles (see page 75).

Obtaining herbs for smudging

Smudge sticks can be bought from stores specializing in natural foods, and from some alternative bookstores. It is nice to buy organic herbs whenever possible. It is also possible to grow, collect and dry your own. This has several advantages. For one thing, you can use herbs indigenous to your local area which can give you a feeling of connection to your own part of the earth. Also, your relationship with plants you have gathered or grown yourself will be personal and therefore much more intense, so that using them in purification rituals will be especially powerful.

When making your own herb bundles for smudging, it is essential to honor the plants at each step of the way—during growing, cutting and drying. Give thanks to the spirit of the plant for its give-away. In Native American tradition, the more you can give, the richer you are, and the more you will be loved and taken care of. It is important to recognize and respect the fact that the plant is sharing a part of itself with you when you are smudging.

When harvesting herbs, never take the whole plant. Always leave the plant enough foliage to go on and live out its life to completion. Bind the stalks and leaves tightly together with string, and hang them upside down in a cool, dry place until they are dry. Then they are ready for use in smudging.

How to smudge

LIGHTING THE HERBS To create smudge smoke, first light the bundle of herbs. When the herbs are ignited, blow the fire out and the bundle will continue to smoke. With your free hand, hold a fireproof bowl underneath the smoking herbs to catch any sparks.

A word of caution about smudging: herbs can continue to smolder for a long time even after they are apparently completely extinguished, so it is very important never to leave them unattended because of the risk of starting a fire in your home. When you have completed your smudge ceremony, tap the smoking herbs firmly in the bowl until the smoke has died out. Then place the herbs inside the bowl in the kitchen sink, just in case they are not completely out.

If you are working with loose herbs, such as evergreen needles or tobacco, you will want to place the herbs in a fireproof bowl which can be set on fireproof bricks. Then you build a little fire with them. (Dry herbs usually ignite easily.) After they are ignited, you can gently blow out the fire and leave the herbs smoldering within the bowl. However, the bowl is likely to remain extremely hot, and you could burn yourself if you tried to pick it up. So it is necessary to leave it on a heat-proof surface and draw the smoke toward you with your hands.

SMUDGING YOURSELF Before you perform a smudging ceremony to cleanse your home, smudge yourself to clear your thoughts, to cleanse the etheric energy of your aura and to provide a base of balance and groundedness. To do this, first light your herbs and offer the smoking herbs to the Four Directions, then to Grandmother Earth below, to Grandfather Sky above and to Great Spirit. Then cup your hands and bring the smoke in toward your body. Start with your eyes. Cup some smoke into your hands and move it over your closed eyes. As you do this, say, "That my eyes may see clearly." Then do the same thing for your head, and say, "That my thoughts might be clear." Move the smoke over the rest of your face and down your body, and over all your extremities. As you do this, dedicate the smoke to the effect that you want, symbolized by each part of the body that you are smudging. Lastly, bring the smoke in toward your chest, and say, "That my heart might be pure and open." This process will leave you in a focused, energized state where you are ready to channel energy into the space you wish to clear.

SMUDGING ANOTHER PERSON   There might be times when you will smudge another person helping you with your ceremony or you may want to smudge household members before they enter into their newly cleansed home. To do this, it is helpful to use a feather. Begin by offering the smoke to the Four Directions, the Earth and the Sky and Great Spirit. Hold the smoking herbs (in your non-dominant hand) and have the person that you are smudging close their eyes. Staying a few feet away, use gentle, short movements with the feather in your dominant hand to direct the smoke toward the person. You are bringing the Spirit of Air into their auric field as they are being purified by the smoke. Go down the front of their body, from their head to feet, with the smoke. Then repeat the procedure down their back, from head to foot.

After you have directed the smoke toward all areas of their body, place the smoking herbs in a safe place (e.g., the kitchen sink) and finish with broad sweeping gestures from head to toe with the feather. The short flicking movements of the feather took the smoke into their auric field and the long sweeping movement takes any etheric impurities and sweeps them down toward the earth where they are neutralized. If there is some place on the body that feels a little sticky or the feather seems to stick, you can spend a little extra time on that place.

Smudging is an intuitive art. Let your inner guide show you what to do and how you should do it. After you have finished the ritual, you can discharge the energy from the feather by touching it lightly to the ground, or by shaking it off.

Feathers for smudging

Feathers are a powerful connection to the world of spirit and deeply connect us to Air Spirit. Feathers are composed mostly of air. Inside the shaft of the feather is a hollow tunnel which runs throughout the length of the feather. When Native American chiefs or shamans wore headdresses of feathers, energy moved from their head through the hollow shafts of the feathers to Great Spirit. Feathers were a way to connect to Spirit. Many kinds of feathers are considered sacred to the

American Indian. In native tradition, wearing or holding a part of the animal connects you to the whole animal and its totem spirit. Birds were thought to fly closest to Great Spirit so they were thought to connect us to higher powers. It is possible to use either a single feather or a whole wing in the smudging process.

If you use feathers for room clearing please honor your feathers and the spirit of the bird from which they came. Keep them in an honored place, occasionally "feeding" them by giving them a pinch of cornmeal. You can do this by putting cornmeal on them and then shaking it off.

In the United States it is illegal to take any part of a wild bird, including abandoned nests and egg shells, without a permit from the Department of the Interior. There are particular regulations restricting possession of owl, hawk or eagle feathers to anyone but a few Native Americans. You may need to check the regulations in your country, or, in the States, apply for a permit through the U.S. Fish and Wildlife Service.

Each type of feather has its own particular energy, and you may want to consider what you are trying to achieve before selecting the type of feather you would like to use in smudging. Eagle feathers are very yang, very strong, and associated with masculine energy. You might want to use this energy for fortifying the productivity or safety of your space. Owl feathers, on the other hand, are associated with yin energy and the feminine principle. Crow and raven feathers are linked to the inner life and the secret ways. Pigeon feathers represent adaptation and survival. Sea gull feathers connect us to the majesty of the sea. All feathers can serve as messengers between men and women and the spirit world. They serve as direct links with that other realm.

Smudging a room

Begin by offering the smoke to the Four Directions, the Earth, the Sky and Great Spirit. Smudge yourself and any assistants. Wash your hands and any tools that you may be using (bells, drums, etc.) in the smoke. Then hold the smoking herbs in a deep fireproof pot in your non-dominant hand. Hold your feather in your dominant hand. Working clockwise starting at the easternmost corner, move the smoke around the perimeter of the room, using little flicks of your wrist with the feather. Make your movements clean and brisk. If you sense any sticky or stagnant areas in the room, feather the smoke rapidly into that area to break it up.

When you have completed smudging the circumference of the room, stand in the center of the room and ask the Spirit to purify and cleanse the room. Here is a smudging prayer:

Great Spirit, may my prayers travel up this smoke to you, that you may bring blessing and peace to this room and all who occupy it. I know that your blessings travel down through this smoke to us and we give thanks for blessings received.

INCENSE

A very simple way to enliven a room is to light a stick of incense while you are purifying it. The scent will permeate your space, not only filling it with a pleasant aroma, but also helping to clear the space. The scents you use are very important. The energy changes from one situation to another, so your needs for different smells change correspondingly. It is good to have at least several varieties on hand to accommodate your changing needs. As you light the incense, take a few seconds to say a prayer of dedication. I believe all prayers are heard.

SACRED BREATH

A potent tool that you can use wherever you are is your breath. You can "breathe a room" to cleanse and purify it with your breath. Your breath is holy and it is one of the most valuable tools available to you to purify your living space. To "breathe a room," first stand in the middle of the room and begin to expand your personal perimeter beyond your body. With each breath allow your awareness to expand until you feel as if you fill the room. Then begin to circle the room feeling for energy blockages with your hands and "blowing" anywhere you perceive that energy needs to be dispersed. As you walk, there may be places in the room where you can't seem to breathe as easily as in others. Blow until you can breathe easily in that location, and continue to walk around the room. Imagine that you are "being" the room and feel the room until the entire rooms breathes easily. This might sound like an unusual way to clear a room, but once you have experienced it, it is absolutely exhilarating.

Invocation

AROMATHERAPY

Who hasn't been instantly transported back to another time and place by a particular smell? The smell of bread baking, the smell of a fresh pot of coffee on the stove, the smell in the air after summer rain evoke associations for almost everyone. Our bodies react emotionally and powerfully to different smells. The smells in your home can contribute to or detract greatly from the way you feel about your home. And aromas can invoke the most pristine subtle energy fields of plants and flowers into your home.

Aromatherapy, essentially "therapy using aromas," can be traced back to over two thousand years ago when Hippocrates spoke of the benefits of aromatics in baths and in oils. Throughout history aromas have been used for therapeutic purposes. The Bible makes reference to healing with aromatic oils. In the Middle Ages aromatics were used to purify the air in times of plague.

In the 1920s, French chemist René Maurice Gattefosse severely burned his hand while conducting a laboratory experiment. He immediately put his hand into a jar of lavender oil that was close at hand. He was astonished to find that the pain immediately eased, and later he noticed that the oil seemed to speed the healing process. (Contemporary first-aid practice is always to plunge burned flesh into cold water, rather than apply oil.) Gattefosse, who became the founder of modern-day aromatherapy, then began to investigate the properties of essential oils (called thus because they embody the essence of the plant's qualities and odor). His research opened the door for the present-day interest in the rapidly expanding field.

More recently, Professor Arch Minchin at the University of Wisconsin discovered what lay people have always known, that smells can affect the way you feel emotionally and *can affect your energy level.* In his research, Minchin exposed individuals in controlled environments to different scents. He found that he could dramatically influence the way a person felt and alter their energy level *just by changing the scents they smelled*!

Recently, I walked into a room which my sixteen-year-old daughter had just left, and was overwhelmed by a cloud of lavender scent hanging in the air. When I asked her about this potent aroma, she said, "Mom, I put lavender essential oil on just before I take a test at school, because then I do better on the test. In fact, lots of the other kids at school put lavender on just before a test. It really does seem to affect our test results in a very positive way." Meadow and the kids at school didn't know that lavender has been used universally as a relaxant. They just knew that it seemed to increase their test results. Perhaps applying this relaxant just before a test helped them to feel less anxious and thereby increased their ability to concentrate.

I cannot stress enough the importance of smell. More than any of our other senses, smell affects our emotional reaction to people and situations. It has been shown that the way someone smells will provoke a stronger reaction in others than the way they look or sound *even if others are not consciously aware of the smell*! Our smell receptors are so sensitive that a single molecule of some substances is enough to excite one receptor ending; our olfactory system can sense less than one hundred millionth of a gram of musk.

Perhaps you have noticed that almost everyone's home has a characteristic smell. Although most people aren't aware of their own home's smell, a house's smell is an important part of the total personality and character of a home. The odors in your home can dramatically affect the way you and your family feel and the way that guests react to you when they enter. You can change the way people are feeling simply by adding (or subtracting with air purification) certain odors. Just by putting a small bowl of cedar chips, rose petals, or pine needles in a closet, for example, you can create an instant uplifting feeling whenever you enter that space.

There are a number of different ways that you can add scents to your home, thus invoking their corresponding energy fields. Here are several simple methods:

Vaporizers

Vaporization is an excellent means to permeate an entire room or even an entire area of your house with scent. There are several ways to vaporize. The most popular is the ceramic vaporizer which has a small bowl on top of the unit which is filled with water to which a few drops of scent have been added. A votive candle—which can last from four to eight hours—is placed in the cavity below. The heat from the candle warms the water which generates a pleasing yet gentle flow of scent to the surrounding area. These vaporizers also come equipped with small night lights in them to generate heat. These work just as effectively as the ones with candles. Special vaporizing ceramic rings or nonflammable rings that can be placed on lightbulbs within which a few drops of scent are added are also available. I don't usually recommend them as sometimes the oil will be scorched by the heat of the lightbulb, creating a harsh smell. However, some rings are better than others, so you may want to experiment.

In our mountain home we have a wood stove, and in the winter I keep a large pot of water simmering on the stove. This not only helps humidify the room, but also by adding several drops of essential oil to the water, usually pine or fir, a fresh wonderful mountain feeling is created. Even adding a few drops of essential oil to your bath can vaporize the scent into the air in addition to making your bathing more pleasant.

Diffusers

I use diffusers when I want to penetrate a large area of a house with smell. There are several ways to diffuse smell. You can use a spray bottle (the type used to mist plants) and add a very small amount of essential oil. You can have a number of these misters prepared with various essential oils. Then, as the need arises, you can mist the room with your prepared scent. I use these in my seminars with very good results. After a deep relaxation exercise I will spray the room with a scent such as lemongrass or rosemary, which are refreshing yet invigorating, to assist everyone in becoming more alert. At the beginning of a meditation I often spray the room with a mixture of lavender and sandalwood to aid relaxation.

In my home I often use electric diffusers. Although they have a humming sound that can be distracting they have the advantage of penetrating a large area very quickly, and without the concern of fire hazard from candles. Because of this they can be used when you are out. They work by a combination of a very fast vibration and a tiny blower which sends out a fine mist of aroma. Another kind of diffuser is a fan unit that blows air through a scent-soaked card, thus dispersing scent.

Additional scent-dispersing methods

There are numerous ways that you can contribute to a home that smells good and thus feels good. You might consider using scented candles, incense, nonaerosol spray perfumes, scented soap, scented flowers and baskets of *naturally* scented potpourri (from essential oils, not chemically produced scent). I also feel that it is worth mentioning that one essential oil I find highly effective for neutralizing animal odors is orange. For severe animal odor you might use an enzyme-neutralizing agent on the stain or odor.

Natural versus synthetic essential oils

In most commercially produced scents, both synthetic and natural components are used. However, when you want to contribute to the overall energy in your home I strongly suggest using natural essential oils, as many people report allergic reactions such as headaches, sore throats, or even nausea when they are exposed to synthetic aromas. Essential oils are a natural product created by the distillation of the essential qualities of the plant or herb. They are extracted by means of steam distillation. The plant oils distilled in this way are 70 percent stronger and more concentrated than the herb or plant of origin.

Essential oils will have not only a superior smell but, more important, they have the energy and the spiritual properties of the plant. They do not have the constancy of synthetic smells, as they vary according to location, climate and soil conditions, but they carry the power and the life force of the plant. Synthetic scents can never duplicate the Spirit of the Plant and it is this spirit that contributes to the overall energy in your home. Though synthetic scents are more economical and more stable they do not have the wondrous connection to the forest and meadow, to nature and the very alchemy of life itself that essential oils have.

Essential oils are often available at health-food stores. Make sure it says essential oil on the bottle and comes from a good supplier. Often less than scrupulous suppliers will dilute a pure essence in a carrier base of vegetable oil and sell it as a pure essential oil. (I have included the names and addresses of some good sources for essential oils in the Appendix.)

Here are some of the essential oils available, and their qualities:

Basil:	uplifting, clarifies thought processes
Bergamot:	uplifting, yet calming
Cedarwood:	relaxing, stress reducing
Camomile:	soothing and calming, excellent to use after an argument
Eucalyptus:	invigorating, cleansing, tonifying
Fennel:	relaxing, warming, calming
Fir Needle:	refreshing, cleansing
Frankincense:	calming, releasing fear
Geranium:	balancing mood swings, harmonizing
Juniper:	purifying, stimulating
Lavender:	calming, soothing, relaxing
Lemon:	uplifting, refreshing, mental alertness
Lemongrass:	stimulating, cleansing, tonifying
Lime:	invigorating, refreshing
Mandarin Orange:	uplifting, refreshing
Marjoram:	very relaxing, anxiety reducing
Myrrh:	strengthening, inspiring
Neroli:	stress reducing, calming
Orange:	uplifting, refreshing
Patchouli:	inspiring, sensuous
Pine:	refreshing, cleansing, stimulating
Peppermint:	stimulating, cleansing, refreshing, invigorating
Rose:	emotionally soothing
Rosemary:	stimulating, cleansing, good for studying, invigorating
Sage:	cleansing, purifying
Sandalwood:	stress reducing, sensuous, soothing, helps release fear
Spearmint:	refreshing, stimulating

Tea Tree:	disinfecting, stimulating, very powerful—use sparingly!
Thyme:	stimulating, strengthening, activating
Vetiver:	relaxing, regenerating
Ylang Ylang:	soothing, sensuous

Here are some suggested combinations for different rooms in your house:

Bedroom:	Lavender, Rose Geranium and Ylang Ylang
Children's bedroom:	very dilute Lavender and Orange
Study room:	Rosemary, Peppermint, Basil and Bergamot
Workroom:	Eucalyptus, Peppermint and Rosemary
Living room:	Orange, Mandarin and Bergamot or Pine and Juniper
Kitchen:	Lemon and Grapefruit
Dining room:	Lemon, Grapefruit and Mandarin Orange (but not during mealtimes)
Bathroom:	Peppermint and Pine or Rose and Ylang Ylang
Meditation room:	Sandalwood and Frankincense

Smell is very personal. We all have very strong associations attached to smell. For example, most people enjoy the smell of lavender and find it very relaxing. But I once met a man who felt upset every time he smelled lavender. It turned out that as a child he had been smelling the lavender at his grandmother's house when a bee had stung him on the nose! It's important to use your own intuition when it comes to smell, rather than always following a prescribed formula.

One of my joys in life is to be a bit of an alchemist with scents. I have a large range of essential oils and I'll mix and match scents until I've made a combination that suits my mood. Usually I will use smells that feel stimulating to me, such as grapefruit, lemon, peppermint during the day and scents that feel more relaxing such as lavender and sandalwood in the evening when I'm in a quieter mood. If someone has been ill in a room I'll use eucalyptus, rosemary or juniper to cleanse the room.

Here are a few suggested formulas, but remember to use your own intuition with scent:

Meditation room:	Sandalwood four drops, Frankincense one drop
Bedroom:	Lavender four drops, Neroli one drop, Mandarin Orange one drop
Living room:	Orange four drops, Bergamot two drops, Frankincense one drop

I'm often asked if vaporizers should be used at the same time as air purifiers. I suggest that you use them separately, as a good air purification system will eliminate the aromas of your vaporizer.

Preservation

CLEAN AIR

When the air in your home is clean you create a conducive environment for air spirits to fill your home with their life-giving properties. It is so easy to forget that the air around us has an affect on the way we feel. We can't see it or touch it, and unless there is an unpleasant odor in a room we usually don't ever think about the air around us. However, the air that you breathe can make a dramatic difference in the way that you feel, and the air around you can dramatically affect your auric field.

Many people who are meticulous about the food they eat and the water they drink don't give a second thought to the air they breathe. We are like fish that don't recognize their environment of water until they are taken out of it. Air is so much a part of our "ground of being" that we often don't even recognize that we are immersed in an ocean of air. The quality of the air in your house has a powerful effect not only on your health but on the overall energy in your home.

Air has substance and weight. In fact, air exerts a pressure of 14.7 pounds on every square inch of your body. That means a section of your body that is only three inches long by three inches wide has 132 pounds of pressure on it! Our bodies are designed to breathe about 2,500 gallons of air every day. Not only does this air contain life-sustaining oxygen but it also contains essential "prana" or life-force energy. Prana is one of the reasons why yogis emphasize the importance of breathing, because breath is a way to access and absorb the life force that is around us. However, our air has become so polluted that it is becoming increasingly difficult to absorb clean oxygen and prana from the air around us.

Even country air isn't pure. One study was done high on mountain-tops far away from the pollution of cities. Snow was gathered from these mountaintops and the snow was melted to examine it for evidence of pollution. Amazingly, lead and foreign matter such as automobile exhaust materials were found.[1] This means that there are very few places in the world where you can breathe pure, sweet air.

Not only can city fumes pollute the air you breathe, but the living spaces in your life can contain airborne contaminates, too. These may include: formaldehyde and other aldehyde vapors from plywood, particle board and even older foam-padded furniture; radon gas from concrete, bricks and the ground; stove emissions such as carbon monoxide and nitrogen dioxide; tobacco smoke which has numerous pollutants.

The air you breathe is being stripped of life by these pollutants. And the pollutants are also stripping the air of a natural healing component: the ion.

The ion effect

Air, like all matter, is made up of molecules. Each individual molecule has a nucleus of positively-charged protons surrounded by negatively-charged electrons. Nature is always seeking a balance of electrons and protons. The continual interplay between the two opposing yet harmonious forces in the universe, signified by yin and yang, occurs even on a molecular level.

The (negative) electron is 1,800 times lighter than the (positive) proton and it becomes easily displaced by pollution. When this unbalance occurs, a positive ion is created. (This is one case when positive doesn't necessarily mean good!) Positive ions are abundant in polluted air and are created by friction, which tends to dislocate negative ions.

The balance of ions is so important that without them we wouldn't survive. In Russia, a group of scientists tried to raise small animals such as mice, rabbits and guinea pigs in air that contained no ions, and the animals all died in a few days.[2]

Scientists from many countries have proved that it is damaging to human physical and emotional well-being when the natural ion balance is upset. Over 700 scientific documents resulting from research done around the world have concluded that an oversupply of positive ions is harmful, while a surplus of negative ions is beneficial.[3]

Researchers in Israel exposed bacteria including staphylococci, streptococci and candida to a negative-ion environment. "Germ counts were dramatically reduced by 50 percent within six hours and 70 percent within twenty-four hours, suggesting that negative ionization is a way of controlling disease."[4]

A study by Dr. Kornblueh in the United States showed that when hundreds of hay fever and asthma patients were put in a negative-ion environment, 63 percent experienced total or partial relief. Dr Kornblueh stated, "They come in sneezing, eyes watering, noses itching, worn out from lack of sleep and so miserable they can hardly walk. Fifteen minutes in front of a negative-ion machine and they feel so much better they don't want to leave." Their relief would last for approximately two hours after their return to un-ionized environments.[5]

A study in Russia researching the effects of a negative-ion environment on the physical performance of men showed remarkable results. After being exposed to a negative-ion environment for only fifteen minutes a day for twenty-five days, the men showed significant improvements in their overall state of health, and in their appetites and sleep. After only nine days, their work capacity had increased by 50 percent. After the twenty-fifth day they showed an 87 percent increase in productivity![6]

Ionizers have been used with positive results on burn victims to speed up healing by reducing the rate of wound infection.[7] It has been suggested that this is because ionizers help increase the decay rate of bacteria such as staphylococci and airborne bacteria that spread common respiratory diseases.

In yet another research study in Israel, electroencephalogram readings indicated that brain-wave activities were altered by being in a negative-ion-rich environment. The research subjects reported that after treatment they felt an initial relaxation followed by increased alertness. Researchers made a connection between these reported feelings and the shifting of alpha waves from the occipital to the frontal area of the brain, which occurred while subjects were being exposed to negative ions.[8]

Some common physical effects of being in a positive-ion environment are:

- Feeling extraordinarily tired and sleepy
- Having trouble getting up in the morning
- Waking up feeling heavy and foggy-headed
- Starting yawning by midday and feeling the need for a nap
- Depression
- Feeling tense and irritable
- Frequent headaches, hay fever, allergies
- Feeling as if it is an effort to breathe

Sometimes nature produces positive-ion conditions and this has a debilitating effect on people. These positive-ion winds are known by different names the world over, but they all spell trouble. They are called the Santa Ana winds in California, the Chinook winds in Canada, the Foehn in Germany, the Mistral in France and the Sharav in Israel. Most people are affected negatively by these positive-ion winds. They will suffer headaches, tiredness, swelling of the extremities, nausea and may even become violent. In a positive-ion wind one's biochemistry is affected. Serotonin levels increase, which causes irritability and tension.

Negative-ion environments occur in nature by the sea, in pine forests, by waterfalls and from lightning storms. You only need stand by a waterfall to notice the difference that negative ions can make in the way that you feel. A negative-ion environment will tend to make you feel relaxed, yet exhilarated. Some might explain this phenomenon by saying that you simply feel uplifted due to the inherent majesty and beauty of the sea, a pine forest, or a tremendous storm. But since falling water and the tips of pine needles are excellent generators of negative ions, some of the exhilaration you feel comes as a result of the beneficial ion content of the air.

To get some idea of the ion saturation in nature as compared with industrial areas here are some comparative charts.

NATURE'S ION GENERATORS	IONS PER CUBIC CENTIMETER
Lightning	100,000,000
Fire	100,000
Waterfalls	25,000
Ocean surf	5,000
Mountain forests	4,000
Country	1,000–2,000[9]

LOCATIONS	IONS PER CUBIC CENTIMETER
City—outdoors	0–500
Home or office	250–500
(without smoking, air conditioning and heating)	
Home or office	0–200
(with smoking, air conditioning or heating)[10]	

A way to create a negative-ion-rich environment in your home is to invest in an ionizer (see Appendix). Get a machine from a reputable company. Poor-quality models will have emitter needles that are not stainless steel or nickel-plated steel, but made instead of some alloy that corrodes with time, so that after a few months your machine will not be emitting any negative ions. Many ionizers will deposit the pollutants that are being neutralized on the surrounding walls or floors so you will have to clean these surfaces periodically. I feel that it is better to have that dirt on your walls than in your lungs.

A number of years ago I sent my grandparents an ionizer. Several months later I had an opportunity to visit them at their home in Los Angeles. When I arrived my grandmother was a bit upset. She said, "I want to show you something, Denise." She took me into the room where they had placed the ionizer and I was astonished to see that the wall near the machine was nearly black. It was almost impossible to ascertain that the original wall color had been a shell pink.

In my own home in the northwestern part of the United States, where pollution levels are relatively low, I had been using ionizers without any noticeable "shadow" on the walls. However, in a few months in Los Angeles, where the pollution levels are legendary, my grandmother was confronted with blackened walls. It was solid evidence that the ionizer was working.

The reason that walls become dirty when an ionizer is used is that dust and pollution particles (which are positively charged) attract negative ions, which transfer their negative charge to the dust particles. The dust then has a negative charge and it attracts more positively charged dust to itself, until it becomes too heavy to stay airborne and falls to the floor. As walls have a slightly positive charge they will also attract the negatively-charged dust. Ionizers can literally "electro-plate" airborne dirt onto walls.

To avoid darkened walls, I suggest you put your ionizer in the middle of a room, rather than next to a wall, so you can vacuum away the neutralized contaminants as they collect on the floor around the ionizer. In a polluted area there may still be a "shadow" on the wall, even if you put the ionizers in the middle of the room.

There are several natural ways that you can generate negative ions in your home (though not to the volume that you can with a negative-ion generator). Ferns are excellent generators of negative ions. I used to keep numerous ferns in the room that I used for giving healing treatments, because I found that a client's emotional releases could literally change the ion balance in a room. You may have heard the expression "the air was charged" after an argument. People literally do give off a positive-ion "charge" during healing releases or during intense emotions. I found that the ferns in the room helped create a balance by neutralizing some of the positive ions in the room. I always gave special thanks to those ferns for their giveaway, for if many people were going through healing crises the ferns would wither and have to be replaced. Also misting a room with water will generate a negative-ion environment.

Ozone generators for air purification

Ozone is a highly unstable form of oxygen with three atoms per molecule rather than the usual two. It is created when an electrical charge divides the oxygen molecules into separate atoms. Oxygen atoms that combine into groups of three (O_3) become ozone. Pure oxygen (two atoms—O_2) doesn't like having a third atom, so it is always trying to get rid of it.

Ozone is concentrated in the atmosphere above the surface of the earth. It is one of the major reasons why life is possible on our planet, as it forms a protective layer between the earth and the sun. Ozone can be generated naturally by lightning, in waterfalls, or even by the sun reflecting on a field of snow. It can also be machine-generated for use in water and air purification. Ozone is one of the most powerful sterilizing agents in the world. It can break down the molecular structure of noxious and toxic gases, as well as bacterial and organic matter. It can be better than a standard air-purification-filter system in some instances because it neutralizes odors, bacteria and gases that are molecular in size and therefore not removed by most air-filter devices.

As mentioned above, lightning is one of the ways that ozone is created naturally, and a good-quality ozone air-purification system creates ozone in a way similar to lightning. Lightning is unpolarized. This means that it is either always positive or always negative. It does not alternate. The electrical current cycle in the United States is alternating, meaning that it switches back and forth from positive to negative at a rate of sixty times per second. (The rate in Europe and most other places in the world is fifty times per second.)

Though ozone generators are still somewhat controversial, scientists agree that ozone substantially neutralizes some chemical pollutants in the air. The extra oxygen molecules interface with toxic gases and neutralize them. Bacteria, mold, mildew and fungus are also effectively eliminated when they come into contact with ozone.

Ozone generators also neutralize odors very effectively and are used for this purpose in fish-processing plants, theaters, pet stores, bars, garages and hospitals. Sometimes when people keep animals as pets, the house can smell more like a barn than a home. Turning on an ozone generator for just a short while in an offending room causes the animal smell to be completely eliminated. Also, kitchen odors such as fish or smoke from a burned pan can be effectively removed in this way.

I use an ozone generator in the bedroom. I usually only use it during the day as it emits a slight hum. However, it is wonderful to enter the bedroom because the entire room smells and feels clean and pure.

Other air-purification systems

A less expensive way to clean the air in your home is to obtain an air-filtration system. These machines will take air in and purify it by blowing it back out through a filter. The most effective filter systems are called HEPA filters and these are used by hospitals to remove airborne pollutants. Another way to contribute to clean air is frequently to replace the filters in your heating and/or air conditioning systems.

All three types of air-purifying machines can fit easily into the home and are not usually any larger than a bread bin.

	ADVANTAGES	DISADVANTAGES
Ionizers	Neutralize airborne pollutants, create an electrical charge in the room that is emotionally uplifting, some models are completely quiet	Difficult to clean walls and surfaces, don't neutralize toxic gases
Ozone generators	Neutralize toxic gases, eliminate odors, kill bacteria and mold	Slightly noisy, don't affect airborne dust or particles, low-quality models could contribute to photochemical smog
Heating filters, free-standing filter units	Filter airborne particles and some bacteria (only larger organisms), often less expensive than the alternatives	Don't affect toxic gases, can sometimes be a breeding ground for mold if filters are not changed periodically; free-standing units are noisy

CALLING THE SPIRIT OF AIR INTO YOUR HOME

To draw the Spirit of Air into your home:

CLEAN THE DENSER ENERGIES IN THE AIR   Use air purification systems to remove toxic gases, pollutants, bacteria and mold.

CLEAN THE MORE SUBTLE ETHERIC ENERGIES IN THE AIR   Use essential-oil vaporizers or diffusers to infuse the air with the etheric spirit of flowers and herbs.

CALL FORTH THE MAGIC OF THE SPIRIT OF AIR TO FILL YOUR HOME   Open a window or a door and ask the Spirits of the Air to enter. When the Air Spirits arrive, even if it is a still day, you can feel an almost tangible breeze as they sail into your home. Also placing windsocks, weather vanes, windmills or wind chimes around the outside of your home or out of a window will attract Air Spirits. The sylphs and spirits of the air enjoy these whimsical things and will communicate with you through them.

7

HEALING EARTH

*"Mother, I feel your heart beat. Mother, I feel you under my feet,"
the chant begins slowly. Families gathered together to honor Mother
Earth, sitting on sweet summer grass in the meadow, begin
chanting softly and slowly. One by one they begin to stand and
sway as the chant builds. "Mother, I feel your heart beat. Mother, I
feel you under my feet." Almost in unison, the chanting stops and
silence spreads across the meadow. Then, as if Mother Earth
sighed in response, a deep ripple of resonating energy from the
earth surges through each person. Tears are shed, old locked spaces
of the heart opened, tattered dreams become new once again, and
murmurs of thanksgiving are heard everywhere. "She is alive! She
heard us!"*

*The golden orb of the sun slowly dips beyond the western edge of
the horizon. Sleepy children are picked up by strong arms.
Sandaled feet head toward home. The day comes to a close, but
in the hearts of those who were there it will not be forgotten for a
long time.*

Of all four elements none has been as revered as the earth. The
earliest cultures honored the earth, which was worshipped as
a living conscious Being who oversaw life in all its phases. Ancient
cultures that lived close to the earth considered Mother Earth to be a
living, fecund provider for all of the earth's inhabitants. There was a

sense of a deep-rooted partnership with the earth. The ancient sensibility was one of living *with* the earth instead of merely on it. The fifteenth-century alchemist Basilius Valentinus said, "The earth is not a dead body, but is inhabited by a spirit that is its life and soul. All created things, minerals included, draw their strength from the Earth Spirit. This spirit is life, it is nourished by the stars, and it gives nourishment to all living things that it shelters in its womb."

The belief in a living earth almost disappeared in modern society. The dismay at the disappearance of the concept of the living earth was passionately expressed at the end of the nineteenth century by Smohalia, a Sioux Indian holy man. He said,

> You ask me to dig in the earth? Am I to take a knife and plunge it into the breast of my mother? But then when I die she will not gather me again into her bosom . . . Then I can never enter her body and be born again. You ask me to cut the grass and the corn and sell them to get rich like the white men. But how dare I crop the hair of my mother?

Perhaps, however, deep in the psyche of all people is a feeling of a mystical unity with the earth. Perhaps deep within each of us is an inner certainty that human life springs forth from the earth, because once again people are beginning to gravitate toward this ancient outlook. Present proponents adhere to what is being called the Gaia theory, after the Greek deity who embodies the Mother Goddess of the Earth. Those adhering to this belief remember that we are never far from the earth, what we do to the earth we do to ourselves. As we honor the earth we are honored.

Elementally the earth is grounding and strengthening. The Earth Spirit brings stability, ancient wisdom and power. From her magnificent mountains to her gentle rolling hills to her sweet meadows the earth brings healing, and power. Calling the Earth Element into your home will generate an energy that is serene and stabile. Your home will become a fortress in times of change. Anyone who enters your home will subconsciously be affected by the earth's energy and will leave your home feeling more grounded and certain of their direction in life. When Mother Earth resides in your home, even those who pass in proximity to your home will be affected and feel more inner strength.

Preparation

To connect with the Spirit of Earth:

1. Sit still and quiet your mind.
2. Hold some earth in your hands. Every piece of earth is imbued with the essence of Mother Earth. Feel the living spirit within the earth.
3. Allow your consciousness to sink into the earth beneath you. (Even if you are high up in an apartment, feel the earth that resides beneath you.)
4. Expand your awareness to fill all of our entire beautiful Mother Earth. Feel her strength and power embrace you and emanate from you.
5. Visualize the Spirit of Earth filling you. Let the power and beauty of the great mountain peaks of the earth fill you. Feel and find the part of you that dwells in the understanding of earth, and your clearing ceremonies will be grounded and healing.
6. Give thanks to the Spirit of Earth for entering you and your home.

PREPARATION FOR ROOM CLEARING
USING SALT—THE POWER OF EARTH

Salt is one of the greatest gifts that the earth has given her children. It has the ability to neutralize negativity and cleanse your aura. An excellent preparation before a room clearing is to take a saltwater bath. Not only will the saltwater cleanse you but it will actually increase your ability to channel energy during your house clearing. Salt added to water increases conductivity of electricity through the water. When we soak in a salt bath our skin, which is a semipermeable membrane, is affected by this salt-rich soaking solution. The salt in the bath interacts with the bio-electricity in our nervous system. I believe that taking a salt bath increases our ability to become transmitters of electrical force fields around us. It increases the etheric ability of our neuro-transmitters and increases etheric bio-chemical transmission across the synapses, which are the gaps between communicating nerves. This creates a greater flow of energy through the meridian system of the body, the system of energy vessels which is the basis for acupuncture.

To take a salt bath, for grounding and for auric cleansing, take two pounds of salt or one pound of salt and one pound of baking soda, dissolve them in your bath, and soak for half an hour. While you are doing this, relax completely, and visualize yourself dissolving into the salt. Imagine that the salt is cleansing every part of your body and every part of your being.

The salt residue left on your skin after this bath can make you feel as if you've just had a swim in the ocean—which is not always unpleasant. But if you want to, it is all right to take a shower afterwards. This will not diminish the effects of the cleansing ritual.

To open your ability to channel energy, take another type of salt bath. Dissolve a pound of Epsom salts in water and soak for ten minutes. *After the Epsom salt bath, rinse in very cold water.* Epsom baths are good to take before a house cleansing when you will be channeling substantial energy through your body.

Purification

The most powerful thing that you can use for home purification comes from the earth. Originating from deep in her womb, crystalline salt is one of the great healers and purifiers of the planet. If there was only one thing that I could use for space clearing, it would be *salt*.

Salt is a valuable resource that has been prized by ancient people who knew of its amazing healing powers for thousands of years. Salt has been known to the inhabitants of our planet from the dawn of time for its great uses as a medicine, a preservative, and as a link to the spirit world. In ancient times salt was considered so valuable that it was traded ounce for ounce with gold, and in early China salt cakes were even used as currency.

Throughout the centuries the value of salt has been evident in many aspects of language and culture. It is reported that Cabalistic tradition considers salt a sacred word because its numerical value is the same as God's name of power, YAHWEH, multiplied three times.

In ancient times, salt was thought to be a substitute for the Mother Goddess's regenerative blood. In both the Jewish and Christian religions, salt was considered a substitute for blood on the altar as it came from the womb of the sea and had the savor of blood.

Because they considered it to be the "Salt Blood of Spirit," the Roman marriage ceremony traditionally included the bride and groom sharing a cake of flour and salt. The flour symbolized flesh and the salt symbolized blood, and this ritual was performed to create a flesh-and-blood bond between the couple, so that they magically became blood kin. The superstition which some cultures have about spilling salt grew out of this connection between blood and salt—when you spilled salt, you had spilled blood.

The Bible speaks of a "covenant of salt" (Numbers 18:19), which is a covenant as binding as blood that can never be broken. Arabs would share bread and salt to create a binding covenant. Semitic visionaries talked of the "salt of the earth" to mean the true blood of the Earth Mother. Christians used the same term to suggest true prophecy. Even in the present day when we want to say that someone is truly trustworthy, we say they are "the salt of the earth." Salt is associated in this way with wisdom, stability and strength.

SALT AS A NATURAL PURIFIER

Salt has remarkable purifying properties. In the ocean it acts as an antiseptic to destroy bacteria. Even though the sea is subjected to the same destructive pollution as the land, salt water rejuvenates itself more quickly. The salt in the ocean is able to neutralize and destroy some of the biological pollution which plagues our planet's coastlines. The ocean is a totally self-cleaning environment, and this can be attributed to the salt in the water.

Salt has traditionally been used in rituals for cleansing and purification of negative energy in many cultures. Church bells were anointed with salt and water to bless and christen them while God was implored to disperse demons through the power of the bell's sound. During baptism an infant was rubbed with salt to repel demons.

The Christian prolific use of salt was thought to have been an imitation of the Romans who used salt to dispel negativity. The tossing of salt over the left shoulder to avert bad luck is an ancient custom. In past times salt was a precious commodity, so why toss away this precious ingredient? It was believed that "evil" was associated with our left side and goodness with our right side. When salt was thrown over the left shoulder it immobilized the evil spirits that were waiting for an opportunity to cause mischief. Whether or not this is true is less important than the fact that salt was known to be a prime element for neutralizing negativity.

In almost every native culture where I have spent time and trained, salt has been used for purification. During my training with a Hawaiian kahuna in the early 1970s, one of the basic skills I learned was the art of space-clearing using salt. In fact, every space-clearing tradition I have studied has included the use of salt.

The power of salt is derived in part from its crystalline structure. Right now we are entering into a period of time where there is an increased number and variety of etheric energies coming into our planet. The use of crystals has proliferated in recent years because they are useful for channelling and realigning with these new energies.

Salt is the most available of all crystals, and its crystalline properties can help us to channel energy within ourselves and within our home environment. Salt is useful not only for realignment of the new energies, but it also serves as a conductor of etheric bio-electrical energy. It increases the flow of etheric energy through us and through our homes.

In performing purification for your own home, it is best to obtain natural salt—either sea salt or rock salt which has not been iodized. Which one you choose will depend on the ends you wish to achieve through your use of the techniques. The use of sea salt will call forth the powers of the sea, which are especially conducive to cleansing and emotional healing. Rock salt, on the other hand, is associated with the powers of the earth, and is very useful for achieving a sense of balance and groundedness. However, these differences are subtle, so that use of either will have a similar effect overall.

SALT PURIFICATION FOR YOUR HOME

Put the salt in a bowl and hold it while you ask for the blessing of the Spirit of Earth to fill your salt. Enter the room that you are going to clear and go into the easternmost corner. Toss a pinch of salt into that corner and say:

> *Sacred Salt, Salt of Earth and Sea,*
> *Clear this Room that We may be Free.*

Or you can say whatever prayer best suits the private needs of your own soul. Let your heart lead you in your choice of prayers.

After you have completed tossing salt in the four corners of the room, move to the center of the room and begin moving outward in a clockwise spiral. Any place where the energy feels sticky or heavy or cold or blocked, sprinkle a little extra salt. Use your intuition to determine where these areas are. Just open your heart and your emotions to whatever information seems to be coming from the room. When you have finished say:

> *Mother Earth beneath us all*
> *Hear us now, answer our call.*
> *Enter this home, this sacred place*
> *Heal all who live within this space.*

Most of the salt you use can be vacuumed up after your ceremony. However, leave a bit of salt in the corners.

Creating a vortex with salt

A quick and effective cleansing can be achieved through a ritual which creates a vortex of energy in the center of the room. For this technique you will need to use salt of a powdery-fine texture. To create this, use a mortar and pestle to grind your salt into very fine crystals. Then stand in the middle of the room and toss salt around your room using wide sweeping motions of your arms. Work in a clockwise direction. This very fine salt will cleanse the air as well as all the hidden spaces in the room.

Salt in the bedroom

If ever there is a time when you feel you are being thrown off balance by outside influences in your life, when you feel you are being negatively influenced by the thoughts or feelings of others, or if you are being troubled by bad dreams, you can use salt in your bedroom to counteract these influences. This method will help you establish your own energy field without interference from others.

Take salt and make a large ring that goes around the periphery of your room, including the corners. Then make a smaller circle of salt right around your bed. It is not necessary to use a large amount of salt to do this. Just sprinkling a fine, small trickle will be effective for creating a protective ring around you in the night while you are sleeping. This method is especially effective because in your sleep you are in a highly suggestive and vulnerable state.

During your night hours, you will be protected from the feelings and thought-forms of others. Sleeping inside the salt circle, your mind will be free to process information in a balanced and grounded way, and to clear out all negative energy accumulated during the day. Your night time will thus be a time of rest and refreshment, and your salt circle will help you wake up feeling safe and full of energy.

Invocation

The earth has given us one of the most powerful tools available for use in energizing and invoking energy into our homes. This offering from Mother Earth is known as clear quartz crystal. This magnificent tool comes from the depths of Mother Earth herself.

Clear quartz crystal is composed of silicon dioxide which, like salt, is one of the earth's most common and plentiful mineral compounds. Silicon dioxide shows itself in our modern electrical technologies as the basic component within computer systems. Silicon dioxide is used as one of the most basic components in the field of computer technology because of its capability of transferring electrical impulses which then become internal communications within a computer. In addition to its ability to act as a transmitter of electrical impulses, quartz has a remarkable ability to vibrate, and to emanate all the color frequencies of the full spectrum of light. Quartz crystals can act as generators and activators of energy.

Crystals have been found and used all over the world in many ancient cultures with an esoteric tradition. In my own tribe, the Cherokee, crystals have been used both for prophesying and for tuning in to the inner dimensions. Crystals were used by many other Native American tribes as well, including the Apache and the Hopi.

When you place a crystal in your home, it has the ability to radiate your intention through it. Although crystals or any stone are not magical in and of themselves, they do act as catalysts for human consciousness. They possess the ability to distill, transform and transmit your intention.

Everything in your home (as well as all life) maintains a particular vibration or frequency. Objects lose their vital force when their optimum frequency lowers. When you place a quartz crystal in a room it can act as a generator to protect energy frequencies that can be absorbed by your home and the objects in your home. Thus the crystal helps things in your home maintain their optimum frequency. A disadvantage with clear quartz crystal is that it does need to be cleansed periodically for it to maintain its transmitting qualities.

Regularly cleansing your clear quartz will keep it vitalized. Without this, it will eventually lose its vibrancy. You need not have a set schedule for cleaning your crystals. Do it when they seem to have lost their "sparkle." You might only need to do this every few months, or if you are in a time of transition you may need to cleanse your crystals every week or so. Definitely cleanse them at the time of your annual spring cleaning and reset or reprogram them at that time.

Place your crystal upon a piece of silk and position it in the light of the sun. Leave it in this location for three to four hours. This method utilizes the healing and sterilizing power of the sun for cleansing and revitalizing your crystal.

You can also clean your crystal with salt and water. Mix together a solution which combines at least one cup of water and half a cup of salt. Bury a bit of your crystal in the salt and let your crystal soak in the solution for at least twenty-four hours. This method is grounding as well as cleansing for your crystal.

Another way of cleaning your crystal is with eucalyptus oil. Take your crystal in hand and rub the eucalyptus oil all over the entire surface. When you apply the oil, do so from the base (this being the bottom or flat surface) to the facet (the top or apex of the crystal where all sides come together). This is a good technique to use if there is no sun for cleansing or you don't have time to wait twenty-four hours for the salt method. The purifying effects of eucalyptus in combination with the stroking movement over the crystal reset your crystal as well as cleansing it.

PROGRAMMING YOUR HOUSE CRYSTAL

To program your crystal to be a house energy generator, begin by putting the cleansed crystal up to your third eye (this is one of the body's major energy centers). If you are dedicating the crystal to the protection and safety of your home you might say:

> *I dedicate you to the safety and protection of this home.*
> *I give thanks for your assistance.*

You might consider dedicating your crystal to spiritual growth for members of the household, abundance and prosperity, love and good relationships, or communication and truth. You can place one crystal in each room in your home, dedicating each crystal to a particular purpose within the room. For example, you might dedicate the kitchen crystal to strength and nourishment for the family. Alternatively, you can have a central house crystal with an overall dedication for the whole home.

You can either have your house crystal out on display or keep it hidden. Do what feels best to you. However, if you have many visitors I suggest keeping it out of view, because crystals are vulnerable to the energy fields around them.

Other stones from the mineral world invoke energy into your home. These stones can be displayed around your home as needed, or they can be tucked away in corners where, even though they may be unseen, they are still emanating their particular qualities.

Linghams

This is my particular favorite stone for the home. Although the legends vary about where this river-tumbled stone originated, the most common theory is that the lingham came from a meteor shower many centuries ago that fell into a particular river in India. What *is* known about them is that their mineral content is quite unusual for the earth and may indeed be from some distant star. The exact truth about their origins may be less important than the strength and vibrancy of these stones. (They are revered in India and in Tibet, where they are used under the lamasery dais.) Whereas a crystal is fluid and light like water, a lingham is solid and grounded like the earth.

Linghams do not need to be cleared often like the crystal. However, they do enjoy being honored periodically. Traditionally they are anointed with sandalwood oil and have flowers laid at their base as they are usually displayed in an upright position. A lingham can be kept on display because its solid grounding nature is not easily affected by the energy fields of others. A lingham in your home brings incredible strength and groundedness; it is very yang. It is good for a home where the occupants are very ethereal but have trouble feeling grounded. It is also a very ferocious protector and will maintain the integrity of your home's energy field, so that it isn't easily affected by outside sources.

Here, briefly, are some of the stones you can use in your home for energizing and invoking life force into your living space. If you would like to do more in-depth study about stones, I have suggested an excellent sourcebook, which is listed in the Appendix.

Agate:	stabilizing and balancing: red agate energizes; blue agate calms
Amber:	excellent for absorbing negativity
Amethyst:	invokes feminine spiritual energy, calming and soothing
Aquamarine:	soothing, calming, Atlantean
Aventurine:	healing, eases breathing
Bloodstone:	detoxifying, healing and strengthening
Carnelian:	focuses and motivates, confidence and action
Citrine:	clears thoughts, confidence, communication, decision-making
Coral:	physical strength and determination
Fluorspar:	creativity and spiritual awareness
Garnet:	activates passion and life force
Jade:	healing, soothing, abundance
Lapis Lazuli:	spiritual awakening
Malachite:	calming, wisdom, peace
Rose Quartz:	love, children, family, creativity
Sugalite:	inner vision, meditation

Smoky Quartz:	abundance, wisdom, good choice for house crystal
Tiger's Eye:	grounding, focusing
Tourmaline:	grounding, neutralizes negativity, psychic protection, purifying
Turquoise:	spirit, strength, success, fulfilment, protection
Moonstone:	feminine, ethereal, love
Pearl:	love, feminine, moon, water
Sodalite:	spiritual awakening

Gemstones are the life of light captured in a pure, visible form. This form covers many colors within the complete color spectrum. Each color maintains a specific vibrational pattern which corresponds to a certain energy and solicits a specific emotional response. They can be placed in bowls in a room or planted in indoor plant soil or planted outdoors around your home. Wherever stones are they bring with them a wonderful variety of vibrational energy from the earth.

Worth mentioning are stones gathered from special locations. For example, if you are in a beautiful place in nature and find a lovely smoothed river stone, this stone will carry the "energy of the river and the trees and sky." In this way you can bring the vibration of a beautiful place in nature into your home.

In purchasing or obtaining a stone, be aware of the energy of the particular stone. If it was ripped from the earth and was not honored in its journey to you, it might not carry the beauty of a "happy stone." For this reason most of my stones are ordinary stones rather than gemstones, but they are essentially "happy stones" and invoke happy energy into my home.

Preservation

GUARDIAN TREES

When I was a child I had a tree that was my special friend. As I was growing up there were many times when I felt the need for a friend, for my home life was very troubled and traumatic. When the pain became too much I would run down the road to the river. Along the riverbank grew a tall magnificent tree with low branches that hung precariously far out over the rich brown, rapid river. The minute my hands touched the rough bark I would feel a wondrous sense of calm fill me. It was as if soothing waves of harmony emanated to me from the tree. I would scale up her gnarled, twisted branches and then scoot down one long branch that hung over the river. There was a place in that branch, smoothed from my many visits, where I could nestle unseen under the leaves. I was safe. It was there, huddled in the arms of my strong friend, that I could finally cry. Hours later when I would shimmy down her disheveled bark I would feel refreshed. I felt renewed hope in myself and the world around me. As a child I felt protected by the loving consciousness of a tree.

TREES HAVE SOULS

The trees next to and around your dwelling can provide a devoted protective energy for your home. Throughout ancient times trees were thought to have souls. Trees were treated as animate beings and were respected as divine sources of wisdom and protection. In ancient Norse tradition the All Father was said to have created the tree of the universe called Yggdrasil, which symbolized all of life. The ancient Greeks worshipped trees as containing the oracular essence of the Gods. Trees were places of prophecy, hence the "talking oak" trees in the sacred grove of the oracle of Dodona. It is said that when priests entered the grove the trees spoke with the voices of humans. One legend states that Zeus inhabited one particular oak tree, which became known as the "oracular oak."

The Cherokees, as well as many other American Indian tribes, considered trees to be holy and sacred. They usually would only use trees that had fallen naturally, rather than cutting down a live tree. If a tree had to be felled its permission was asked and gifts were given in return for its gift of life to the tribe.

The Maori of New Zealand, like most tribal people, consider each tree to have a soul. They despair because as trees are cut down, the souls have nowhere to go, so they are returning to the stars and we on earth are poorer for their loss.

Perhaps the people best known for veneration of trees are the

Celts. Trees, particularly the oak tree, were sacred to ancient Celts. The spiritual advisers of the Celtic tribal leaders were called Druids. The word *Druid* means "men of the oak trees." Druids communicated using a secret alphabet of twenty-five letters. Fourteen of the letters were named after trees. Each tree expressed a particular spiritual quality that was conveyed through the alphabet letter named after it.

There are a number of stories of the dryads (the spirits of the trees) leaving their tree homes to go into battle in defense of the Celts. A Spirit of a Tree could leave its tree, but only for short periods of time, and it could not go very far away from its tree, for to do so would mean death. Often during the Celtic battles the Spirits of the Trees would be away too long and would die in their effort to help their friends.

TREES AS PASSAGEWAYS TO MYSTIC WORLDS

In some shamanic traditions trees serve as doors or passageways for earth dwellers to go through to other worlds. While in a trance the spirit of the shaman journeys through the root systems of the trees. Tree roots are the pathways that are used to travel to the inner realms and the underworlds. The tree acts as a transition between ordinary reality and mystic realms. Californian Indians used a tree stump to embark on their sacred journeys. The Arunt of Australia also use a hollow tree. The Indians of the Amazon follow the roots of the tree into the underworlds.

PLANTS HAVE CONSCIOUSNESS

It has been documented that plants are capable of "intent." They respond to the environment around them. Take the example of the dandelion. In the wild, the dandelion will grow to several feet high. However, in the environment of a garden they will grow only high enough to stay beneath the lethal blades of a lawn mower.

One of the first scientists to describe plants as having consciousness was a Viennese biologist named Raoul Francé. He stated that plants were capable of extraordinary perception and even communication. He further felt that plants reacted to abuse and were grateful for kind treatment. Scientists in the early twentieth century largely ignored Francé's findings, but in the 1960s his research was confirmed by researchers who proved that plants do indeed have intent and can in fact communicate with humans.[1]

Another scientist who understood the consciousness of plants was Luther Burbank (1849–1926). He was well known for plant cross-pollination and selective breeding. He was able to achieve results which were unavailable to traditional scientists at the time. He stated that "the secret of improved plant breeding is love." A well-known example of this approach was the development of the spineless cactus, which was desired for the feeding of livestock. Burbank spoke gently to the cacti, thereby letting them know they would not need their thorns. By creating an environment of love and trust, he was able to eventually breed a new thornless variety.[2]

TREES OF LIGHT

Having a Guardian Tree can be a *very important* source of healing, strengthening and light. Trees are going to become increasingly important in the years ahead, for trees are contact points for energy. Trees are entrance points for energy harmonies and frequencies, since they have the ability to distill and transmit energy. The honor and love that you give your tree will make it become an even more powerful vortex to bring in energy and light. Your Guardian Tree can also be a powerful transmitter of energy and healing for your entire household, as well as the entire environment around your home. I've seen some trees that were transmitting energy up to a one-mile radius in all directions.

To call upon the energy of the trees to preserve energy within your home, find a tree you can connect with in your garden, or perhaps in a nearby park. The tree you choose does not need to be right next to your home. Find a tree that makes you feel good when you are next to it. This feeling is a strong indication that it will be a good Guardian Tree for your home.

Tree-of-light meditation

Sit or stand next to your chosen tree. Sit comfortably with your spine straight and up against the tree, or put your arms around the tree. Breathe, relax, and let go. Allow your consciousness to merge with the tree. Feel the energy surging up through the tree. "Feel" the roots deep in the ground and the branches high in the sky. Ask your tree its name. Ask that the dryad or Spirit of the Tree envelop your home.

Give thanks, leave a gift, a token, a gesture of goodwill for your tree. This is important. In native tradition you always give something in return. (I know a Blackfoot Indian who always leaves a shiny copper penny whenever he visits his tree.)

FAIRIES, GNOMES, ELVES, SYLPHS, UNDINES, AND SALAMANDERS

As we have moved into a world of modern technology, the elemental realm of fairies and elves have receded. I am sad to look across a field and see no elemental beings, or fairies. It is especially important that your garden be an environment that welcomes all living beings, including fairies and elves. It was the philosopher Paracelsus who called the beings in the invisible planes "elementals," although most cultures have stories of fairy folk. The elemental beings are divided into four groups: the earth spirits—elves, gnomes, and trolls; the water spirits—nymphs, undines and water sprites; the air spirits—sylphs; and the fire spirits—salamanders. All of these elementals are forms of fairy folk, although when most people speak of fairies, they are only referring to the flower and plant fairies.

I used to go into the tropical Hawaiian forest with my Hawaiian kahuna teacher. She was a gentle and gracious woman. The Spirit of Earth resided deep in her soul. We would bring with us into the forest a large basket of papaya, mangoes, bananas and pineapple as a gift to the Menehune King (Fairy King) and his people. I would stand "on guard" waiting for her as she would venture deeper into the forest. She would return with the basket empty and tell me of her conversations with the Menehunes. She had the gift of sight and could see and talk to fairies.

Attracting fairies into your garden
Fairies are real and there is great value in creating an environment around your home that is attractive to the elemental energies.

Create a garden that is conducive to life, not just plant life but all life. Put up birdhouses, birdbaths and bird feeders, bat houses and hummingbird feeders. Plant flowers and plants that are attractive to bees and butterflies. Fairies are attracted to any place where there are butterflies. Plant a night garden to attract nocturnal creatures such as bats, owls, and crickets. Put nuts out for the squirrels. Even in the center of a big city, wildlife abounds. Whatever you do to bring life into your garden will bring fairies and elementals as well.

Here is a short list of plants that are "open invitations" for the beautiful butterflies (and fairies) to visit your garden:

Achillea millefolium   (common yarrow)
Aster novi-belgii   (New York aster)
Chrysanthemum maximum   (shasta daisy)
Coreopsis grandiflora/verticillata   (coreopsis)
Agastache occidentalis   (western giant hyssop or horsemint)
Lavendula dentata   (French lavender)
Rosemarinus officinalis   (rosemary)
Thymus   (thyme)
Buddleia alternifolia   (fountain butterfly bush)
Buddleia davidii   (orange-eye butterfly bush, summer lilac)
Potentilla frutiosa   (shrubby cinquefoil)
Petunia hybrida   (common garden petunia)
Verbena   (verbenas, vervains)
Scabiosa caucasica   (pincushion flowers)
Cosmos bipinnatus   (cosmos)
Zinnia elegans   (common zinnia)

For a night garden, alba or white flowers are used because their iridescent color will stand out in the twilight and evening darkness. Also a night garden can include noctiflora, flowers that bloom only at night. Especially helpful in a night garden are flowers that have a strong sweet smell particularly at night, such as *Nicotiana affinis*, tobacco plant, *Mirabilis jalapa*, four o'clock flower, *Hesperis matronalis* (alba variety available) or dame's violet or sweet rocket.

Install a small fountain or waterfall or put in a fishpond. You might want to include statues of angels or Saint Francis; these, and other garden statuary, attract landscape angels. Anything that reflects light (like shiny garden globes) or is colorful and moving (like banners) particularly attracts the gnomes and elves. Both fairies and water sprites like the splashy sound and sight of a fountain.

Leave one area of your garden a bit wild and not too cultivated. Elementals like this. It need not be a large space, but having one area that is dedicated to the fairies will make them feel very welcome.

Ask fairies and elves to come into your garden. "Where Intention goes, energy flows." Whatever you place your conscious awareness on, you will pull into your life. As you put your attention on fairies and gnomes and the elemental realm, they will respond by being drawn into your garden.

GARDEN OF ENERGY

If you are fortunate to have a garden as part of your home, the energy generated by it can help sustain your home's energy. You can create a garden of energy. It does not need to be big. Even the tiniest garden of just a few feet square can generate a fantastic energy field.

It is valuable to decide what energy you want to generate in your garden, because it will affect the energy fields in your home. If you want your home's template to generate passion and activity and movement, then let your garden be a symphony of sound, color, scent, and visual stimuli. Plant vivid reds, oranges and bright sunny yellows. Be wild and madcap. Have large splashes of color and dramatic vegetation. On the other hand, if what you want is a spiritual, serene template for your home, then cultivate a meditative atmosphere in your garden. Plant lavender, delicate bluebells, delicate Sterling Silver roses and other softly colored flowers. No matter what template you want your garden to project, it can become a garden of energy so that all who enter into it are uplifted and energized just by being there.

Planting your garden

In planting your garden, it is valuable first to spend time connecting to the Spirit of Earth beneath you. Spend time with each plant you bring into your garden, sensing where it would be happiest and where it would be most in harmony with the other plants. Thank each plant, as you put it into Mother Earth, for adding beauty and energy to your home.

Just as each person has a totem animal, we all have totem plants. Totem plants are particular plants that make you feel good and strong just by being there. (For how to find your totem plant see Chapter 14.) Your entire garden will become much more dynamic and energized when you have planted your personal totems, as well as the plant allies of other members of your household.

Insects

It is best to protect the energy environment you have created in a natural and organic way. It is valuable to yourself and your plants to use organic methods of controlling the insects which need to feed on your plants. One natural approach to pest control would be to introduce ladybirds, nematodes, or praying mantises into your garden. Also, placing certain plants such as marigolds around the border of flowerbeds can help to repel damaging insects. Use natural soap sprays on aphids. If you are willing to let the insects have a bit of the garden for themselves, it creates a much more natural energy field than using chemical pesticides.

Scientific research has uncovered some interesting information about the relationship between the plant world and the insect world. Some insects see in the ultraviolet spectrum. Flowers also radiate in this spectrum. Color acts as a kind of language between the plant and the insect. For example, if a plant is under stress due to root shock, draught, dampness or root rot, its natural radiant color will change. An insect seeing this change in the color spectrum will sense that this particular plant is under stress, and therefore vulnerable. In the wilderness, the principle of "survival of the fittest" creates maximum life force by weeding out weaker animals. This is also true in the plant world. Aphids and insects will be drawn to a plant experiencing "stress" and devour it, making way for stronger plants. It is important to honor all living things—even the insects eating your plants. If you do decide to destroy insects that are devouring your garden, bless them as you do it.

Indoor plants

When you bring a plant into your home it becomes a part of you and your energy field. Aside from the soothing effects that a plant will bring both through color and a heightened sense of nature, plants can bring a positive, invigorating life force into your home. Each plant carries a particular energy field. For example, ferns bring a soft gentle radiance and respond strongly to energy fields around them. Cacti have a grounding energy field and can absorb negative emotions without being diminished themselves.

Here is a ritual you can perform with a house plant that contributes to maintaining a strong energy in your home.

- Specify one plant to be your House Guardian Plant.
- Name this plant, or ask the plant its name. The name is important because what you are actually doing is establishing a relationship with this plant. As with any relationship, acknowledgment is a key to the bonding process.
- Say an affirmation—this might be a dream, wish, or a specific intent for you home's energy. You can bring this Intent into the physical dimension by assigning a tangible object, e.g., a stone (upon which a symbol may be painted or carved), to your desired reality. For instance, you might have the Intention that your home be a place of healing. Find a small stone and imagine placing your Intention for healing into the stone.
- Place this object into the soil, just below the surface. Or if you wish the object can be visible as a constant reminder of your Intention.
- Every time you water the plant, restate your Intention. Know that when you water the plant, you are nurturing your Intention or your dream. After it is watered, the living plant then emanates your Intention into the room.

COPPER

One of Mother Earth's great tools for energizing a home is copper. Copper is an excellent conductor of the new energies. To energize your bed, so that you are absorbing and integrating energy during your sleep, take copper wire and make clockwise coils by wrapping the copper seven or twelve times around a circular object. If you use small copper wire then you can wrap it around a pencil. The larger the wire, the larger the coil needs to be. Place one coil at each bedpost and put one right in the center of the bed underneath it. If you feel that you are absorbing too much energy too quickly to assimilate it all, then use smaller coils or only put one coil under your bed. To increase the effect of the copper coils, wear a copper necklace or bracelet while you sleep.

If you want to draw energy into the place where you meditate, take very fine copper wire and either run it back and forth across the ceiling or under the carpeting. (Ideally put the wiring both above and below you.) The connected lines of copper wire should be about one foot apart.

If there is a location in your home where the energy seems very low, place a copper coil in that area of the house. To overlay your home with an etheric energy template, place four large copper coils in the four corners of your home (either on the outside or the inside of your home). If you have a means of placing a copper coil in your attic or on top of your home, this is an excellent way to "call" energy into your home.

CALLING THE SPIRIT OF EARTH INTO YOUR HOME

To draw the Spirit of Earth into your home:

HONOR THE "EARTH" THAT IS IN YOUR HOME   Bless the wood and stone and bricks that have come from the earth from which your home is made. You might place your hands on a wooden wall and say:

> *Thank you, Earth Spirits.*
> *May the Earth Energy that flows through you bring blessings to*
> *this family.*

INVOKE THE SUBTLE ETHERIC ENERGIES OF EARTH   To invoke the subtle etheric energies of earth, place crystals and stones and living plants throughout your home.

CALL FORTH THE MAGIC OF THE SPIRIT OF EARTH TO FILL YOUR HOME   Focus your awareness on the earth that is beneath your home, no matter how high up your home is. Call forth the Earth Spirit to bring grounding, stability and healing into your home.

8

SACRED SOUND

*Only the sound of my breath infringes on the stillness in the Zen
monastery. I'm facing the wall, observing the rhythms of my breath.
Suddenly, the fragile tranquillity of the moment implodes as the
Zen priest strikes the temple gong. The sound seems to vibrate from
inside me. My whole body seems to resonate with the potent sound
of the gong. The walls disappear. I disappear. I feel myself sinking
deeper and deeper. Beyond form, beyond time. The deep resonance
of the gong carries me to the center of stillness; to the void, to unity
with all things.*

My experience of listening to the gong in the Zen monastery
was one of the most profoundly validating experiences in
my life. The vibration of the gong allowed me to transcend time and
space and enter into another reality. Bells and gongs are used in
monasteries throughout the world because it is believed that the
sound of either of these can carry you to satori, or enlightenment.
Not only does sound allow you to descend into different dimensions,
it is also a powerful tool for clearing home energies and for invoking
healing energies into your home.

There are two aspects of sound: audible sound and silent sound.
The sound that you can hear audibly has the power to illicit emotions
as well as create a physical vibration so dramatic that it can "bring
down the walls of Jericho." However, the most commanding sound is

the sound that you don't hear. There is an energy template for sound to which audible sound clings. Sound templates are around you always, even in stillness. Some of the most beautiful and powerful sound occurs in complete silence. For sound is energy, it is vibration. And whether or not you hear sound with your ears, the energy of sound is all around you. Sound has color and life force and consciousness. Sound can be used to establish a sacred temple that reposes over your home. Not only can sound cleanse and clear the energies in your home, it can speed up the vibratory rate in your home so that your home sings with light and life. Sound can influence not just the molecules of your home, *but can also impact the space between the molecules*. The instruments that you use for clearing the energy in your home are activating templates for octaves both heard and not heard.

Everything has sound. Every blade of grass, every cloud, every mountain has its own sound, its own vibration. Your rocking chair and toaster and kitchen table all have sounds. When you are using musical instruments to cleanse the energy in your home not only are you breaking up stagnant energy, but you are also attuning every board, every nail, every tile and each and every part of your home with sound.

Your home will absorb the octaves that it needs to be in harmony from the sound that you create.

You do not need to worry if you do not know the "sound" of your study or your sofa when you are creating sound. Your home will absorb the octaves from the sound that you create, just as a plant pulls from the soil those nutrients it needs to be in balance. Your home and objects in your home will absorb frequencies, harmonics and octaves from the sound that you create with your musical instruments.

Objects can be out of harmony just as much as people can be out of harmony, and sound can assist them to move back into harmony. A professional seamstress told me scissors aren't as sharp immediately after they have been dropped. She said that they didn't feel right for a while afterwards. I believe that the shock of the drop puts the scissors out of harmony. Their essential sound vibration begins to wobble a bit after they are dropped. However, sound can put them back in harmony. I suggested to the seamstress that she ring a bell next to her scissors after they fell to see if it improved the cutting edge. She said she tried my technique and noticed an immediate difference.

Native Americans understood the concept of "silent sound" very well. They used this skill to "call" animals to the hunt and to find plants for gathering. My teacher Dancing Feather taught me how to call animals using silent sound. He said that every animal and plant has its own sound vibration. Most of the sounds of animate and inanimate objects we cannot create with our vocal cords, but we can create them with our energy fields. For example, to use silent sound to call a crow, first imagine the crow. Allow your consciousness to merge with the imagined crow. Then imagine or feel the animal's vibration and sound. Then project the silent sound vibration of the crow outwards. This is sending out the call to crows in the area. After doing this, don't be surprised if crows begin to gather near you.

I believe that the power of sound has only just begun to be explored. The capacity of sound to heal, to be an entrance point to other dimensions and to shift energy fields is an area of study only in its infancy. As you use sound to cleanse your home's energy and invoke energy into your home, keep in mind the silent sounds . . . the sounds that you don't hear.

Clearing a Room Using Sound

When using sound to clear a room, any musical instrument can be used. You can improvise or create your own space-clearing sound implement. In some native cultures spoons are banged against pots and pans to rid a room of "evil spirits." (The term *evil spirits* usually suggests stagnant energy but can extend to earthbound spirits.) However, whatever tools you use, start with larger and louder sounds and proceed to smaller and more refined sounds.

The instrument you use is less important than the way that you feel when you are using it. As you are using an instrument to clear a room, shift your consciousness so that you can feel and become sound. When you create sound in a room, feel the sound vibrate inside of you. Imagine that the sound is radiating out from you to fill the room. Imagine that you are the instrument and you are the sound. Enter into the place where you are not separate from the sound, or the room or the instrument. As you "sound" the room, *be* the sound.

Everything in the room has a sound. As you become sound, allow waves of sound to emanate from you and all the sounds in the room will begin to harmonize. It's as if you are the conductor and every sound in the room is tuning under your direction. A room that has been harmonized can be compared to a great symphony—all objects in the room exist in harmonious relationship. A room that has been harmonized will seem to glow and sing with light.

BELLS

My Zen Master told me that the sound of a bell continues to resonate far beyond the time when you can hear it. He said that it carries into eternity as it resonates throughout the universe.

I love working with bells to clear energy. If possible, I always like to use bells for clearing a room before a seminar because it leaves such a crystal-clear energy field in the room. In addition, whenever a bell rings not only is sound vibration emitted into the room but also beautiful *color* vibrations. These colors are not visible to the human eye but many will notice a difference in the colors in a room after a bell has been rung. People who see auras can often see the colors of sound. But even if you cannot see them, you can *feel* them with your heart and soul.

Bells have always been associated with religious services. They originated in Asia. Archaeologists have found bells as far back as 800 B.C., although most certainly their use pre-dates this. The Celtic tribes who were famous for their metal-casting techniques are credited for bringing bells from Asia to Europe. Bells were introduced into France in A.D. 550 and into England a hundred years later.

Size of bells
It is best to have a series of bells, from large to small. This way you can start with the larger deeper sounds, which are good for breaking up stagnant energy, and then gradually move on to the smaller bells, which bring a refined purity into a room. A good beginner set of bells should be all of the same approximate shape, ranging from a three- to four-inch-diameter bell to a one-inch-diameter bell.

Kinds of bells
When I observe the energy produced in a room when a bell is rung, I notice differences depending on the metal used, the size of the bell, and

the energy of the bellmaker. Some bells have energy fields that seem to move out like luxurious slow waves. Some will emit energy fields that are similar to small waves, interspersed by deep dips and then returning to the small wave pattern. Some bells' sound will ascend before abruptly descending. Some bells' frequency even folds back on itself. Each bell will affect the energy of a room in a different way.

The kind of bell you obtain is a highly individual matter. The first measure of a good bell to use for house clearing is how the bell feels to you. A bell that you love and honor will clear your home faster than the most pristine, valuable bell in the world. The affection with which you hold your bell will imbue it with a special sacred energy. There is a kind of alchemy that occurs between you and an object that you love. I've included some suggestions regarding different kinds of bells but the deciding factor should be how *you* feel about the bell that you use.

Silver bells have a lovely purity of sound and have a very feminine nature. They invoke the energy of the silvery light of the moon. They are excellent to use in a house that is very yang or a home where the occupants are very active and outgoing and need to take time to turn inward to discover inner dreams and the quietude of self. Silver bells can help bring magic and innocence into a home. In some traditions newborn babies are given a silver bell as a baby gift, for silver bells have the spirit of innocence and purity.

The therapeutic effect of specific combinations of metal has long been recognized in Eastern civilizations. Tibetan bells are usually made from seven base metals: iron, copper, tin, silver, lead, gold and zinc. I love using these bells as the energy and colors that radiate from Tibetan bells is multidimensional.

It can be difficult to find solid brass bells that are consistent in sound. However, if you find a good brass bell it can be good for generating a go-for-it energy. Brass bells cast forth a sparkling vibrant energy which is outgoing and very yang. If home occupants have become too inward, reserved and stagnant, a brass bell is an excellent bell to use.

Bronze bells, such as the ones used in Japanese monasteries, are very good for grounding energy. It is quite remarkable to watch the effect that a bronze bell has on a room. The sound will emanate from the bell over a room in a silken wavelike form and then suddenly sink to the floor. If occupants in a home tend to be flighty and scattered, a bronze bell will instantly bring a more grounded energy into the home.

Some bells, such as the kind used in churches, are molded in a single piece from a molten metal called bell metal consisting of copper and tin. It is an interesting coincidence that most church bells have copper in them, because any bell that has copper in it is excellent to use in energy work. The copper attracts life-force energy (see pages 113–14), which then meshes with the sound vibrations of the bell, forming a powerful harmonic. Use a bell that has copper in it if you are working with energy or wanting to step up your vibratory rate.

My favorite bell is a Balinese temple bell that is made of brass and 22-carat gold. Though the sound is excellent and the bell itself is very beautiful, the reason I love this bell so much is because of the love and care that went into its creation. My bell was hand-crafted by a family of bellmakers who live on the side of a mountain in Bali. These bells are usually only created for Balinese priests. However, a friend of mine who lives in Bali became close friends with the bell-making family. They made me a bell with the strict understanding that the bell would only be used for sacred purposes. Immense care was taken in its creation. The two-month production process was begun at the properly prescribed time (full moon), and offerings were made to the Balinese deities at every stage of the highly skilled process to ensure that the bell was "alive" as the Balinese put it. Finally, an hour-long consecration ceremony was held on an auspicious day by a highly respected Balinese priest to bless, charge and dedicate the bell to sacred usage.

Another favorite bell that I use was a gift from a special friend. It comes from the monastery of Saint Francis in Assisi. Although the sound isn't perfect and it isn't the most beautiful bell, I love it because I feel that it carries in its soul the energy of the monks and Saint Francis.

If at all possible, obtain a bell that was made by someone you know; or at least try to find out all you can about the bell's origin. These kinds of bells can be powerful additions to your space-clearing tools.

Bell care

Keep your bells (and all your space-clearing tools) in a special place when not in use. Treat them with respect and love. If possible, keep the bells elevated as a mark of respect (for example on a shelf rather than on the floor). Don't keep them in a junk cupboard or in the bathroom, or any area of your home which you think of as being more functional than spiritually oriented. If you take your bells from your home, keep them wrapped in cloth that is only used for this purpose. This protects the bell in transit and will also insulate it from emanations of everyday objects until it is used. If possible, carry your bell in a separate bag when in transport.

It's a matter of choice whether you let others handle your bells or not. However, it is important to maintain the purity of their vibrations by feeling good about anyone who handles your bells.

How to ring bells

There are two ways to ring a bell, either by striking or by ringing. You can either ring the bell using the clapper inside, or you can create your own external clapper. When you strike a bell externally, you have more control of the sound than when you use the clapper. However, when ringing a bell with the clapper you have the advantage of being able to swing your arm while ringing which helps get energy flowing. Also, by using the clapper method you can create a continual ringing, which can be of great advantage if you are working in a large room or have many rooms to clear.

To strike a bell, you can use a wooden stick. (For the larger bells you can use the large end of a wooden kitchen spoon.) You can use it as a plain stick or you can cover it with a light layer of leather. Experiment with different strikers because each one creates a different sound.

In some esoteric traditions many months are required to learn how to hold a bell accurately if it is to be used for religious purposes. However, any way that you find to hold your bell comfortably, so that your fingers and wrists don't tire, is sufficient. Always hold your bell lightly with a loose and relaxed hand rather than a hand that is clenched and tight.

Using bells for room clearing

When you first unwrap your bell to clear a room, take just a moment to hold the bell in your hand to reacquaint yourself with it. This can be likened to greeting a friend that you haven't seen for a while.

Start by standing in the center of the room that you are going to clear. Strike your bell once and listen very carefully. This first ring will tell you much about the energy of the room. If the room is stagnant, the bell will sound almost muffled. If there is erratic energy in the room, the bell tone will sound tinny and shrill. You need to know the varying sounds of your own bell so you can decipher its different moods and responses to various kinds of energy. In the beginning you may not be able to detect the difference between rings. However, just as a connoisseur of wine can tell the difference in vintages that taste the same to the uninitiated, so you will, after practice, begin to hear the subtle variations in the sounds. Even if you are uncertain about what you are doing, just ringing your bell as you circle the room will help to clear the energies in the room.

Move toward the easternmost corner of the room while holding your largest bell. With a clarity of movement make a sharp clean strike. Strike four times. Listen very carefully after each strike. The sound should become sharper and clearer with each ring. If this doesn't happen after your initial four strikes then continue to strike. Wait between strokes to let the bell ring until you can no longer hear it.

Even in rooms that are relatively clear you should still notice a variation between the rings, although it will be less dramatic. In places in the room where energy has collected and pooled over time you will notice a more marked difference between rings, as the sound is dissipating the stagnant energy. Continue to strike or ring your bell with crisp, clean movements until the sound becomes very sharp and has a clear resonance.

After you have cleared the first corner, continue walking slowly around the room in a clockwise manner. Even if you live in the Southern Hemisphere, working clockwise around the room seems to work best in the majority of cases. Counterclockwise has had merit too in some rare circumstances. If you keep getting the feeling as you walk clockwise that it just isn't right, try walking counterclockwise.

As you walk, hold your left hand out while your right hand holds the bell. With your left hand you are feeling for the energy fields in the room. Everyone seems to feel these variations in a different way. To some people, an area of stagnant energy might feel sticky. Another person might perceive the same area as fuzzy. Some feel that it is cold and even sends shivers up their arm. You will probably need to experiment to see how you best experience the difference between stagnant and clear energy.

As you circle the room, continue striking the bell until each part of the room has a clarity of sound. Some places may seem more muffled than others. As you move around the room you should increasingly feel clarity filling the room. Usually it takes fewer strikes of the bell near the end of your room circling than at the beginning. If you encounter any area that feels stagnant, just stop and strike the bell until you get a clear, clean sound. Continue around the entire room until you return to where you began.

Often I find stagnant energy not only in the corners but also around electrical outlets and electrical equipment. Trust your intuition about where to ring the bell—if you are uncertain about whether to ring the bell or not, then by all means ring the bell. Your uncertainty often is reflective of inner knowledge.

After you've gone around with a large bell, then continue to circle the room, each time around using smaller and smaller bells. Each time listen carefully until you get a really clean, clear sound. This indicates that the energy in the room is flowing freely. With each bell you are refining the energy in the room. You can complete the room using a small bell or jingle bells or druid balls. Druid balls are spherical balls, usually silver in color, that have an ethereal, delicate sound when you shake them. They sound almost fairylike. By the time you have completed the room, you will have created a lovely, fine-tuned energy.

A special feature of some bells is that you can make them "sing." To do this, take a smooth stick of wood, and as you run the wood around the surface of the bell it may begin to vibrate with a pure ringing tone. Many Tibetan bells are made to be used in this manner. You can use singing bells the same way you use ringing bells in clearing a room.

Sometimes it is valuable to keep a window open while you are "ringing a room." Though you don't actually need this in order to allow the stagnant energies to release, an open window is an important symbol for the subconscious mind, so that you can really *feel* at a deep level that the stagnant energy is flowing out of the window.

When you have completed your last circle around the room, take your hand and move it in a large infinity sign in the same corner where you began. (To do this, draw a sideways figure eight in the air with your hand stretched out toward that corner.) What you are doing is closing the circle. You started the circle in the easternmost corner, and now you are closing it by connecting the beginning to the end.

GONGS

There are two kinds of gongs. One is a hammered metal percussion instrument that is shaped like a circular metal plate and hangs on a stand. Another kind of gong is also made of hammered metal but is shaped like a bowl. Most gongs are made in China, although some of the flat gongs are now being made in Europe as well.

Hanging gongs

Hanging gongs can be quite dramatic in sound. Their tones can vary from a deep vibration that feels as if it emerges from the center of the earth, to an extraordinary wind gong that sounds like shimmering star dust. A gong produces a rich sound that changes with the type of mallet used. Most mallets are made of rubber or wood that is covered with cloth, felt or wool.

There are two ways to use hanging gongs for room clearing. One method is to circle the periphery of the room holding and striking your gong, using the same technique described above for use with bells. Because gongs can be physically heavy to carry, if you wish to use this method, I suggest you use a gong no more than sixteen inches in diameter.

The second method is to keep the gong in the center of the room. Gongs are so powerful that it is possible to do all your work from the middle of the room, because the sound of the gong will fill every crevice. Larger gongs can be used with remarkable results. When a large gong is struck, the entire building will feel as if it is vibrating.

To gain the maximum vibration from your hanging gong, begin with very soft, gentle taps around its periphery. You will feel a vibration begin to build as you do this. Gradually bring the circle inward until the entire gong has increased in resonance; then strike once in the middle of it. Quiet your mind and allow the vibration to fill you and the entire room.

Working from the largest and deepest sounds to lighter and more refined ones, you can complete a room in the same way as you did with the bells. End by making the sign for infinity.

Bowl gongs

You can use bowl gongs in a similar way to bells and hanging gongs. If you are using a very large gong that is too heavy to carry, you will need to place it on the center of the floor while you are striking it, as in the second method described above for hanging gongs. As you proceed in your room clearing to using the smaller gongs, you can then place the gong in your left hand and strike it with your right hand as you circle the room.

Strike your hand-held gong along the edge of the rim as you are walking around the room. When you encounter an area with stagnant energy, strike the gong and, while it is ringing, move the entire bowl in a horizontal or a vertical circle. This intensifies the power of the sound. At the completion of your circling, remember to complete your ceremony with the infinity sign.

I keep a variety of bowl gongs on display in my home so they can be struck when family members pass by. This occasional sound vibration continues to clear and energize the rooms.

TUNING FORKS

Tuning forks can be used for very fine tuning of the energy in a room after the denser energies have been cleared out. They can also be used for personal preparation before clearing a room.

To use tuning forks to attune your energy before clearing, hold the tuning fork lightly in one hand and strike it firmly on the palm of the other hand. As it is vibrating, take the tuning fork and very slowly move it in front of your face in an arc from your left ear to your right ear. Then extend your arm and swing the tuning fork down to point at the earth. Hold for one second, then, arm extended, swing your arm up so the tuning fork is pointed toward the sky. Hold for a second, and then return to moving from your left ear, and right ear. As you do this exercise with a tuning fork the sound will begin to adjust your subtle energy field.

Use tuning forks for room clearing only *after* you have cleared the much denser energies. Tuning forks can subtly adjust the etheric room energy because of their delicate refined nature.

SINGING BOWLS

Singing bowls are bowl-shaped instruments on which you run a mallet around the inner (or outer) edge to create a tone that builds in density and volume. They usually are made of metal and come from either Tibet or Nepal, although some are made by spinning silicon into crystal-glass bowls. The energy fields generated by singing bowls are quite remarkable, for the sound begins to spiral outwards in ever widening circles from the bowl, while at the same time spiralling back down into the center of the bowl.

These cannot usually be carried around with you as you clear a room because they must remain stationary to gain full volume. The spinning energy that these instruments emit creates a sacred spiral that can attract a deluge of cosmic energy to your home. Negativity and stagnant energy is whirled away in ever-expanding circles while the center of the bowl "calls" etheric luminous energy into the home. Singing bowls are among the few instruments that can clear and invoke energy at the same time.

WIND CHIMES

To create an energy of protection around your house, it is valuable to invite the Spirit of the Wind. You can do this by placing chimes around the circumference of your house. Wind chimes will create a circular energy of sound which is very protective and healing, even when they are not playing.

You can also hang wind chimes inside the home (see pages 200, 201 and 211). Place them where an occasional gentle touch can bring forth their delicate sound. I have electric wind chimes in my home that are set to chime occasionally, as if a light breeze had found its way into my living room.

For very fine tuning of a room you may want to use a calibrated set of chimes which are hung in a row. The sound is ethereal and almost mystical. Remember to strike them in order from the deepest to the highest tone.

DRUMS

Drums carry the heartbeat of Mother Earth. Drums carry the Spirit of Life. There is an ancient Cherokee saying that says, "The Sun and the Moon are the drumsticks playing upon the Earth, bringing harmony and peace to all the Earth's children."

From ancient times to the present, people inhabiting every corner of the globe have incorporated the drum into their culture. Because of its ability to alter and synchronize group consciousness, the drum has been used for a variety of cultural purposes. The drum has roused warriors to battle and led initiates into a state of deep ritual trance. It has been used in religious ceremonies and for secular diversion.

In almost all earth-based cultures, the percussive sound of the drum or two sticks clicking together is used for clearing energy. There are two reasons for this. The first is that the rhythmic sound has been found to put the shaman into an altered state of consciousness. The sound literally alters brain waves. This has been verified in scientific research. The beat of the drum puts medicine men or women into an altered state of consciousness where they can be more in touch with their intuition, God, the spirits and their ancestors. In this altered state of consciousness, they can hear advice that is given to them while they are clearing the room or space.

The second reason that shamans use drums for room clearing is that the vibration of the drum is so powerful that it instantly gets energy flowing. The beating of the drum clears unwanted energy or "unwanted spirits," even as it also calls in the "good spirits." Drums can banish and invoke. They can carry you to the stars and return you to your roots.

The drum itself is feminine; the drumstick is masculine. When you bring these two together in rhythm, you assist the harmonizing of the two opposing yet harmonious forces in the universe, yin and yang. With every beat of the drum you help harmonize the male and female energy within yourself, as well as the male and female energy within your home and within the universe. This is the medicine of drums. Drums are circles of power that can realign the energy of your home powerfully and quickly.

In native cultures, drums are considered to be holy objects that are "alive." They are thought to have consciousness and spirit. Woe to anyone who touches the shaman's drum without permission. An Apache medicine man told me that in his ancient tradition, if a drum were touched without permission, the offender would be put to death.

When I was in a Zulu village in Africa, I asked if the Zulus had a similar tradition. I was told by Credo Mutwa, Most Holy Shaman of the Zulus, that the old tradition was to kill anyone who touched the shaman's drum, but now they just extract money (200 rand) from the offender. He told me that when a drummer dies his drum "is stabbed and killed and pronounced dead, and is buried in a holy place, a drum burial place." These traditions are illustrative of the power and reverence that was assigned to the drum.

Every drum has its own personality and feels very different from all other drums. Some are reserved and focused, some are outgoing and exuberant. The Zulus believe that drums are "born" either male or female, and that they should only be made under the most peaceful conditions because then only peace will come forth from the drumming.

When I drum, I sometimes feel as if time stands still. I feel as if I can reach into the past as well as touch the future. Colors vibrate, life springs forth from my pores and an energy awakens inside me that reminds me of ancient promises and future fulfillments. When I hold my drum I feel as if I am home.

Kinds of drums

The materials that drums are made of and the methods by which they are made varies throughout the world. In Melanesia the drum maker climbs the tree that is to furnish the wood for the drum and remains in the tree until the drum is finished. In Africa the Banyankole make a daily offering to the drum. A sacred herd of cows yields milk to a woman known as "wife of the drums" who carries the milk early in the morning to the drum hut (the drums have their own special enclosure). The milk remains outside the hut until about nine or ten o'clock, by which time the drum spirits are thought to have taken the essence of the milk.

Drums are often made of animal skin tied to wood. They are also made of hollowed logs which are rolled onto their side, or hung from trees, and then struck with mallets. The Confucian temples in China had drums that were six feet wide. In the Greek Dionysus cult, women used small hand-held frame drums in their ceremonies to the moon. Some drums had one side and some drums were two-sided, which created a double vibration. Materials used for the drum varied with whatever materials were at hand.

Today, the most common drums used for space clearing are the hand-held frame drums. The most typical of these is in the Native American style, where an animal skin is stretched over a circular wooden hoop. However, any kind of drum can be used for space clearing.

How to drum

Before you begin drumming, hold your drum close to you and allow your consciousness to expand into the drum. Take your hand and slowly rub around the drum in a circular manner as a way of greeting it. Many drums have an individual name, so in your mind you may want to address your drum by this name. The Ojibwa Indians address their drum with an expression of respect, calling it "Grandfather," so if your drum does not have a name, you might greet your drum with the reverent title of "Grandmother" or "Grandfather."

After you have greeted your drum, be still and allow energy to build inside you. When you feel the energy reach a peak, allow that energy to be expressed in a great yelp. This spontaneous sound is calling Spirit. You are asking Spirit to assist you in your clearing. Then you can begin drumming, keeping your drumstick hand very loose. Let your wrist be very limber so the movement comes from your wrist rather than your arm. Using your arm for long periods of time can be quite exhausting.

Different drumbeats are used for different purposes. A very good drumbeat to start out with is a heartbeat, which is a two-beat rhythm. This is perhaps the most primal sound known to human beings. It is what you first heard when you were in the womb. This sound is the aligning and balancing of the two opposing yet harmonious forces in the universe, the yin and yang—male and female.

After you begin drumming a two-beat, allow your breathing to deepen, and allow your body to relax. There will come a point where an energy or feeling inside you begins to take over. So instead of deciding what rhythm to drum, allow the drum to tell you what beat is needed. Each room has different energies and will call forth different rhythms of the drum. You might find when you are clearing the energies of the bathroom that you are drumming a fine, fast beat. And then when you enter into a bedroom the beat has changed to a slow three-beat. Trust your intuition. You may even feel as if you are being drummed as the rhythm surges through you. The best drumming is where you get out of the way and allow yourself to be drummed—allowing a natural drumbeat to move through you. If there's any place in your body, or any emotions where there is a congestion or blockage, then not only will the drumming clear the room, but it will also be clearing your energy as well. The less you think about the right drumbeat, the more the rhythmic surges from the universe can move through you. (For specific directions on how to clear a room using a drum, see pages 253–55.)

When you have completed your space clearing using the drum and the room feels clear, complete your ceremony as you began. Once again allow your energy to build until you don't feel that you can contain it any more, and then let a great yelp come forth from you. This is your way of thanking Great Spirit for assisting you. I learned this technique of beginning and ending a ritual by issuing a shout to the heavens from a Havsupai Indian who lives in the Grand Canyon. He said it wasn't the traditional way of his people but it came to him on a Vision Quest. He told me that when he touches his drum "a blessed feeling fills me and allows me to have entrance into spiritual realms." With his permission, I incorporated his technique into my teaching because it is very powerful.

The drum is an excellent instrument to use if the room energy is very congested. Drumbeats can break up thick energy quickly. Working with bells and incense can be good for the more fine, subtle energies, but if you need to clear a space that has heavy, dense energy, the drum is one of the most effective tools for doing this. Drumming is particularly useful in clearing emotions. If there's a room where an emotional charge has been released or there's been anger or great sadness, or if there has been a death or sickness in the home, the drum can be one of the most powerful tools to clear the emotional energy in the room.

Drum care

A drum made of animal hide will change in tone according to the moisture in the air, the temperature, and the energy of the drum's location. The skin will expand and contract during the day, creating different sounds. Sometimes you will even hear the drum contracting and expanding. Many people say that their drum talks to them. If it is a moist day and the drum sounds thud-like, you can warm the drum by holding it near a light source. (Some modern Indians even use a hair dryer.) If it is an extraordinarily dry day, your drum may sound tinny. Using a light misting of water on the face of the drum will usually adjust the sound, as the moisture will expand the drum.

Place your drum in an honored spot. Hanging it on the wall is usually preferred. It is not advisable ever to place your drum facedown on the earth, as it shows disrespect for it. When you are in transit with your drum, it is preferable to have a special drum carrying bag or a cloth to wrap your drum in that is used only for that purpose. If you use a drum for ceremonial purposes it is best not to use the same drum for drumming popular tunes or for jamming at a party.

RATTLES

The rattle complements your drum for room clearing. Use the drum for your initial clearing work in a room, and then complete your ceremony using the rattle. (Use the technique described on pages 256–58.)

The rattle has a very soothing sound and creates a gentle energy field. It is excellent for "sealing" a room after it has been cleared. The sound of the rattle, like the drum, has been shown to alter brain waves. It can put someone into a very deep relaxed state. It is no accident that mothers use rattles to soothe their babies.

Kinds of rattles

Rattles come in as many shapes and forms as drums. They can be made of seeds rattling in a dried gourd. They can be made of pieces of leather laced together into a sphere with small pebbles inside, or sand-filled, hollowed wood. Rattles can also be made of deer hooves or hollow seed pods that rattle against each other as they hang in grapelike clumps. Perhaps because of my Native American blood, I prefer to use Native American rattles for space clearing, although any kind of rattle can be employed.

How to rattle

Begin by blessing your rattle. Offer some cornmeal or tobacco to the Four Directions and to Great Spirit. To do this take a small bowl filled with cornmeal or tobacco and another bowl to place the blessed offering in. If using cornmeal, take a small pinch between three fingers. Bring it close to your mouth and blow gently on it. Then hold it in the direction of the east asking for blessings from the Spirit of the East. Then place the blessed cornmeal into the offering bowl. Do this in each of the Four Directions and finish by taking a pinch of cornmeal, blowing on it and keeping it close to the center of your chest as you ask for a blessing from Great Spirit. Then take your rattle and rattle in each of the Four Directions and close by you. Place the cornmeal in the center of the room as a gift for the spirits who have responded to your invitation. (See Chapter 16 for additional information about this.)

When rattling, allow your wrists to be very loose and hold the rattle with a relaxed hand. I suggest using a rhythm of about 200 beats per minute, which is a very rapid fast beat. To break up blocked energy, hold your rattle at about eye level and do quick, rapid, woodpecker-like movements. Continue until the area you are rattling into feels lighter. Your hand should move quickly enough so that you can't focus on your fingers. If you want to seal the room when you have finished with room cleansing, go to the door (or doors) that open into the room. Stand outside the door of the room that has just been cleared and do the woodpecker movements, but go down the length of the door as though you were zipping it closed.

CLAP STICKS

Clap sticks can be found around the world in many native cultures, though they are perhaps most closely associated with the Australian

Aborigines. They can be used in the same way as the drum and rattle. Clap sticks (sometimes called click sticks) consist of two sticks which are between eight and twelve inches long and about one inch in diameter. When you click them together they produce a wonderful resounding sharpness of sound. Each part of the stick has a different sound and a different energy. I love working with clap sticks because they can call forth the spirit of the trees for your energy-clearing work. (See information on trees in Chapter 7.) You can direct energy with clap sticks. When you find stagnant energy in your home, click down the length of one clap stick with the other stick. After your last click, flick the stick in the direction of the energy that you want to get moving.

CLAPPING

Clapping dissipates energy. Think of a time when you've been at a very powerful performance. Remember when the clapping started? Often it is at that point when the energy generated by the performance began to dissipate. It is said that in ancient China at the end of an artistic performance, they would never clap, because they knew that clapping would dissipate the energy created by the performers. So the audience would leave in silence in order to take the energy of the performance with them.

I use clapping for room clearing when I don't have any other tool available but my own hands. It is a very effective method. When you begin "clapping a room," clap a few times at your beginning corner. Make sure that your body is relaxed, your legs are spread slightly apart, and your knees are bent. Use small fast claps to test the energy and use larger, louder claps to clear energy. The clapping should sound clean, crisp and clear. If your clapping sounds muffled or mushy, it usually means that the energy is stagnant. To disperse stagnant energy clap all the way from the floor up to the ceiling, with your arms spread apart after each clap. You are uplifting the energy of the room as your clapping gets closer to the ceiling.

Continue walking around the room, doing small claps, until you get to the next corner or the next place where you feel the energy is blocked. If some object in the room is in the wrong place, you might find that your clapping sounds muffled near it. It doesn't necessarily mean that object has negative energy. It just might not be the right place for it. Try moving it to another place in the room, and then clap again. You may find that the energy has cleared.

TONING

Toning means using the power of your own voice for activating energy flow. It is holding one note for an extended period of time. Anyone can tone. You do not need musical training. If you can talk you can tone.

To tone, you need to go inside yourself to find your own very natural sounds. These sounds have power. To find your own sound, first loosen up. Shake your whole body from side to side; bounce up and down. Let your body become as loose as a rag doll. Open your mouth wide and yawn. Loosen your jaw muscles by rotating them from side to side.

Take a few deep breathes and allow yourself to become still. Imagine that you are going deep inside yourself until you find your sound. You *do* have a sound. In fact, you have many sound vibrations within you. Every animate and inanimate object has a sound. Each of us has an essential sound, and within that sound are a multitude of vibrations. Each of these vibrations has a unique power. You can create magic in your life by learning to use your tones.

You can begin toning by saying, "Ahhhhh" or Ohhhhhh" or any of the vowel sounds. Keep your jaw loose and easy. Make sure your body is relaxed and imagine that you are breathing into your belly rather than your chest. Your first reaction might be to think, "Oh, no! This doesn't sound very good." But that's all right. Just keep allowing those sounds to come through. Be willing to make whatever sound is there without judging whether it is a beautiful sound or not. Once you have become used to toning, you are ready to clear energy in a room using your sounds.

First go to the easternmost corner of the room that you wish to clear. Be still and use your imagination to get a sense or a feeling of the sound of that area of the room. Now you might say, "How could I possibly know what the sound is of a particular area of a room?" If you are very uncertain, say to yourself. "Well, I know that I don't know, but if I did, what sound would it be?" As you ask yourself this question, begin to listen inside yourself. *Imagine* that you could hear the sound or the tonal vibration of that part of the room. Then after you have found and connected with the "sound" of the room area, move inside yourself and find your sound. Begin to tone. Be aware of your personal sound and the sound of the area of the room merging. Allow sound to come through you and flow through you into the room. The less you think about it, the easier it is. It can be an exhilarating experience. You may even begin to "see" colors associated with the sounds that you are making.

Continue toning until you can feel a clarity and strength begin to fill you. Move around the room and continue allowing your toning to come through. You'll know when an area is clear because the sounds coming through you will sound clear, like running spring water. (If you are trained to create harmonic overtones, this can also be very effective in room clearing.)

As you tone, go around the room, starting at the periphery, then begin walking around and around, in ever-decreasing circles. (Of course you may need to make adjustments in your walking pattern if there are obstructing objects in the room.) This is a very slow meditation. Often you'll notice that when you hit an area of the room where there's stagnant energy, you can feel the tone change. It might become a less clear, less vibrant tone. So you might need to spend extra time in that location. Otherwise, just keep walking in an inward spiral. Continue your circles until you come as close as you can to the room's center. When you reach the center of the room, continue toning until you feel that your toning is vibrating out to all the corners of the room, filling every part of the space. This can be a very holy experience for you, as well as for the room.

CHANTING

Chanting a room can be used in a similar way to toning a room but instead of toning you can chant a mantra. Mantras can be the repetition of holy words or the name of God or even just the dronelike repetition of words such as "peace" or even your own name. The nineteenth-century English poet Alfred, Lord Tennyson, regularly used mantras. He once wrote in a letter, "A kind of walking trance—

this for lack of a better word—I have frequently had, quite up from boyhood, when I have been all alone. This has come upon me through repeating my own name to myself silently, till all at once . . . individuality itself seemed to dissolve and fade away into boundless being, and this not a confused state but the clearest, the surest of the surest, utterly beyond words."

A wonderful, often used chant is the Sanskrit word *om* (also spelled *aum*). I usually find chanting in Sanskrit or another foreign language can be better than one's own language, because many of the words in my own language have emotional associations attached to them, and it is best to keep chanting as unencumbered as possible. For example, the word *peace* might have many connotations (not all of them positive, e.g. "I gave him a piece of my mind") from each of the times that we heard it. All of the associations that we have for words are subconsciously activated whenever we use them.

OTHER SOUNDS FOR HOUSE CLEARING

SINGING Singing can have such a powerful vibration that it can break glass. To sing a room, follow the same instructions for chanting a room. Sing sounds that move you. Sing songs that fill you with joy and with power and this will emanate from you as you "sing the room."

SQUEAKIES Squeakies are any toy or tool that make a squeaking sound. Use these for inserting humor into a room where people have been very serious and the atmosphere needs some lightening.

FLUTE Playing a flute can bring crystal clarity to a room. Flute music is better for calling energy into a room rather than breaking up blocked energy. Even if you are not musically inclined, you can obtain a very inexpensive bamboo flute and practice playing it until you are able to achieve some clear tones.

MUSIC Live and recorded music can dramatically affect a room's energy. For a soothing effect on a room, Schubert's "Ave Maria," Pachelbel's *Canon*, and any music by Bach and Albinoni are good. Flute music is excellent. To bring an energy of childlike innocence, children's lullaby music is good. For creativity, life force, and strength, African drumming music is very good. To call forth a powerful dynamic spiritual energy, Gregorian chant is good.

Music is highly personal, so when you choose music for tuning the energy in a room, find something that makes you feel the feeling that you wish to create in the room. For a general tune-up of a room, you can used a progression of recorded music. Start by playing something rousing like one of the classical marches, then play some uplifting yet soothing music (Baroque music is good) and complete with soft, ambient New Age music.

9

MYSTIC SYMBOLS
FOR THE HOME

*T*he symbols in your home have a life and spirit of their own, and they are constantly affecting the energy in your home. You can literally change your life by harnessing the power of the symbols around you.

Symbols have been essential for understanding and relating to the world since the beginnings of the human species. Throughout human history, symbols have been used as a way to harness and focus the mysterious forces around us and humans have used and honored the power of symbols. From the earliest cave drawings to Egyptian hieroglyphs to the Star of David, symbols have given meaning to the mysterious forces around us. They have allowed us to distill our intention through their meaning. In ancient cultures, using symbols in one's home was considered essential to the well-being of its inhabitants.

Though specific symbols have changed through the ages according to culture and fashion, some symbols have remained constant despite the shifting winds of time. These symbols have a power of their own. Not only does the individual shape of a particular symbol affect the flow of energy but, also, the hundreds of years of use strengthens its power on the etheric planes. For example, the particular shape of the symbol has its own power, such as a circle which represents wholeness and completion; but in addition every time someone draws a circle, *holding the idea of completion and wholeness*, this energizes the energy of "Circle" that exists on the etheric planes. Every time you draw a circle in ceremony and ritual not only are you calling upon the power of the shape but you are also accessing the power of the collective consciousness.

A symbol can act in two ways. First, it can be used to focus and project your energy through it. Second, a symbol can function as a magnifier and transmitter of energy, *even if you are not focusing attention on the symbol.* Symbols do have a life force of their own. They are mini-transmitting stations for subtle energies that are infused in our reality. Each symbol interacts with your energy field, constantly generating a force field that strengthens you.

To input the power of symbols into your home you can draw the symbol on a piece of paper, wrap the paper in silk and tuck it into places, such as underneath your bed or in your chest of drawers. You can have paintings or drawings of symbols on your wall, or you can have sculptures or structures in the form of symbols. For example, I have a brass Egyptian ankh (symbol for unquenchable life force) that I keep on my desk.

One fascinating aspect of symbols is the advent of crop circles. Within these unique shapes are symbols that seem to trigger a deep remembering within many people. Although some of these symbols imbedded in crops around the world have been proven to have been created by hoax, there is also overwhelming evidence in support of some of these symbols having been created without human intervention. To facilitate the activation of inner codes, some people draw the symbols exhibited in crop circles and place them in their home.

After you have made or obtained symbols for your home it is important to consecrate them. Metal symbols may be passed through fire or bathed in clear, "charged" water. Paper symbols may be held to the wind or passed over smoking incense. While the symbol is being consecrated it is important to state your Intention aloud. Here is a short list of just a few symbols with a brief description of some of their meanings.

CIRCLE   The circle is one of the most potent symbols. It represents eternity, completion, unity, the universe, wholeness, perfection and the Great Mystery. All of Native American culture revolved around the circle. This was because their conception of life was circular, rather than linear. The Power of the World always goes in circles. The great round sun rises and sets in an enormous circle, as does the moon. The power of the people comes from the sacred hoop of life which represents birth, death and rebirth.

TRIANGLE   The triangle embodies the power of the pyramids. It relates to the combined power of body, mind and spirit, of mother, father and child, of past, present and future, of the Holy Trinity. It is an active symbol for Spirit and for aspiring to higher realms. Two triangles—one in normal position and one inverted and super-imposed on the first—form a six-pointed star (called Solomon's seal) and constitute a symbol for the human soul. The triangle has the power of protection.

SQUARE   The square symbolizes the four elements: air, water, fire and earth, and the four directions. It represents stability and strength, the four seasons. Whereas the triangle (expression of the ternary) is activity and dynamism (or pure spirit), the square (expression of the quaternary) represents the material world. To the Egyptians the square signified achievement. The square is a good symbol to use if you desire your home to be a template of prosperity, abundance and achievement.

CROSS   The symbol of the cross pre-dates Christianity and is perhaps the oldest talismanic symbol in the world. The cross symbolizes eternal life, resurrection and divine protection from evil. It also represents Jesus Christ.

PENTAGRAM   The pentagram symbolizes the human body with each point representing one part of the body's extremities—the head, hands and feet comprising each point of the star. It is used for protection and to invoke the powers of goodness with the single point upright.

INFINITY   The symbol for infinity looks like the number eight laid on its side. This is a very powerful and cosmic symbol to use in your home. I once returned home after a walk and noticed immediately that the energy of my home felt charged in a very positive way. I instantly felt refreshed, exhilarated in fact. I asked the woman who was visiting my home if she had noticed this. She explained that she had been going through the house making the sign of infinity in the air with her hands shortly before my return. The difference in the energy of the whole house was palpable!

*   *   *

The meaning for symbols will vary dramatically from culture to culture and will change during different historical periods. For example, the swastika is an ancient symbol that is sacred to the American Indians and has been found in ancient Viking, Celtic and Aztec ruins, as well as other ancient cultures throughout the world. This very powerful and beautiful ancient symbol now represents fear and suffering to many and is a difficult symbol to work with for that reason.

In order to fully activate the power of symbols in your home, it is necessary to spend some time visualizing their form, while at the same time focusing on your Intention for using the symbol. Your connection with the symbol in this way causes you to become a kind of channel whereby the energy and power of the symbol can flow through you to energize and enlighten your entire home, and your life. Once you have activated the symbols in your home you don't need to keep visualizing them. They will continue to radiate energy and strength.

Other Symbols for Your Home

Throughout your life, you will find that you are attracted to various symbols which will have personal significance for you. These symbols may come to you in dreams, or perhaps you are always noticing them whenever you see them in the world around you. The attraction that you feel is an important clue from your subconscious that these symbols have important meaning for you. If a particular symbol makes you feel hope, empowerment, joy, courage, or any other emotion that you wish to expand in your life, using such a symbol in your home would be a powerful and effective way of accomplishing this. It is not necessary that you fully comprehend the significance of this symbol for you. Just go with the way it makes you feel, and incorporate its meditative qualities into the physical presence of your home.

Numerology

Symbolically, numbers are not merely expressions of quantities, but each number also carries its own spiritual power. Understanding the significance that numbers play in the energy of your home is very important, for the numerology of your address affects the energy of your entire home.

Essentially, numbers are symbols. Each number has a spiritual essence and capacity. It is not known exactly where the art of numerology began, but research can trace its source back thousands of years. Ancient Mayans were known to practice the art of numerology as well as the Mesopotamians, who originated the idea that numbers can explain the structure of the universe. The Cabbala—an ancient Jewish mystical system of understanding the universe—maintains that God created the universe using letters and numbers. Many believe that the pyramids in Egypt and Mexico contain numerological secrets in their architecture and structure.

PYTHAGORAS

Pythagoras was a Greek philosopher, metaphysician and mathematician who pursued the mystical significance of numbers as a science in the sixth century B.C. He not only venerated numbers for their mathematical qualities, he also believed that each number had a mystical significance. Pythagoras thought that numbers were an expression of the fundamental laws of the universe. He stated, "Were it not for Number and its nature nothing that exists would be clear to anyone either in itself or in relation to other things. You can observe the power of Number in all the acts and thoughts of man."

Century by century, the secrets of Pythagoras were passed from master to student. As the student became a master, he would teach the mysteries to a new initiate, and this tradition has continued. Most cultures with esoteric traditions have honored this understanding of the symbology of numbers. Famous people such as Napoleon Bonaparte allegedly used the science of numerology to evaluate his senior officers.

NUMBERS FOR YOUR HOME

Over the last twenty-five years, I have used numerology to help me decide what apartment or home to rent. In fact, I assign so much importance to the numerology of my home that sometimes the numerology has been the sole deciding factor in a move. For example, when I was having financial difficulties I moved into an Eight house. When I wanted to spend time alone working on my spiritual path, then I looked for a Seven vibration house. I learned about numerology from my grandmother on my father's side, who was an astrologer. It was through her that I came to understand the power of numbers. She trained with the metaphysician Manly Hall, who gave her a depth of understanding of the mystical power of numbers.

When clients consult me about purchasing or renting a new home the first thing I do is to calculate the house's numerology and see if the number vibration is in harmony with my client's energy. For example, I was consulted by a young professional woman who was very stressed in her life and complained that she was always on the go and wanted to feel some peace. I asked her when she began to develop the stress, and she responded that it had corresponded with her move into her home. I worked out the numerology of her home and found that it had a Five vibration; Five has an energy of activity and movement. It can be a difficult energy to live in if you need a home that is completely peaceful (although Five homes are great for excitement and adventure and no one will stagnate in a Five house).

Of course, there are many factors that will affect a home's energy, but certainly a house's numerology is important. There were a number of things that I could have done to shift the energy in this woman's home, but as she said she was ready for a move, we focused on the numerology of her prospective choices for a new home. The first home she wanted me to consider was also a Five vibration. This was completely the wrong numerology for someone wanting her home to be a sanctuary from a harried life. The second house she asked me about was a Six vibration and this was perfect for her. The vibration of Six is good for harmony and family. She took my advice, moved into the Six vibration house and reported that she felt more relaxed and at ease than she had for years.

Another story illustrates just how dramatic a part numerology can play in changing the energy field of a home. A family I know has a second home which they use as a kind of retreat from the pressures of urban living. Until recently, they had used this country house almost exclusively for private family activities, seldom ever inviting any guests to it. The house number was 24, which adds up to Six energy, a very private, harmonious kind of vibratory energy.

Recently, their habits regarding this getaway place changed dramatically. Both the husband and the wife began taking business associates out to this home to spend time on work-related projects at weekends. Their children began inviting schoolfriends too. In short, this once very private refuge became almost overnight a bustling center of sociability and enterprise. My friends had told me about this, and I was puzzling over the matter, until later in the conversation they mentioned that the small town where their house is located had recently renumbered all of its streets. Their new house number was 211, which adds up to Four energy, which is a productivity and service-oriented number!

HOW TO CALCULATE
THE NUMEROLOGY OF YOUR HOME

To discover the numerology of your house, take the numbers of your address and add them together. For example, if your house address is 710 Elm Street, you would add 7+1+0=8 so your house would be an Eight vibration. If the total is more than 9 add those numbers together until you reach a number nine or less. For example, if your address is 783 Main Street, you would add 7+8+3=18; then add the numbers of the total together. 1+8=9. So the numerology for 783 Main Street would be a Nine vibration.

Here is another example of how to calculate a home address:

9295 Oak Tree Lane is a Seven Vibration
9+2+9+5=25
2+5=7

There are three exceptions and they are the numbers 11, 22, and 33 which will have the energy of Two, Four, and Six respectively but they also have their own vibration (see page 152). If you live in a block of apartments and the entire block has a numbered street address but you also have a apartment number (for example your address is 457 Jones Street, apartment 27), you are affected by both your address and your apartment number. However, the strongest influence is your individual apartment number. The address 457 Jones

Street is computed thus: 4+5+7=16; 1+6=7; Seven is the vibration of the street address. Seven energy is spiritual growth through the path of individual apartment retreat and solitude. Your apartment number is 27 which reduces to a 9 (2+7=9); Nine vibration is the energy of contributing to humanity. So you would find the energy of this apartment would be concern and dedication to others (Nine) through the path of solitude and spiritual retreat (Seven).

If your address has a letter on it, for example, 328C Fern Lane, convert the letter to a number (A=1, B=2, C=3 and so on). 328C Fern Lane would reduce to 3+2+8+3(C)=16; 1+6=7. Here is a chart for converting letters to numbers:

A	B	C	D	E	F	G	H	I
J	K	L	M	N	O	P	Q	R
S	T	U	V	W	X	Y	Z	
1	2	3	4	5	6	7	8	9

If your home doesn't have a number but only a name, work out the individual letter-number equivalents and then reduce them to the base number. For example,

OWL HOUSE
6 5 3 8 6 3 1 5

(OWL) 6+5+3=14   (HOUSE) 8+6+3+1+5=23

14 + 23 = 37   3+7=10
OWL HOUSE=10

Your home's main number is only one part of a house's numerological energy, just as your astrological sun sign is only one component of your entire astrological profile. Although your home may reduce to a Five vibration the numbers that reduced to the Five will affect the overall energy. For example, 77 Maple Drive reduces to a Five vibration (7+7=14=5). But since the two numbers that are reduced are 7s (a very calm influence) the Five energy of the house is softened. Using the similarity of this to astrology as an example again, consider how a person with an Aries sun sign might be pioneering, outspoken and sometimes rash. However, if the moon sign and rising sign as well as some of the planets were gentler signs such as Libra or Pisces, the dynamic energy of Aries would be lessened by the other planetary influences. The influence that the various individual numbers have on one another in a combined number works in much the same way.

Below is some general information to help you understand the particular numerology of your home.

One

ESSENCE OF ONE Independence; new beginnings; oneness with life; self-development; individuality; progress; creativity.

A HOME WITH A ONE VIBRATION is excellent for a person who wants to embark on an individual creative venture. A person living in a One house will learn from experience rather than instruction and advice from others. A One house is conducive to someone who wants to follow their own instincts and express individuality with creativity and originality. Strong emotions can sometimes be felt in a One house, especially if there are several strong individuals sharing the home. But the emotions are healing and can even spur inspirational creativity. A One house is not a house that will always be neat, as sometimes minor details are secondary to the creative process. If you have been a caretaker for others and have come to a place where you need to be number one in your own life, then move into a One house. You will feel more assertive, independent and willing to take risks in this home.

CHALLENGING ASPECTS OF A ONE HOME Sometimes in a One house you may feel isolated and alone, even if there are others around you. Others may view you as selfish, but you are only isolating yourself so that you can make the decisions that you know are right for you.

Two

ESSENCE OF TWO A balance of the yin and yang energies of the universe; polarities; self-surrender; putting others before yourself; dynamic attraction one to another; knowledge comes from the balance and marriage of opposites.

A HOME WITH A TWO VIBRATION is an excellent home for two people who are going to share space as close roommates, lovers, or as wife and husband. Two vibration could be likened to lighting two candles from the same source; they are separate yet share the same light. People living in a Two house can be as connected as peas in a pod. You will be strongly tuned into the energies and feelings of the others with whom you share your home. Living in a Two home you will have a strong desire for peace and harmony through diplomacy. You will often find yourself standing back and tuning into situations rather than advancing your point of view. You'll find that you can fully and lovingly understand the perspectives of others. In a Two home you will begin to develop a sensitivity to subtle energies of nature and music and even the auric fields of others. Gardens, music, art and magic all flourish in a Two home. You will develop your gentle nature and a desire for harmony. This is a perfect house to explore and develop your psychic and intuitive abilities. It is an excellent house for a marriage or partnership to grow.

CHALLENGING ASPECTS OF A TWO HOME   Because the Two vibration can expand your sensitivity, you may find a tendency to sometimes become oversensitive or to care too much about the feelings of others. Should this happen just take time to be still and listen to your inner voice. Also the energy of a Two home may sometimes seem to exclude others because the occupants of the house can be very self-contained.

Three

ESSENCE OF THREE   The Trinity: Mind, Body, Spirit; the threefold nature of Divinity; expansion; expression; communication; fun; self-expression; to give outwardly; openness; optimism.

A HOME WITH A THREE VIBRATION   is a home where you can feel and be positive about your life. It is also a home where you communicate with flamboyance. This a home where you can expand your vision for your life. Positive thinking produces positive results. A Three house fans your enthusiasm and enhances your warm nature. It is a great house for parties and entertaining. Three houses can be conducive to generating sexual/spiritual energy. Move into a Three house and find your social life expanding. It is a home where people from different cultures and different backgrounds can meet and relate to each other with warmth and love. The power of the Trinity is strong in this house as well as the energy of the triangle and the pyramid.

CHALLENGING ASPECTS OF A THREE HOME   There can be a tendency in a Three house to expand too quickly, scatter your energies and spread yourself too thin. Be careful about finances because in a Three house there is a tendency to enjoy now and pay later. Also sometimes there can be a tendency to be overly optimistic. But certainly the fun that you will have in a Three house can make up for any challenges.

Four

ESSENCE OF FOUR   Security; four elements and the Four Sacred Directions; self-discipline through work and service; productivity; organization; wholeness and unity.

A HOME WITH A FOUR VIBRATION   is a stable and secure energy. Four represents the four walls or boundaries that provide security. It symbolizes solid foundations and protection. If you have been experiencing instability and uncertainty in your life, move into a Four house. You will find your practical, secure, earth nature coming forward. A Four house is very grounded and very connected to Mother Earth. It is in this home that you can find your roots and plant the seeds of your dreams. In this home you will find certainty, stability and strength. You will also be able to relish the fruits of your labor. Kahlil Gibran says in *The Prophet*, "Work is love made visible." Your work can offer you satisfaction and can be a source of security. A Four home lends itself to steady employment and building foundations for the future. Often those who are drawn to a Four house will be involved in areas of service to others, such as nursing. This is an excellent house for a group of people to live in who are working together toward common goals. For example, groups of people working to help Greenpeace would find a Four vibration house conducive to their common goal. Call the assistance of the Four Elements, the Spirit of Air, Water, Fire and Earth, into your home. Ask for the sacred winds from the four directions to further enhance the Four vibration of your home. If you are interested in gardening and connecting with the earth energies, a Four house will suit you.

CHALLENGING ASPECTS OF A FOUR HOME   Sometimes living in a four home can feel like work, work, work and no play. If you find this happening, take a day to be madcap and carefree. Be silly. There can also be a tendency to hoard or to be stubborn. Remember, there is always enough. Loosen up! Life is not as serious as it sometimes seems.

Five

ESSENCE OF NUMBER FIVE   Feeling free; self-emancipating; active; physical; impulsive; energetic; adventurous; resourceful; well-traveled; curious; excitement; change.

A HOME WITH A FIVE VIBRATION   is vibrant, alive and ever-changing. Hold on to your hat if you have moved into a Five house. If you feel that you are stagnating in life this is the perfect house for you, for Five is activity, movement and change. Life becomes a merry-go-round of going to meetings, answering the phone, attending parties, out-of-town trips. It is all exciting and adventurous. This is good house to move into if you want to increase your communication skills. A Five house is all go, go, go with lots of people coming in and out. Five houses tend to be hubs of activity. Five energy lends itself to mental stimulation, gathering information and experiences and sharing it concisely and quickly. This is a great house for a journalist who works at home. A Five house lends itself to having experiences from a vast variety of areas. You might also think of a Five house as a place for Wine, Women(Men) and Song. If you are planning on being celibate this is *not* the house for you. Your sexual appeal will increase in a Five house and this is a good house for romantic flings.

CHALLENGING ASPECTS OF A FIVE HOME   Sometimes living in a Five home can make you feel that your life is a whirlwind. Slow down. Take time to smell the daisies. Also, there is sometimes a tendency to make snap decisions. Usually your instincts are right in a Five home. But if it is a very important decision, take a second breath and deliberate carefully before you decide.

Six

ESSENCE OF NUMBER SIX   Self-harmony; compassion; love; service; social responsibility; beauty; the Arts; generous; concerned; caring; children; balance; community service.

A HOME WITH A SIX VIBRATION   is a center for harmony and balance. This is an excellent vibration to have for a family, especially when there are children in the home. Living in a Six house can contribute to feelings of community service and wanting to help others less fortunate than you. It is an excellent house for someone wanting to develop their artistic abilities. A very good home for a counselor who works at home, for the energy of Six is nurturing and caring. And a counselor working in a Six home will find it much easier to go directly to the heart of the matter with their client, but in a compassionate caring way. The sense of family is all-important in a Six vibration. Close loving relationships with your partner, roommates, friends and family come to life in a Six house. Also the beautifying of the home, as well as the surrounding area, will be important in a Six house.

CHALLENGING ASPECTS OF A SIX HOME Because a Six vibration is so geared toward giving, sometimes there might be a tendency to give too much of yourself. Seek a balance between giving to others and taking care of your own needs. Sometimes the comfort of a Six house can make one inclined toward being reclusive. If this happens, push yourself to get out and see the world.

Seven

ESSENCE OF NUMBER SEVEN The inner life; a mystical number symbolizing wisdom; seven chakras; the seven heavens of the Hawaiian kahunas; birth and rebirth; religious strength; sacred vows; tendency toward ritual, particularly spiritual ritual; the path of solitude; analysis; contemplation.

A HOME WITH A SEVEN VIBRATION is a sanctuary for contemplation and retreat. It is a place where you can analyze past experiences and present situations, with an emphasis on spiritual development. A Seven house is perfect for someone who lives alone who wants to retreat and meditate and seek divine inspiration. It can be a bit difficult for more than one person to share Seven space, unless others in the home complement your contemplative mood. This is an excellent home for a student or a researcher, in that a Seven vibration lends itself to focused investigation. Seven vibration contributes to intuition, dreams, visions, telepathic experiences, philosophical and metaphysical studies—all helping you find your path in life.

CHALLENGING ASPECTS OF A SEVEN HOME This is not a home for those who want to advance in the material world. The energy is focused on the spiritual rather than worldly goods. Also if you are desiring a relationship a Seven house isn't the best to live in, since there is a tendency toward being alone and even aloof in this vibration.

Eight

ESSENCE OF NUMBER EIGHT Infinity; material prosperity; self-power; abundance; cosmic consciousness; reward; authority; leadership.

A HOME WITH AN EIGHT VIBRATION is abundance in all areas of life; abundance of friends and family and material possessions. If you want to get the material side of your life in order, move into an Eight vibration. Eight contributes to organizational and managerial skills which contribute to growing material success. Through discipline and hard work you can achieve a position of power. If you find that you have been working too hard on your spiritual and emotional development and you just don't seem to have it together in the material world, this is the home for you. Power and financial abundance are all possible in this vibration. Awards, honors and public recognition are possible here. Eight is the vibration of wholeness. Your relationships can develop more than just one aspect—they can embody physical, spiritual and mental characteristics. You can command respect and equality.

CHALLENGING ASPECTS OF AN EIGHT HOME You must be careful to consider the welfare of others and be wise with your finances. Otherwise an Eight house will mean that you are always having to deal with abundance issues.

Nine

ESSENCE OF NUMBER NINE Humanitarianism; selflessness; dedicating your life to others; this is a number of completion and of endings; release; universal compassion; tolerance; wisdom.

A HOME WITH A NINE VIBRATION is a home to reap and harvest from past efforts. It is a home where your love and compassion for humanity expands. This vibration allows you to see beyond your own boundaries. You give to others freely because you recognize how much you have gained in your own life. You can develop a breadth of wisdom that can even be prophetic in a nine vibration. Because you know that you are part of a universal family, you have the ability to release the small things in life—you won't take offense easily. Old friendships are important and you might hear from people from your past while living in a Nine house. You will find people drawn to you because of your compassion and wisdom. This is a good home to live in to tie up loose ends in your life. Live your truth because you will be an example for others.

CHALLENGING ASPECTS OF A NINE HOUSE   In your effort to be aware of what the greatest good is for the greatest number of people, you may fail to see the needs of the individual. In addition you may fail to see the particular need of one aspect of yourself as you are overly concerned with the overall picture for your whole self. For example, you may be aware that candy is not good for your overall health, but you may fail to see that the inner child inside you needs the comfort of candy now and then.

MASTER NUMBERS

Master numbers can be reduced to smaller numbers (Two, Four, Six, etc.) and carry the energy of the smaller numbers. However, in metaphysical traditions the following numbers are thought to have a special power and significance of their own:

11   Especially good for developing intuition, clairvoyance, spiritual healing, and other metaphysical faculties. This would be a good home for someone who wanted to develop these capacities.

22   Unlimited potential of mastery in any area, not only spiritual but physical, emotional and mental as well.

33   All things are possible.

I believe that every moment our life is guided, and I believe that wherever we live is one part of a greater plan for our life and evolution. We often have no choice in the home we live in or the subsequent numerological vibration. However, every vibration has its own beauty and will *give you what you need at the time*. For example, you may think that you want to be alone and develop spiritually, and then you find that you have to move into a Three vibration house, which is the energy of communication, expression and expansion.

Even though this might not seem like what you want at the time, I would suggest that this is exactly what you need. I don't believe that there are accidents in where you are living. You chose a vibration that you need at the time for your spiritual growth. However, if you want to offset the numerological vibration of your home, add a letter to it (only in accordance with your local postal authority's regulations, of course) and include that new address in all your correspondence. Although the vibration of the old address will still affect the overall energy of your home, you can mitigate the original energy through personal choice and change.

10
MOVING INTO A
NEW HOME

*M*oving day can be one of the most important days in your life. It can be the beginning of a great and grand adventure or it can be the start of your worst nightmare. The seeds that are planted in the first few days of moving into a home can make all the difference in the years ahead.

Homes are like people. They have a personality and a consciousness. When you first meet a person, if you ignore them or, even worse, if you criticize them, this can taint the rest of your relationship. However, if you begin a relationship with love and care and kindness, then the years to come will often be rewarding. To prosper and be healthy and happy in your new home it is important to take a few simple first steps.

Moving into an Already-Lived-In Home

FORMAL GREETING

When you are anticipating a move and are looking at a number of homes, it can be difficult trying to decide which one is the best for you. Give a "Hello!" in your mind to each home that you visit. (To say it aloud might bring a startled response from the real estate agent!) Listen to the response that you get from the home—open your mind and heart to how a particular house makes you feel. Take time to really imagine yourself and your family and/or friends living there. Try to evaluate how close a connection you feel to the various places you visit, and try to visualize how the individuality of each home might affect different areas of your life.

Once you have made your decision, take a little time getting to know your new home. You can say, either aloud or in your mind, "Greetings. I'm [your name], and I am very happy to be moving here. I'm looking forward to getting to know you and spending time with you." This particular greeting might seem silly to you, so find the words that feel best to you. But the basic idea behind this process is to start off your relationship with your new home with the feeling that you are happy to be there, that you are looking forward to caring for and being sheltered by your home. A simple greeting can bring joy and life into a home that initially seemed inanimate and dull. A home can be like a seed, dry and dormant for many years, that when given the right conditions begins to sprout and grow into vibrant new life.

·

GETTING TO KNOW THE PERSONALITY OF YOUR NEW HOME

Before you move any furnishings into your home, get to know the personality of your home. Start off by spending some time alone in the house. How does it feel? What sort of "pulls" on your spirit and your energy field do you perceive? Walk into each room. Sit and "listen" to the energy in it. In meditation connect with the spirit of the home and see if there is anything the home would like you to know before you move in. Wander from room to room. Stop in each one and close your eyes. Open your heart, your ears, your nose, your skin. What images come to you?

Observe the basic structure of your new home. Decide how its layout can best be used to further the aims you want to pursue during your time there. What overall feeling do you want your home to convey? How can each room contribute to the overall energy that you desire for your home? What feels like the best use of each room— which room will you use for socializing and where will you go for a time of seclusion? Where do you feel the most propitious energy for meditation? Voice out loud your intentions for each room.

If possible, try to sleep in your new residence before you move anything in. Notice the dreams you have. Your dreams can provide valuable information which can guide you in later design decisions. Even if you are not consciously aware of what is occurring subconsciously during your dreams, the information will be stored in your mind, and you will begin to act upon it in your waking life.

HOUSE CLEANING AND CLEANSING

Before you move in give your home a complete cleaning. Wash the windows. Mop the floors. Wash down the walls. Completely clean everything. Not only are you cleaning dirt but you are also cleaning residual energy emanations from the previous tenants. This doesn't mean that previous occupants' emanations are bad; it just means that you are establishing your personal energy field in the home.

When you have finished cleaning, do a very thorough house clearing using the methods described in this book. *The clearing that you do before you move into a home is very important.* Not only are you clearing energy but you are establishing an energy field for the future. The intention that you establish at the beginning of your relationship with your home will create a context for the form and energy that develop in your home in the future. This is very important. Just as the attention that you give a child in the early years will set in place patterns for the rest of the child's life, the intention that you create at the inception of your move into a new home will create an energy that will be felt for the duration of your stay.

As you are packing all of your possessions, do so with attention and care, for this will imbue them with positive energy. Likewise, when you are unpacking them, clean them with the same loving attention, so that they will radiate their beauty with joy into the atmosphere of your new home.

NAMING

It is valuable to find the name of your home. In ancient metaphysical tradition everything had a name, and to know the name of a thing was to form an intimate connection with it. To find your home's true name, first go into the room that feels like the heart center of your home. (Homes have chakras [energy centers] just as humans do, and to discover the heart center of your home, simply ask yourself where in the house it is that you feel the most love.) When you are in the heart center of your home, go into a meditation. Allow yourself to imagine that your home has a personality and a human form. Gently and lovingly request to know the name of the being who appears to you as the personification of your home. It might be that you are not given a name but receive a feeling instead. If this is the case, then try to name the feeling. Perhaps an overall name for a home will come forth, as well as additional names for different rooms. The more you use your home's name and relate to the Spirit of your home, the better the overall energy will be in your home.

MOVING-IN CEREMONY

In ancient times the Moving-In Ceremony was very important. In some tribes the entire village would gather together for the ceremony. Priests would bless the home and ask for the Spirit of the Home to bring blessings to its occupants. Afterwards there would be a celebration where the new occupants would provide a feast for the villagers.

In some traditions the Moving-In Ceremony was done only on an auspicious day, which meant that the stars and the moon were in favorable location for the move.

You can design your own Moving-In Ceremony in whatever way best suits your own beliefs, needs, and personal style. The details are not the essential thing. What is important is that you find some way to mark and honor the fact that you are beginning a new cycle in your life.

Constructing Your Own Home

FORMAL GREETING WITH THE LAND

Building your own home presents you with a unique opportunity for connecting with your home literally from the ground up. From the moment when you first conceive of the idea of building your home, you can decide on and bring into being the kind of energy your home will be imbued with for as long as it exists.

Once you know where you are going to build your home, spend time on the land. Walk the land. Sleep on the land. Talk to the land. Reach your hands into the soil and feel the land. Once you have established contact with the land, formally introduce yourself and explain what plans you have for the area. Ask for the support of the land in your venture and for the years ahead. This first step is essential because once you gain the support of the Earth Spirit, the construction will go more easily and there will be continual energy flowing up from the earth during your years in the home.

CHOOSING HOME LOCATION

The arts of geomancy and Feng Shui can be helpful in picking out the place where your home will be placed on your land, but the greatest guide should be how a particular spot feels to you. Once you have connected with the earth, you will have a stronger sense of just where the best place to build is. Even if all the Feng Shui signs and the geomancy signs are right, the whole thing can still be wrong if it doesn't feel right to you. When Native Americans were choosing a place to put their teepee, hogan or lodge, they did not look at all the Feng Shui rules. They just knew when a place *felt* right. This is a most profound method for planning the location of your home too. Trust your intuition.

ARCHITECT, BUILDER AND BUILDING SUPPLIES

Since you are creating energy as well as a physical structure, it is very important to feel good about the people who will be working on your home. This doesn't mean that the architect and builders have to meditate every morning. (You might be waiting a century before you could find a meditating construction crew.) However, work with people you feel good about, because their energy is a part of the evolving energy of the home. Homes made in joy have a wonderful energy. A home made with arguments and anger often has a feeling of disharmony.

Everything that makes up your house has its own history and significance. Take some time to observe and honor the sources from which everything in your home comes. Look at what materials make up the parts of your house. When you look at the golden grain of a polished wood floor, see also the mighty strength of the oak tree from which the wood came. Thank the tree for its gift of life and spirit to make shelter, warmth and enjoyment for you. When you look through the clear panes of your windows, imagine the golden sands lying warm in the sun, sands which were then melted and transformed into glass for your benefit and vision. Connect to the source of the building materials in your home and the spirit from which they have come. As you do this, it "calls" Spirit into the materials.

FOUNDATION CEREMONY

On the day that the digging begins, give a gift to the earth. You might follow the Native American tradition of sprinkling cornmeal or tobacco on the earth in thanks. The morning that the actual foundation is laid it is valuable to have a Foundation Ceremony. The Foundation forms the support for your entire home, so you want this to be as strong and balanced as possible. In ancient times, sacrifices were made at the time that a foundation was laid. This was done out of respect for the importance of the foundation laying. To bless the foundation sprinkle a bit of "charged" water into the foundation mixture, saying, "May the strength of the firmaments fill you. May the blessings of Mother Earth fill you. May this home stand firm and strong in the years ahead."

After the foundation is poured but before it is set, put something of value into the mixture. You might place a crystal that has been blessed or a photograph of your family completely happy together. I knew a family that placed coins into the mixture because they wanted prosperity in the new home. (It worked. The family business flourished while they lived in the home.)

MOVING-IN CEREMONY

In some native cultures when a family moves into a new home they take sticks and drum on the walls for hours. This is their way of connecting with the Spirit of the House and celebrating together with it.

Before you move into your new home, you should try and follow the steps described above in the section on older homes for getting to know the personality of your home, and about house cleaning and clearing. Even though your home is brand-new and you will be the first people ever to live in it, going through these steps will help you to define your vision for living in your home, and will help clearly to establish the energy that you want there. After following these steps, you can invite friends and family into your new home. Ask them to spend a few moments in silent blessings for your new home. If you have friends who like to be very verbal you can ask them to share aloud their blessing for the home and its occupants. Then have a huge celebration with food and music. You have worked hard, you have brought a new home into existence, you made it happen! Rejoice! Your new home will be rejoicing with you!

11

YOUR HOUSE
AS METAPHOR

*E*verything around you is a reflection of your inner being. The visible realities surrounding you are symbols of your invisible world. In every moment of your life you are walking in a "forest of symbols" which are constantly reflecting your personal reality. In order to understand this, it's valuable to know the underlying dynamics.

We all have conscious and subconscious beliefs about ourselves and the life around us. The beliefs that specifically dictate the quality of life are our *subconscious* beliefs. Each of us has subconscious programming that directs the way we see the world and also influences the way others see us. This programming has come from the way others related to us when we were children. It also comes from decisions that we made in past lives. In addition, our beliefs come from the collective consciousness of the society within which we live. If you are not sure what your subconscious energy field is projecting into the world, just look at your life. Your life is an absolute indication of the energy and subconscious beliefs that you are projecting.

Perhaps you've heard the expression "You are what you think." This doesn't mean only what you *know* you think consciously. It also refers to what you *don't know* you think (your subconscious beliefs). A young boy being repeatedly told that he is selfish is an example of how subconscious beliefs begin to occur. The child's critical faculties are not developed enough to reject this negative programming, so his subconscious accepts the idea of his being selfish. This belief of self-ishness begins to become a part of the boy's reality so that he begins to feel as if he really is a selfish person. *Whatever is expected tends to be realized,* so the child grows up acting selfishly. His inner programming is so deeply embedded in his mind that it becomes part of his "ground of being."

When a subconscious belief becomes part of your "ground of being" this means it doesn't seem like a decision or belief—it seems that it is "the way it is." Sometimes our inner-core beliefs can be likened to gravity. Gravity is so much a part of our ground of being that we don't have any conscious awareness that many pounds of pressure are being exerted on every square inch of our body every moment. Gravity is such a fundamental part of what we take for granted as reality that we almost never think about it.

Core beliefs become so much a part of our view of ourselves and the world that we don't even know that they are beliefs. They are glued or embedded into our personal energy field. And these subconscious beliefs continually coalesce into form in the manifest world. As your energy projects from your body in undulating waves all around you, it projects your beliefs into the world. Then the beliefs in your energy field act as magnets, pulling to you situations and people that are congruous with your subconscious beliefs.

This means that your personal world is created or manifested by the core beliefs in your subconscious about yourself and life. For example, if you have the subconscious core belief that no one will ever truly love you, you will continue to create relationships where you are never truly loved—even though consciously you may desperately want to be loved.

Or if you have a subconscious belief embedded in your personal energy field that you can't trust anyone, this subconscious belief is constantly projecting out of you; this occurs even when you are feeling calm and peaceful. The emanations from your energy field will act as a magnet pulling people into your life who can't be trusted.

Many people are beginning to realize that they can change their inner core beliefs, and by doing this their life changes. When you change your inner reality it naturally follows that your outer reality reflects that change. Less commonly known, but just as true, is the fact that *if you change your outer reality, your inner reality can change.*

You can dramatically alter the conditions of your life simply by implementing changes in the energy fields in your living environment!

Creating the Template in Your Home

By changing the energy in your home you create an energy template. Working with your Intention and your furnishings, you can create a new pattern or template that will penetrate deep into your subconscious. This template can help change deep subconscious negative programming.

As your inner programming is altered by your home template you begin to project a new energy field. Life and people around you will respond to this new energy field and the universe around you will coalesce to match the energy that you are projecting. For example, if you create a template of adventure and drama within your home this becomes absorbed into your auric field. Then wherever you go, even when you are not in your home, your auric emanations will be saying, "Hey! I'm ready to go and have fun!" and you will draw adventure to you.

If you want to create abundance in your life, create an abundant template in your home. If you want to feel a deep inner peace, create an environment that projects an energy of deep inner peace. Thus your home can be a living affirmation of what you want to create in your life now and in the future. Here are some suggestions you can use to create templates that can positively influence your life.

TO BE MORE ORGANIZED IN YOUR LIFE

If your life feels full of confusion, the simple task of cleaning out your dresser drawers and making them spectacularly neat will spill over into the rest of your life. The sense of control and order that you gain from organizing your drawers can give you a sense of power and order in your life, and you may suddenly be able to solve problems which you felt completely befuddled about previously.

Go through each and every drawer with this motto in mind: "Use it, love it or *get rid of it!*" Clear out every drawer with the ferocity of a warrior. If something needs to be mended, mend it or get rid of it.

To keep this from becoming an overwhelming job, start with one small drawer or one small area and slowly work one area at a time. Dumping all your drawers in the middle of the floor to begin your task of reorganization would only increase your feelings of indecision and confusion. Even if you are only able to organize one room in your home, accomplishing this task will create a powerful template for you to begin to gain control of your life.

TO CREATE MORE ABUNDANCE IN YOUR LIFE

If you want to create abundance in your life, start by creating the illusion or the feeling of luxury in your personal space. This can be done with little money if you use your creativity. Buy things which, although inexpensive in reality, nonetheless feel abundant, like a richly colored fabric. Visit shops that sell nice things secondhand at a fraction of what they would cost if new. Pick up items that appeal to your sense of self-indulgence.

Then start with one room, perhaps your bedroom. Drape your bed and your walls with the rich-colored fabric. Add lots of pillows. Make everything exude a sense of deep comfort and well-being. Put on the wall photos or paintings that portray abundance.

You may also want to create a "treasure map" to hang on the wall to help reprogram your subconscious. A treasure map is a collection of photographs or magazine clippings you have pasted together that create a picture that conveys the image of what you want to manifest. For example, if your old car keeps breaking down and you want a newer car, find a picture of the car that you want. Paste it on a large poster board (approximately 18 by 20 inches). Then find a picture of yourself in which you look really happy to paste on the board near the car. Then paste pictures and words that convey abundance and prosperity. You might paste pictures of big bunches of flowers or beautiful carpets and luxurious food. Make sure you paste something on your board that represents Spirit as a way to remember the creative loving principle at play in your manifestation. Then place your treasure map somewhere so that it can begin to infiltrate into your subconscious mind. This is often the bedroom. Creating a base of abundance in your private space will alter your consciousness in such a way that you will begin to know that abundance can actually flow into your life.

A young man contacted me about clearing the energy in his home. He had been made redundant from his job and was struggling with prosperity issues. He hoped that clearing the energy in his house might help to change his fortune. He said money seemed to leave his life just as fast as it entered. When I entered his home, as I walked around each room I was aware of energy leaking out of the home. Energywise, his house was like a sieve. Upon querying him I found that he was often very tired in his home and people who came to visit often left early because they felt tired. After closing up the energy leaks using space-clearing techniques, I suggested that he create an environment that felt abundant. (I also suggested that he explore and resolve his feelings of unworthiness so he could realize that it was all right to be abundant and so he could discover that he was worthy of prosperity.)

To create a more abundant atmosphere we talked about what felt abundant to him. I then had him close his eyes and go on a creative visualization journey to imagine that he was walking around inside an abundant home. As he went on his inner journey, he said that he saw bottles of wine in a wine rack, a good quality olive oil on the work surface, and fresh garlic in a basket in the kitchen. His images all seemed to center around the kitchen and on good quality ingredients.

He came out of his meditation and we talked about what he had seen. He really enjoyed cooking and he realized that many of his associations for abundance had to do with ingredients used in recipes. He realized that in some cases his perception of his financial state was reinforced by the way he shopped. For example, he would use powdered garlic in his cooking rather than fresh garlic (although he could easily afford fresh garlic), because he had the subconscious thought form that only abundant people can use fresh garlic.

After our meeting he went shopping and bought a nice bottle of olive oil, some good wine and fresh garlic. This course of action may seem silly or trivial to some people, but to him he was breaking a pattern of poverty consciousness. He later told me that he felt very abundant whenever he cooked after that. He created a kitchen that felt and looked abundant to him. Every time he entered his kitchen he was symbolically breaking his old pattern. This wasn't an overnight success story, but slowly and surely he began to break a lifetime pattern of poverty consciousness and began to build an abundant and prosperous future.

TO CREATE MORE LOVE IN YOUR LIFE

Look to see what symbolizes love to you and then fill your home with that. A woman who came to me wanted to have love in her life. We cleared her home and then installed an indoor waterfall in the relationship area of her house (see Chapter 13). I asked her to tell me what else represented love to her. She replied that the color pink (pink roses and hearts) represented love to her. At my suggestion she planted pink roses in her garden. Lots of them! She painted her bedroom wall a soft shell pink and she put all shapes and sizes of hearts in her home, from photos of hearts to heart-shaped pillows. I also suggested that she put up photos of people who looked happy together. In much less time than she expected she met a professor at a local college and fell head over heels in love. They developed a wonderful relationship.

TO GENERATE MORE CREATIVITY IN YOUR LIFE

Creativity comes from being able to see something ordinary in a different way. Look at a basket and see a lampshade. Take things that others are throwing away and see what you can do to be creative with them. I knew of three brothers who were all dustbin men. The three of them lived together and had created a wonderful magical environment in their home just by using the things that other people had thrown away. Take what someone throws away and find a way to turn it into an object of beauty.

You can use your home as a canvas for your creativity without spending a lot of money. Get an old secondhand sofa and a large amount of inexpensive canvas or heavy muslin. Get a paintbrush and create designs on the canvas. I have used watered-down latex combined with acrylic polymer to bind it to the canvas (or fabric paint, which is a bit more expensive). Throw it in the washing machine and voilà—instant designer fabric filled with your creative spirit! Sew the fabric into a big square and drape it over the old sofa. To keep the cover from slipping make a long tube of fabric and use it to tie around the base of the sofa.

Paint a plain paper lampshade with your own designs. Paper your walls with torn brown paper bags layered over each other. Papier-mâché an old set of drawers with newsprint or glossy, colorful magazines. Take tiny white Christmas tree lights and string them through a tall branch and stick this in a corner of your living room to make it seem full of magic.

These are just a few ideas to get you going. Be creative in your home, and you will find that you have begun to create a template of creativity for your life.

TO CREATE MORE PEACE IN YOUR LIFE

To create more peace in your life fill your home with the energy and feeling of peace. Paint a room blue. Replace reds and oranges with blues and pastel colors. Get rid of any object that you don't like or anything which makes you feel irritated. Play soothing music. Dedicate your house crystals to peace. Have pots of ferns about your home. Invest in an aquarium with slow-moving, graceful fish. Create an indoor waterfall so you can listen to the relaxing sound of water flowing. Put up photos and paintings of peaceful nature scenes. Soften sharp corners by draping or hanging fabric there. Spray lavender aroma throughout your home periodically. When your home feels like a sanctuary of peace, peace will fill your heart.

TO CREATE MORE PASSION IN YOUR LIFE

Purple velvet curtains, luxurious pink towels, candles everywhere, tassels, tassels, tassels. Let overlong curtains fold onto themselves as they lay languid on the floor. Throw an assortment of pillows everywhere. Mix and match colors and fabrics. Place bowls of flowers—let them wilt, all stages of a flower can be beautiful (tulips go through so many wonderful curling and turning stages before the last petal drops). Toss your shoes over your shoulder when you take them off. Throw an old paisley shawl over a sofa. Put a burgundy silk scarf with long dangling tassels over a lampshade. Put an oversized nude painting, slightly askew, as the central focus in your living room. Spray flowered perfume throughout your home. Play Billie Holiday music.

Of course, passion means something different to each person. Find out what passion means to you and create this feeling in your home. I was invited to clear a middle-aged woman's apartment. When I was talking to her about her life and her desires and goals, it became clear that she was lonely and wanted to be in a relationship. When I looked around her home, I saw that although it was very attractive, it was almost too neat. Everything was in its place and looked as if it had been carefully placed there. One table had small intricate porcelain figures, each placed an equal distance from the others. Another table had a small bunch of flowers in a tidy arrangement. Although the effect was pleasant, it did not feel as if there was room for anyone else in her home or in her life. It was a closed circuit.

Asking her forgiveness, I went over to the arrangement of flowers and took them out of the vase. I took them into her kitchen and began to haphazardly stuff them into a drinking glass so that they cascaded over the edges in a whimsical and fluid manner. I then asked her to look at the flowers and tell me how she felt. She said that looking at them made her feel awkward and uncomfortable. We talked more about her life and she said that she had been feeling very confined and restricted.

She agreed to let me make some more changes in her home after I had cleared its energies. There wasn't much to clear—only a bit of stagnant energy here and there. But after the clearing I began to push furniture around and toss throws and pillows haphazardly about. I took a painting off the wall and set it on the floor, leaning it up against a wall. I also gave her some suggestions of additional things that she could do on her own to loosen up the energy in her home.

The energy in this woman's house was so precise and confined that it made it difficult for anyone else to enter into her home and feel comfortable there. By creating disarray it opened up the circuit. Although she said the changes made her uncomfortable, she agreed to live in her rearranged home for a while to see what happened.

A few days later I received a very excited phone call. She said that men at her work who previously hadn't even noticed her had begun to pay attention to her, even though she was acting exactly the same as always (or so she thought). She was so encouraged that she went home and messed up her home some more. I told her that it wasn't really necessary to mess up her house completely. What we had done was to begin breaking up old patterns of behavior reflected in her home that had precluded her ever being in a relationship. I am happy to report that a number of months later she told me she had entered into a relationship. Create a template of passion and form will follow.

TO CREATE MORE
FUN AND HAPPINESS IN YOUR LIFE

If you are suffering from a lingering sense of depression, a heaviness on your soul, try opening up your environment to light in every way. Throw back the curtains. Fill your room with candles. Try suspending gauzy fabric from the ceiling. Consider a bird for a pet! You will be amazed at the startling effects these actions will have on your mood.

Use happy colors. Use bright yellows and clear cheerful colors on your walls and in your home furnishings. Open the windows to let in as much light as possible. Put toys on your bookshelves. I find that one of the best ways to cheer up a home is to have the old-fashioned wind-up toys on display. These inevitably bring a smile. Put up a windsock, colorful banners and bird feeders. Throw soft toys on to the beds. Put a whimsical sculpture in your living room. Paint one dining room chair with stripes and another with polka dots. Have whimsical, madcap and carefree household accessories and this will spill into your life.

TO CREATE MORE SIMPLICITY IN YOUR LIFE

Get rid of absolutely everything that you don't need or don't completely love. Be ruthless. If you haven't used it within the last two years, get rid of it. If you haven't worn it in a year, get rid of it. Unclutter your walls. It's better to have one good picture than a whole cluttered wall of paintings and wall accessories that you don't really care for. Clear your coffee table. Leave one favorite perfect object on it. Clean your closets. It is better to have ten good outfits than thirty you don't really like or use. Revel in the bare, simple form of your home and your life will begin to become more simple too.

TO RELEASE A NEGATIVE PAST

To release a negative past, release objects in your home that carry the energy of your past into your present life. For example, a client told me that she always felt ill every time she entered her bedroom. She asked me if I would clear the energies there for her. I tested the energies in her bedroom and they were fine. I began to question her about what it felt like when she got ill. She said it felt exactly like when she had morning sickness when she was pregnant two and half years earlier. I then asked when she started feeling ill in her bedroom. She responded that she had felt ill whenever she had entered her bedroom for the past year. I asked her if there was anything in her current bedroom that was the same as in her bedroom when she had morning sickness.

Suddenly her entire face lit up. She said, "I was sick almost my entire pregnancy and usually I would stay in bed because I felt too ill to get up. The bedspread was the blue-green covering that you see on my bed now. After the birth of my baby I was given a new bed cover. Then about a year ago the new cover became stained so I put the old blue-green cover on the bed. That is exactly the time I began to feel ill every time I entered the bedroom." She realized that she had associated morning sickness and nausea with the blue-green bedspread, so that every time she entered her bedroom she activated a subconscious nausea response. We promptly removed the offending cover and she said that she felt great. In fact, ever since removing the bedspread, she never felt ill when she entered her bedroom again.

The Zulus will burn clothes that someone wore when going through a difficult time to release the emotional residue left on the clothes. Some cultures will burn the clothes a woman was wearing when giving birth so that she and the baby are symbolically stepping into a new cycle. If there are objects in your home that have bad memories associated with them or that were given to you by someone you don't feel good about, get rid of them! (Or if you can't bear to get rid of them, then cleanse them thoroughly.)

The objects in your home should be associated with good memories. Otherwise, negative associations will drag down the energy in your home. When you purchase something for your house be aware of the fact that how you feel while shopping for the item will affect how you feel about it once it is in your home. If your experience is good and joyous, your associations with the object will be good ones and it will continue to emanate that happy experience. Whereas if you purchase something and the salesperson is rude and you feel disgruntled, you will probably never enjoy that object as much as if the shopping experience felt good.

A young woman called me who had been divorced the previous year. She was suffering a mild depression and wondered if maybe there was bad energy in the apartment she had moved into after her divorce. When I went to her apartment I noticed unusual emanations from a number of the objects in her home. In answer to my queries she said, "Oh, Ted and I bought that in Hawaii"; "Ted and I got that in a cute little antique store." Every item that had an unusual energy field was a purchase made during her difficult marriage. (She had been married for only a year following a short courtship.)

I told her that the basic energy in her home seemed fine. I did suggest that she hang some mirrors and place crystals in her windows, but my primary suggestion was that she remove all the objects that she had acquired during her short marriage. She didn't want to do that, so I suggested that she put them in storage for two weeks and see if it helped lift her depression. She reluctantly put the objects in storage for two weeks. I called two weeks later to see how she was doing. She told me that the depression had lifted. She said she had realized that she was holding on to the past and that every time that she looked at the objects she and Ted had bought together she subconsciously felt like a failure. Removing the constant affirmation (in her mind) of her failure had opened the space for her to evaluate her relationship objectively. She decided that she wasn't going to put the objects back in her home and that she was ready to step forward in life rather than keep looking backwards.

TO BE HEALTHIER IN YOUR LIFE

To use your house as a template for excellent health there are two areas you can work with. The first area deals with steps you can take to change directly your physical environment. Check the EMFs (electromagnetic fields) in your house and eliminate as many of them as possible; stay away from the rest of them (see pages 191–94). Invest in an air-purification system (see pages 90–92), and drink purified water or invest in a water-purification system (see Chapter 5). Check to see if there are any allergens in your home, such as carpet glue, asbestos, or radon gas from bricks (to name only a few) and investigate ways to neutralize these allergens.

Another way to create a template of health is to create an environment that feels vibrant and healthy. Put plants everywhere. (Make sure that they are healthy—an unhealthy plant is not a good template for health.) Color the walls bright clean colors, rather than muddy colors or gray. (Clean clear colors are much more healing than murky colors.) Put up photos and paintings that either show healthy people or that have a vitality to them. (In other words, no gray drizzling scenes of London streets in the winter; rather, put up a photo of a mountain meadow resplendent with flowers on a bright sunny day.) Completely clean your home and completely cleanse the energies in your home. Then lightly clear the energy of your home at least once a week. The more vitality and health that your home projects, the easier it is for you to stay healthy and well.

TO BE MORE SPIRITUAL

Find photos or paintings of special spiritual teachers or people on a spiritual path that you admire. Place these photos in places where they will imprint on your subconscious. Placing a spiritual teacher's photo near your bed where it will be the last thing that you see before bed and the first thing that you see when you awake is a good idea. Not everyone likes the idea of gurus, in which case you can place images of God's creations around your home, such as a painting of a forest or a mountain. Another good way to create a more spiritual template is to put affirmations or inspirational quotes throughout your home. Find a quote that resonates with your spiritual aspirations and have it copied out by a calligrapher. Place it in a frame and hang it someplace where it will begin to imprint your subconscious. One of the best places to put quotes or inspiraitonal sayings is in the bathroom or bedroom.

Another way to create a spiritual template in your home is to create a home altar. What an altar is like is a matter for personal choice but, at its most basic, an altar is a small shrine of physical objects that are symbolic of your connection to Spirit and objects that help you remember why you are here on the planet. Of course, not all people have the space for an entire meditation room for their altar, but a small one can be created in even the tiniest apartment—on a table top, on a shelf, or anywhere that you consider to be a place of honor in your home. My current meditation room with an altar is in a converted cupboard. When we previously lived in a very tiny house, I placed my altar underneath a decorative table. I made a cover for it which covered the table and came to the floor, and which created a wonderful intimate location for a small spiritual retreat for me.

Your altar should be the spiritual center of your home. The energy created by your altar radiates to the rest of your home. If you have a guru or other spiritual teachers you might put their photos on your altar as a reminder of the qualities that you perceive within them for which you are personally striving. If you find your connection to Spirit in nature then you might put objects from nature on your altar. It is good to have one object that is a focal point for your altar. This might be a symbolic object (such as the Star of David), or it could be a photo (of some place in nature or of someone who helps you to connect with your spiritual source), or an object (such as a crystal, a bell, a feather or a flower). It is important continually to energize, dust and clean your altar since it fulfills such an important function in your home.

TO BE MORE BEAUTIFUL

To feel more beautiful, create beauty around yourself. Take time to be still and be aware of what represents beauty to you. For one person, beauty is a bowl of pink roses, while for another, beauty is sunlight streaming through a window with the curtains gently blowing on either side. Buy one perfectly beautiful sheet for your bed and every time you get into bed feel yourself being enveloped by the smoothness of this beautiful sheet. Create an environment that feels beautiful to you.

The more you see and perceive beauty around you the more beautiful you will become. Wherever you are, even if you are not in your home, perceive, see, feel, smell, hear beauty all around you. Involve all your senses. Even if you are in a crowded smoggy city, wherever you are there is always beauty somewhere. Perhaps a beautiful small plant has forced its way through the pavement, or a small cloud is wafting between tall buildings. Perceive beauty wherever you are, in your home and in your environment, and you will become more beautiful.

TO HAVE MORE ADVENTURE IN YOUR LIFE

I have a friend who lives in the center of London, yet when you step into her small apartment you feel that you have stepped into an adobe home in the Southwest of the United States. She has adobe walls and cactus plants. She burns sage for incense and plays Native American flute music on her stereo. She has Indian dream catchers on the walls and photographs of wolves and Southwest-style carpets. You almost feel that if you looked out of the window you would see the great plains with buffalo stampeding across them, instead of Portobello market. I asked her about her home and she said that it filled her with a sense of adventure and the pioneer spirit. (It is interesting to notice that her life is filled with adventure.) Although she works in a London office, she has traveled to the United States to participate in a sweat lodge and made a Native American drum. Form follows Intention, and as she had the Intention for adventure and the Spirit of the West she has begun to create that in her life.

To have more adventure in your life put up photos or paintings of exotic places. Create an environment that says, "I step beyond personal boundaries. I'm willing to go for it in life." No color-coordinated furnishings for you. Be daring. Mix traditional Queen Anne chairs and delicate Wedgwood cups and saucers with a heavy metal poster or a fluorescent orange lamp.

Are you one of those people who doesn't want to use their "good stuff"? Do you never use the towels on display in your bathroom, but have a grubbier version for actual use? Or do you never use your good china? If you want more adventure in your life then break loose. *Use* your best china! *Sit* on your best chair! (Take off the plastic cover!) *Use* your best towels! Take risks in your home environment and this creates a template for you to step into madcap adventures in life.

WHAT IS YOUR CURRENT HOME TEMPLATE?

Examine the template that you have created for yourself in your home now. What overall energy does your home project? Does your home look and feel spartan? Does it portray comfort and a relaxed view of life? A spartan home is fine if you want to have a precise approach to the world. However, if you want more comfort in your life, then make your home environment more comfortable. If you want more precision, clarity and organization in your life but your home looks like a tornado hit it, change your home to change your life.

Does your home project the template that you want for yourself? Are you happy about the messages your house conveys? If you were a stranger walking into your home, what judgments would you make about the person who lived there? (Usually the judgments that we assign to others are a true indication of our own subconscious feelings.) If your home doesn't project the template that you desire, change it and watch your life change.

House as Self

The sense of order revealed by the way in which we organize our homes reflects our personal sense of order in the universe. Your home in many ways is a symbolic representation of your self. In fact, many dream experts concur that whenever a person's house appears in a dream it is often a symbolic representation of one's self. The basement in a dream usually represents the subconscious, whereas the attic often represents higher aspirations. Every part of your house has a symbolic correlation to a part of your life. In order to change your life or strengthen one aspect of your life, pay attention to the corresponding part of your home. Every room in your home represents a part of you. Though I've given a few examples below, it is best for *you* to find what each room symbolizes in your life.

FRONT ENTRANCE

The front entrance of your home is very important since it not only creates a first impression and sets the energy for the entire rest of the house, but is also symbolic of how you present yourself to the world. Your home needs to be a nourishing space for you to come into, and the more welcoming your entrance is the more your home will nurture and sustain you. Make your entrance an expression of the intention of your entire home. Place healthy flowering plants at the entrance and pictures which inspire you inside the doorway. Good lighting is also important and mirrors can help to bring light and add dimension, especially if your entrance hall is small.

If you want your personal presentation to the world to be expanded and welcoming, create a feeling in your entrance that is expanded and welcoming. Make sure that your entrance way isn't cluttered or dirty. Clutter in the entrance way and especially clutter which prevents the door from opening fully needs to be cleared so that beneficial energies can flow into the home. When your first experience entering your home is one of having to push through obstacles, this can symbolize creating obstacles that you need to push through in your life. Clear the obstacles in your entrance to help clear the obstacles in your life.

BEDROOM

Your bedroom is your place of retreat and it can symbolize the way you perceive your inner self. This is different from the entrance, which symbolizes how to present yourself to the world. If you have a low sense of self-esteem and your bedroom is dark and dreary, then you may want to use more lighting, hang mirrors and use lighter colors. This communicates symbolically to your inner self that your inner space is bright and uplifting. However, if you are always giving energy out to everyone and never leaving anything for yourself and your bedroom is bright and light with lots of windows, then you may want to create more of a nest and use dark warm colors and pull the curtains. This creates a template that says you have an inner sanctuary within yourself.

BATHROOM

Your bathroom can symbolize release and letting go of what you don't need in life and it also represents cleansing and renewal. A bathroom can be symbolic of letting go of the old and embracing the new. If you have difficulty in letting go of things that you don't use any more and letting go of relationships that aren't supportive, then go through your bathroom and clean the cupboards. Get rid of anything in your bathroom that you don't need. This can create a template of releasing things from your life that are not serving your best interests. If you feel that your life is stagnant and needs renewal, then clean your bathroom. The simple act of cleaning it generates a template of renewal and purification in your life.

HOUSE SYSTEMS

Not only do the rooms in your home represent aspects of you, but the systems within your home and the materials in your home also represent aspects of you. Although it is important to come up with your own symbolism for the various systems in your home, here are some examples to consider.

Water represents emotions and feelings, so the plumbing in your home can represent your emotions. If your plumbing is clogged, it could be a sign that your emotions are blocked. If a toilet overflows, it could be a sign that your emotions are overflowing. Frozen pipes can symbolize that your emotions are frozen. A leaky tap can represent a constant drain on your emotions. Of course a leaking tap could just mean that you need new washers, but often there is a correlation with plumbing and one's emotional state.

Electricity in your home can represent your life force or your personal energy field. If the circuits keep overloading in your home, take a look and see if you need to downgrade your life a bit. Maybe you are taking on too much. If lightbulbs keep blowing maybe you are giving out too much energy and not taking in enough energy.

The floors in your home can represent your foundations in life. If your basement floor begins to crack or your floor begins to buckle, see if there is some area of your life where you feel on "shaky ground."

The walls in your home can symbolize your structure and support in life. If termites are eating away at your walls, notice if there is anything in your life that is eating away at your support systems.

As you explore the symbology of your home, remember everything around you including your home is your reflection. In every moment the universe is whispering messages to you. These messages come in your dreams, from the situations you are involved in, and from the powerful symbolism that surrounds you in your home. Just as the high mountains, the deep caves and the golden rivers all dwell in our soul, so your home is a macrocosm of you, and this inner biology exists in your home. Within your home is the spirit of the mountains, valleys, the oceans and the stars. Your home is a myriad of overlapping vibrant energy fields, reflecting you and whispering to you in so many ways. Your personal living space can either be a spiritual template that contributes to your inner path so that you can spring into the future with glee, or it can stand lifeless and inanimate. As you create templates in your home that are rich and full of life and love, so your life becomes fuller and richer.

12

INTO THE LIGHT

Our planet and all her creatures have evolved under natural healing sunlight. Our body cycles and our skin color and even our personalities, to some extent, have evolved according to the amount of light in our environment. Our body requires oxygen to breathe, food to eat and light in order to live. Not only is light one of the most basic components essential to the survival of our species and the world, but light may be one of the most potent (but least recognized) sources of healing available to us on the planet.

Exciting research is developing that shows what civilizations of sun worshippers knew for generations. Light can be used to heal physical and mental problems. The light in your home can drain you or it can contribute to healing you. Not only is the light around us symbolic of the inner light of Spirit, but it is essential to our physical well-being as well. It is not a coincidence that we use the term "enlightenment" to describe a profound spiritual experience. In the deepest level of our being we have the recognition of the potency and power of light. We use expressions such as "I saw the light," "He is the light of my life," "Living in the Light," or the Biblical statement "Let there be light," indicating the power that we assign to light. Step into this exciting area of discovery.

Color

One of the most obvious ways that we observe and relate to light in our environment is through color. Every part of life is affected by color.

The color you use in your home has the most direct and most powerful effect on you of all the colors in your environment. Even if we are not consciously aware of it, we do acknowledge the power of color on our life. We use such expressions as "I'm feeling blue today," "It was a blue Monday," "She's really feeling in the pink," "He looks at life through rose-colored glasses," "He saw red," "She was red with anger . . . or green with envy . . . or purple with rage." The list goes on and on. Color continually plays an important role in every area of our lives. To understand the power that color has in our homes it is valuable to understand what color is.

WHAT IS COLOR?

Color is a part of the radiations from the sun. The light from the sun is comprised of numerous electromagnetic waves. Of all these waves only one percent of the total electromagnetic spectrum reaches the earth's surface. Among this percentage are found electric waves, radio waves, short-wave infrared, visible electromagnetic waves (colors), ultraviolet waves, X-rays, gamma rays and cosmic waves. Visible light (color) is only a very small part of the electromagnetic spectrum of wavelengths. The difference is that color is visible to our eyes while radiations of the other electromagnetic waves are not. The fact that humans have developed the ability to perceive color (and not the other wavelengths which are less plentiful on the planet) signifies that the human response to visible light has been evolving slowly since the beginning of human existence and *our response to light is very deeply ingrained in our nervous system.*

Within the visible electromagnetic spectrum the longest wavelength (lowest frequency) is red light and the shortest wavelength (highest frequency) is violet light. All other colors can be placed between the extremes of these two colors. There are no definite borders between them. They meld together like the colors of the rainbow. Each and every color and light in its totality has an enormous affect on us physically, emotionally and spiritually.

HOW DOES COLOR AFFECT US?

Albert Szent-Györgyi, Nobel Prize winner and the discoverer of vitamin C, experimented with color with some profound results. In his research he exposed certain enzymes and hormones to different colored lights and ascertained that selected colors caused the enzymes and hormones to go through molecular changes.[1] If different colors can affect the molecular structure of enzymes, might they not have a powerful effect on us? Other researchers found that while some colors could increase the rate of enzymatic reactions, others would deactivate enzyme reaction. Also, some colors can affect enzyme movements.[2]

Dr. Max Luscher, a color scientist, studied people's color preferences. He came to the conclusion that individuals' reactions to color have meaning transcending cultural differences and are rooted deeply within them. He concluded that color preference could indicate a person's state of mind, as well as possible glandular imbalances.[3]

Even blind people are affected by color. Research done in Russia has shown that some blind people can identify colors *through their fingers*. Some people who are blind say, for example, that they perceive red as warm, rough and tingling (surface temperatures on all the colors were measured to be the same) and blue colors feel smooth and cool. This suggests that color not only affects us visually but also affects our energy fields, even if our eyes are closed and we are sleeping.

Repeated research has shown that exposure to the warmer colors of red, orange and yellow increases blood pressure, pulse rate and respiratory rate, while exposure to green, blue and black decreases blood pressure, pulse rate and respiratory rate.

COLOR HEALING

The ancient Egyptians are thought to be among the first to use color for healing, while the Greeks specified different colors to be used for different ailments. In our time, color is being used medically. Maternity wards use blue light for the treatment of neonatal jaundice. Sixty percent of premature babies have jaundice, which is a result of a yellow chemical that accumulates in the body and causes the skin to turn yellow. Left untreated, it can cause brain damage and even death. The blue light works very effectively for treating this condition. Previous to the discovery of color therapy, the only treatment option was a risky procedure called exchange transfusion.[4]

The pink rooms used to sedate prisoners in the United States are examples of the effect that color can have on the way a person feels. These rooms, painted a bright bubble-gum pink, have the effect of calming violent prisoners in a matter of seconds. Within seconds there is a reduction of muscle strength, showing that the color has a physical as well as emotional effect. This has been an innovative discovery because before this discovery, sedative drugs or even brute strength was used to sedate aggressive inmates.

COLOR AFFECTING EMOTIONS

I was once called to do a house clearing in one family's home because the parents were concerned that there was an entity or ghost in their child's room. The young boy, a very sensitive lad, was having nightmares and had become uncharacteristically hyperactive. When I questioned the family about the history of this condition, they stated that the problems started after their child had been moved into an unused study. His own room was very small and they had decided to use his room for their new baby.

My immediate thought was that the child was having a difficult time psychologically adjusting to the new baby and having to move from his room. Although the family was certain of entity interference (it is all too easy to blame difficult situations on ghosts), I thought that perhaps the boy felt that he was being displaced from the family by the move, hence the nightmares. Talking to the young child didn't seem to reveal any (conscious) abnormal apprehension about the new baby. And when I examined his room I didn't find any residue of a ghostly presence. However, I was immediately aware of the maroon-red walls. The color seemed oppressive and draining. Feeling that I had reached the source of the problem, I asked the family (while involving the child in the decision-making process) to paint the child's walls a bright, clean, clear blue.

I am happy to report that immediately following the redecoration the child returned to his previous calm and happy disposition. He was able to sleep well and had no recurrence of nightmares. Looking at the situation psychologically, it might be said that the attention his parents gave him by painting his room made him feel more secure. However, I personally feel certain that the simple change of the room's color made all the difference.

COLOR IN THE HOME

Our spectrum of consciousness is not separate from the spectrum of light.

Red

Red stimulates the physical body to respond with direct action. Strength, courage, steadfastness, health, vigor, and sexuality are all attributes closely associated with the color red. It can be extremely vitalizing and stimulating and can assist in overcoming inertia, depression, fear or melancholy. It is a great aid to those who are afraid of life and inclined to feel like escaping. Red is power. It is dynamic and tenacious. It is the color of adrenaline, fire, zest and drive. It is physical energy. It is passionate and courageous and exciting. It supplies the energy and motivation necessary to reach and accomplish goals. Red is a "doing" color. It is a "get the job done now!" color. A study of athletes at a university in Texas showed that viewing red light increased strength 13.5 percent and prompted 5.8 percent more electrical activity in muscles. This suggests that the color red can activate activity and physical strength.

Red is not the best color for a bedroom, for you will have difficulty finding rest in this stimulating color. However, you might find that your desire for sensual excitement expands in a red bedroom. A red dining room will stimulate appetite, so if you are on a diet this might not be the best color for your dining room. Red in a workroom or exercise room, or even a living room stimulates movement and activity. If you are a procrastinator or in a sluggish time in your life, paint a wall red (use a crimson, scarlet or even a hot red or rust, rather than a dark maroon or muddy red) and get ready to take off!

Orange

Orange is a warm, stimulating color but it is lighter and higher in vibration than red. Orange is a happy, social color. It is used by clowns the world over. It stimulates optimism, expansiveness, emotional balance, confidence, change, striving, self-motivation, changeability, enthusiasm and a sense of community. It is flamboyant and warm-hearted. It is tolerant and sociable.

Orange is good in any room where you will be having group gatherings or where people will gather to socialize and have fun. It is a great color for any room in which you have parties. My dining room was a cream/gray color and my family never wanted to eat there. We either ate informally in the kitchen or in the living room. I painted the dining room a warm pumpkin color without telling anyone my reasons for doing so. Almost immediately kids began studying in the dining room. Projects were done in the dining room. It seemed to be the room were everyone hung out, not to mention that subsequently everyone wanted to have their meals in the dining room. Though I'm aware of the power of color, it was astonishing how quickly everyone reacted to the change in color in this room.

Yellow

Yellow stimulates the intellect as well as communication. It is the last of the warm, extroverted color rays. It is associated with mental discrimination, organization, attention to detail, evaluation, active intelligence, academic achievement, discipline, administration, praise, sincerity and harmony. Thus, yellow gives heightened expression and freedom. It is good for concentration and clarity of thought. It is a color that stimulates flexibility and adaptability to change. It is also associated with good luck.

Yellow is an excellent color to use in a home office. It is good to use in any room where you want to feel mentally uplifted and wish to stimulate conversation. Yellow kitchens tend to be gathering places for family and friends and usually generate a feeling of well-being. Yellow is also a good color to use in a room where you do counseling in your home. It gets people talking and at the same time brings forth uplifting feelings and optimism. Bright clear yellow is also a good color for a young child's room as it promotes a positive feeling and at the same time contributes to the development of thought processes.

Green

Green is the balance between the warm extroverted spectrum of red, orange and yellow and the cool introverted colors of blue, indigo, and violet. Thus, green stimulates feelings of balance, harmony, peace, hope, growth and healing. It is found everywhere in nature, symbolizing the abundant, replenishing forces of the universe. Green reminds us that there will always be enough. Often in hospitals the medical professionals wear green. This is a very good color because it is restful and healing.

This is a good color for any room. It is restful yet energizing. I often like to have some green in the bathroom—either green towels or green plants, or even green trim or a green wall. Since the bathroom is a room symbolic of purification and renewal, green is perfect in this room. (For more information about room symbology, see Chapter 11.) The green you use in a bathroom should be either a bright spring green or a clear and clean leaf green, rather than a khaki or muddy green.

Blue

Blue is the first of the cool spectrum colors. It stimulates you to seek inner truth. Blue helps you to attain inner peace and to live out your ideals. Blue stimulates inspiration, creativity, spiritual understanding, faith and devotion. Blue allows for gentleness, contentment, patience and composure. It has also been used for pain reduction. In 1982 Dr. Sharon McDonald conducted a study with 60 women who were afflicted with rheumatoid arthritis to see if color could affect pain. It was concluded that exposure to blue light could substantially reduce pain.[5]

A warm, light blue bedroom is good for relaxing a hyperactive child. Blue is also excellent for a meditation room or a bedroom, or any room where you want to have a feeling of peace pervade the entire atmosphere.

Purple

As with blue, purple's effects are calming, soothing and comforting. Very often, purple is associated with psychic awareness and intuition. When a person chooses purple as a favorite color, he is usually abstract, inspired, trusting in the future, and able to tune in to the inner world of others. Purple stimulates our spiritual perspective and intuition.

Purple is so powerful that I suggest not painting an entire room in this color. It is best to use it for accents to a white room or green or even a yellow room. Or it can be diluted with white paint to make a soft shade of lavender or violet—this is excellent for a meditation room or for a room where you do healing, particularly spiritual healing. For me, the exact shade for a meditation room is important, for the color of the room can influence how you feel when you are in that room. I ended up repainting my mediation room three times until I "felt" I had exactly the right shade of purple, a light blue shade of amethyst. In my meditation room I also have vibrant splashes of gold, which is a good balance to purple. Lavender rooms are also beneficial to use for convalescence.

White

White encompasses all colors. White vibrations are the fastest wavelength of the color spectrum. Its effects on our being are divine realization, humility and creative imagination. It can also be purifying. It is the energy and the power to transform the focus of the imagination. White leads us toward higher spiritual attunement and divine love. White is purity and perfection. This can be a great healing color for all rooms, for it holds within its energy the power of transformation.

White can be used successfully in any room in the house. However, if you have an all-white room with all-white accessories, it can feel too sterile—it may not seem friendly and inviting. White feels clean and clear, but unless it is a room used for meditation only I suggest that you always have colored accessories and pictures for your white room, or that you tint the white with peach, gold or blue. We rented a furnished home for a short while that had white walls and white carpeting and even white furniture. It was an exquisitely beautiful home and I loved how very uplifted I felt in it, but my friends said they didn't feel comfortable in the home because it seemed unfriendly. The overwhelming predominance of white made the house seem too sterile and unapproachable.

Black

Black is the mystery, the unknown. It is the realm of the visionary and the dreamtime. It is inward, whereas white is outward. It is constricting, whereas white is expanding. Black is the darkness of winter where life lies dormant and germinating. Out of the blackness comes new life. Black absorbs, while white repels. Black is silent and still. It is endings and beginnings. Our day ends and begins with darkness. In some cultures, nuns, monks, priests and people in mourning wear black, for it is an inward color. Black focuses attention into the inner world, whether to pursue the spiritual realm or to process feelings of grief.

To use black predominantly in a room can be overwhelming and even depressing. Black room accessories, however, can bring drama and power to a room and can accent and define a room the way that outlining colors in a picture can highlight and bring definition to the color. There are no bad colors. Each has its own special qualities and power. When I was at college I went through a difficult period. During this time I painted the walls of my basement room, my closet and my desk black. Even my bedspread and almost everything in my room was black. As I was living in the basement and had no window, you can imagine that this room was very black. I loved my room and felt good when I was there. Looking back at that time in my life, I think that my room was offering me a haven. It was a place where I could go and incubate, away from some of the life issues that seemed to be assaulting me at the time. It was a place where I could draw into myself and be still. However, for most homes a predominantly black room can be difficult to live with.

SHADES, HUES AND TINTS FOR ROOMS

Obviously, there are more colors than the seven that can be seen in the rainbow. What about silver, gold, pink, turquoise, brown and gray, for example? And what about the many different shades and hues of the colors? Color is very personal and individual. A shade lighter or darker of a particular color can make an enormous difference in the way that it feels to someone. I offer the above information about color as a starting point.

The best thing to do when you are considering painting a room is to use your imagination. Sit quietly in the room and feel its energy. Then imagine (or sense, if you are not visually oriented) different colors of different hues and shades in the room. Imagine how each color makes you feel in that particular room. You might even ask the Spirit of the Room its choice for colors. Then go to a paint store and go through their sample color swatches to find colors that are similar to the one you have chosen. It is a good idea, once you have chosen your color, to buy a small amount of it and cover a small portion of a wall to see how it looks before you invest in a large amount of paint. It is often hard to tell how a whole room will look from only a small paint sample.

KINDS OF HOUSE PAINT

Although oil-based paint has the potential to be environmentally damaging, in terms of its overall energy quality, oil-based paint absorbs and holds energy much better than water-based paint. The downside of this is that, if you move into a house with oil-painted walls, those walls will hold the energy fields of the previous tenants more and will need a more stringent cleansing than a water-based paint. As cleaning-up is more difficult and the mineral spirits' odor can be unpleasant, some people prefer latex.

Ideally, when you paint a room, take just a moment to energize the paint. Hold the Intention that energy will emanate from the painted walls filling the entire room. To energize your paint, place your hands over the open container and feel the energy flowing from your hands into the paint.

The quality of the paint you choose will make some difference in the overall feeling of your painted walls. Inexpensive paint tends to fade more quickly so that the color you have chosen so carefully will change more quickly, particularly if it is a darker color. Also, some good-quality paints tend to come in richer colors and have better coverage.

STAINED GLASS

Another wonderful way to bring the magic of color into your home is to have stained-glass ornaments hanging in a window. Or you might even consider installing a stained-glass window. The power of color is magnified when it is comprised of sunlight through stained glass. To use stained glass to its best advantage, if possible have the colored glass in a location where the sun actually falls on the glass bringing the radiant color into your home.

RAINBOW LIGHT

Another way to bring the power of color into your home is to place prisms or lead crystals in your windows. This is color in its purest, most brilliant and beautiful form. It is the radiant array of infinite light. Your aura will instinctively pull out the colors it needs from the rainbow colors. Stand in the rainbow light and know that your body and your aura are pulling in the colors that you need at the time. Not all areas of the world are blessed with sunshine, so modern technology has developed an electronic rainbow machine that can generate rainbows even on a darkest night. These can also be pleasing to place in a child's bedroom as they don't light up the entire room, but just display a beautiful shimmering rainbow of colors on a far wall or ceiling. I will often place a cluster of cut lead crystals in a sunny window to flood a room with rainbow light. This is especially good to do in a healing room. The best kind of cut crystals for making large clear rainbows are flat ones with large facets, rather than spherical ones with smaller facets.

COLORED WATER

Another way to combine light with color is to put colored water into bowls or vases. Simply adding a few drops of food coloring to a clear glass container of water and placing it in a window can pull the power of that color into your home. Adding coloring to water and oil, for the purposes of healing, has been developed into an art form by the Aura-Soma and Aura Light companies (see Appendix).

Full-Spectrum Lighting

The type of lighting that you have in your home can make an enormous difference to the way you feel. The contrast between the way you feel in a room lit either with a fluorescent bulb or in a room with soft incandescent light is marked and obvious. Moreover, studies show that not only does fluorescent lighting affect your emotions but it also affects your physical health.

Dr. John Ott, a respected light researcher, did a study on the effects of full-spectrum lighting on humans. In a Florida school, two different kinds of lighting were installed in two otherwise identical classrooms. One classroom had the usual fluorescent lighting and the other had a Vita-Lite, the full-spectrum light that Dr. Ott developed.

The students exposed to the fluorescent lighting displayed hyperactivity, irritability and fatigue, and had difficulty paying attention to the teacher. The students in the full-spectrum lighting classroom had much better academic performance, were calm, and developed *one third the cavities in their teeth than the children in the cool white fluorescent classroom.*[6]

Similar research by other scientists has produced the same results. Chickens who live under full-spectrum lighting live twice as long, lay more eggs, are calmer and produce eggs that are 25 percent lower in cholesterol than chickens reared under other forms of lighting. (Human cholesterol levels also drop under the influence of sunlight and full-spectrum lighting.)[7] The light in your home can have a powerful effect on your health and your emotions. Incandescent lighting, though better than fluorescent lighting, is a poor substitute for full-spectrum lighting because it is missing part of the spectrum of light, and it gives off practically no ultraviolet (UV) light.

UV light from the sun is damaging in large amounts, of course, but small amounts are essential to our health and well-being. The typical brightness on a summer day is 100,000 lux (a lux is approximately equal to one candle), while a typical indoor environment is approximately 600–700 lux. When we spend so much time indoors we are receiving only a small percentage of what our bodies are designed to receive. In his book *Sunlight*, Dr. Zane Kime declares that a series of exposures to sunlight will decrease heart rate, blood pressure, blood sugar, respiratory rate and lactic acid while increasing strength, energy, tolerance to stress, and the ability of our blood to absorb and carry oxygen.[8] UV light also contributes to lower blood pressure, increases the efficiency of the heart, reduces cholesterol, increases the level of sex hormones, and activates the synthesis of vitamin D, which is a prerequisite for the absorption of calcium.

Most incandescent lights have prominent yellow, red and infrared light, and this is unnatural. This is why the lighting in your home can make it look dingy or yellowish at times, and can contribute to your feeling exhausted. Though expensive, it is valuable to augment the lighting in your home by obtaining some full-spectrum lights (see Appendix). You will immediately begin to feel the difference in the energy of your entire home.

SAD

Recent research has been done into the affects of diminished light which causes Seasonal Affective Disorder (SAD). This is a syndrome that reportedly affects five million Americans. It occurs during the winter months when people are indoors and not exposed to much light. It is marked by depression, fatigue, weight gain, and sometimes severe withdrawal. In 1987 the American Psychiatric Association listed SAD as a true affective disorder.

The prescribed treatment for SAD is light therapy. It was found that by exposing patients to intense, bright, full-spectrum lighting far brighter than normal household light for a total of two hours a day, remarkable results could be achieved. Usually with a week of treatment or less, patients dramatically improved, saying that they felt up-lifted, productive, alive again.[9] I mention this because even if you are not affected by SAD, you can still benefit positively from the amount and kind of light that you have in your home. The best way to remedy SAD is to obtain a bright full-spectrum light. (See Appendix for source and further reading.)

Electromagnetic Fields in Your Home

I spent my teenage years in the Midwest of the United States. I loved the summertime. I loved looking at the glowing waves of golden wheat rippling on a warm afternoon. I loved the soft glowing fireflies suspended over a meadow on a languid warm night. And I loved the compass plant (called pilot weed in some areas). The compass plant is a wild sunflower. It has yellow, daisy-like flowers and grows up to ten feet tall. The unique thing about this plant is that the lower leaves tend to line up edgewise in a north-south magnetic axis.

This phenomenon of aligning to the earth's north-south axis is not seen only in plants. Many animals and bacteria also orient themselves to the earth's electromagnetic fields. Scientists have found magnetic sensors in the brains of some birds and bees, as evidenced by minute deposits of magnetite. Other researchers contend that humans also respond to the electromagnetic fields of their environment.[10]

Subtly, and sometimes overtly, we are influenced by all of the electromagnetic fields around us. They constantly sustain and influence us. The medicine women and men of times past did not need scientific research to prove this. Throughout the world shamans felt the magic and the mysterious forces available in the four directions. They honored the four directions in ceremony and ritual. They intuitively felt the pull of the earth's axis and knew that the electromagnetic fields of the world affected all of life. They did not have scientists to tell them that beneath their feet flowed a subterranean stream of energy that formed patterns, electrostatic fields and negative-ion concentrations. Nor did they know that waterfalls, mountaintops and electrical storms had beneficial electrical effects. They just knew that these were a sacred part of the living universe.

Every minute of every day we are influenced and impacted by electromagnetic fields (EMFs). EMFs are generated by the electricity flows in your home. They are generated by lights, appliances, home office equipment and the power lines into and out of your home. I began to be aware of the effect of EMFs during a seminar I was conducting for about two hundred people. During this seminar I noticed that there were two areas of the room where a number of people were becoming emotional during the guided meditation. I noticed that these two areas of the room corresponded to the placement of the audio speakers.

For the next meditation I moved the audio speakers to different locations. Again I noticed that the people near the speakers were the only ones in the room to become upset. Assuming that it was because the sound was louder by the speakers I turned one of the speakers off for the next guided meditation. However, people around *both* speakers still continued to become emotional during the exercise. No matter how I moved people around the room, so that different people were next to the speakers, I always got the same results. I concluded that people were being influenced by the electrical fields of the speakers.

Of course, normally people don't become emotional when they are near speakers, but when someone is in a very deep meditation state, he or she becomes much more sensitive to energy influences.

Again and again in my seminars I found that when people were in deep meditation they were dramatically affected by electrical circuits. Even if those circuits were in the wall and not visible from the surface, they had a negative effect on them.

Our homes have a myriad of electrical circuits infiltrating through them due to the enormous dependence we have on electricity. Our bodies are made of a diverse number of fields. The inner universe of our body and the outer universe around us are in constant interplay. When our body comes into contact with a strong external electromagnetic field, it influences the weaker components of our internal physical energy fields. When our integral energy fields move toward the same frequency of the stronger field this is called biological entrainment. Spiritually, the effects can be devastating, because our subtle energy fields are particularly susceptible to electromagnetic energy. In a purely physical way, this can affect our vision, hearing, emotions and our immune system. Results of a Swedish study involving children exposed to elevated EMF levels revealed that their risk of cancer was two times higher than normal. The incidence of multiple sclerosis and other serious diseases has been linked to increased exposure to EMFs.[11]

Although there are many gadgets on the market which claim to neutralize EMFs, I'm not convinced. I do know of two things that you can do to diffuse the amount of EMFs in your home. One way to reduce them is by reducing the use of electricity in your home, especially televisions, fluorescent lights, microwave ovens, computers, home appliances, motors, telephones, hair dryers and electric blankets. The second way is the most practical, and that is to stay away from the source of the electric fields. You are much more at risk if you are close to electrical items than if you stay away from them. You are safer ten feet away from your television than three feet away. And it is much better not to sleep with your head or body in close proximity to an EMF. For example, don't keep your digital, electronic alarm clock right by your head while you are sleeping.[12]

The best way to find out about where there are EMFs in your home is to obtain a gaussmeter. This is an easy to use, affordable tool that can accurately measure the EMFs in your home. The tool will allow you to see where the strongest EMFs in your home are and will show you what the minimum safe distance is for your family for every field. (For information about where to obtain this tool see the Appendix.)

As we move toward a new millennium, the understanding of light in all its forms, and the understanding that we are light beings melded with form will begin to expand. As we move into the recognition of our own light, our ability to utilize and absorb the light around us will expand. We embody light ... from light we have come and into light we go. The renowned physicist David Bohm said it best—"all matter is frozen light."

13

THE ART OF
PLACEMENT

I sat in the middle of my first apartment. An odd array of second-hand chairs, lopsided lamps, unopened boxes and worn carpets surrounded me. Suddenly, I began pushing and shoving furniture this way and that. I stuck a plant in one corner, threw a rug to another end of the room, and dashed posters and paintings up on to the walls.

Abruptly I stopped and looked around. It was done! I felt amazed by the change in the way the room felt. It seemed that perhaps there was one perfect place for every item and that, in a magic moment, I had found this mystically correct place for each thing. I felt as if I had "tuned" the room as though it were a fine violin, where only by tuning every string perfectly could a perfect pure sound be created.

My apartment was singing. Everything was in its perfect place. The threadbare furnishings which previously had appeared limp and unattractive, now seemed to glow with inner beauty. This was my first experience of what I call the Instinctive Art of Placement.

The Art of Placement is not new. This mystic art has been practiced for thousands of years in ancient China. It is called Feng Shui (pronounced Fung Sway), and it dictates the physical placement of Chinese homes, as well as the placement of objects within them. Feng Shui literally means wind and water. The Chinese do not consider buildings to be inanimate objects. They believe that buildings radiate an energy field and that the underlying energy of all things is called chi.

People often intuitively recognize the energy field of a building when they enter. It might feel like a cold, tingling sensation, or perhaps it might arouse feelings of constriction, relaxation or expansion. Even people who don't believe in psychic phenomena will register a measurable response to the energy of a house. The longer that you are in a building the more the chi of the building will influence you, so the Art of Placement is considered very important.

Many ancient cultures practiced the Art of Placement, although the Chinese system is the most widely known now. The systems of different cultures all agree that placement is important, but they disagree when it comes to details. A Korean person, for example, would likely rule out any home with more than three steps leading up to the entrance. And a Japanese would not even consider a corner joining two streets as an acceptable location for a home.

Even different regions in China have different Feng Shui traditions. One region may consider that an east-facing door is the most auspicious entrance, while another may consider only a south-facing entrance door. The Art of Placement grows out of individual cultures and their geographies. Often some aspects of the Chinese Feng Shui system are not effective when used in the Western world because of the different energies, traditions and belief systems. Nevertheless, it is valuable to gain an understanding of the basic principles underlying this ancient art form.

Different Approaches to Feng Shui

In China, each of the different approaches to Feng Shui has its own advantages and beauty. Here is a brief synopsis of several of these schools of thought.

LAND-FORM APPROACH

The land-form system is based on the building shapes and arrangements of rooms in conjunction with the surrounding terrain. Every shape emanates a life force and these shapes affect the energy fields of a home. An example of this is understanding how the different shapes of a table can affect the energy of the people at the table. Squares and rectangles are considered yin (see yin and yang chart, page 199). Since yin shapes are thought to hold energy, people will sit longer over a business meeting at a square table rather than a round table. A circle is thought to be yang and spins energy away, so people won't linger as long around a circular table as a rectangular table.

COSMOLOGY APPROACH

Another school bases its theory on cosmology and uses a special geomancy compass, called a luo pan, to see how a home is situated in relationship to the solar system, the stars, the sun, the moon, the elements and the directions. The Feng Shui master attempts to situate the home and the objects in the home in such a way that they are favorable to the universe and the energy of heaven and earth. The directions and elements are very important in this system. For example, the direction your front door faces has great significance. A door facing east means involvement with family, a door facing south means professional success, a west-facing door will mean joy and children, while a door that faces north means the unfolding of one's inner destiny.

SYMBOLIC APPROACH

The third approach looks for the meaning of the objects and symbols with which a person surrounds herself. Every symbol, whether the Christian cross, an Indian mandala, or even a triangle drawn in a painting, is considered to have a particular power. Every time an individual enters the room with the symbol, then the power of the symbol is activated. After repeated entrances into the room, the symbol will activate its presence in the person's life.

THE CHI APPROACH

A fourth system is called the chi approach. This is an approach in which the practitioner enters the home and "reads" the energy of the room or house in much the same way as an acupuncturist reads the pulse of an individual in order to make a medical diagnosis. Modern Feng Shui practitioners will also read electrical waves such as EMFs or microwave emissions. The chi method stresses a more direct interface with the house, rather than reliance on specified rules.

When a Feng Shui master using the chi approach is asked to select an auspicious site for a home, factors such as the shape of the land, the positioning of trees, the situation of water, neighboring buildings, and the history of a particular site are all taken into account. In designing a new building or studying an existing one, the Feng Shui master will give attention to the shape and arrangement of the house and its individual rooms, as well as the positioning of doors and windows. After a home is built, the master will give guidelines for the positioning of beds, desks, and stoves.

In China a house is likened to the body of a living spirit. The windows are the eyes and the doors are the mouths. Chi (energy) is inhaled into the home and flows according to the interior structure. The layout of the rooms, as well as the positioning of the furniture, will either be favorable to the flow of energy or will impede it. If the energy flow through a house is good, then the occupants will be healthy and have good fortune.

YIN AND YANG

To understand Feng Shui it is important to understand the Chinese philosophy of yin and yang. This philosophy sees life as a dance between the two opposing yet harmonious forces in the universe. It is believed that to be in balance one must be in harmony with these two forces. In addition, for one's house to be in balance, there should be a balance of yin and yang in each room. Here are some examples of yin and yang attributes.

YIN	YANG
female	male
inward	outward
dark	light
still	moving
sinking	rising
contracting	expanding
cold	hot
black	white
mountain	valley
meandering	straight
moon	sun
cyclical	linear
receptive	projecting

An example of a room being too yin would be a room that is a very dark color, is always cold and has little light. In this room you would feel very restricted and inward and could become ill. On the other hand, if you spent time in a room with lots of windows, full of light, painted stark white, and very warm in temperature, you would be in danger of becoming too yang and of losing too much energy. In this room you would also be susceptible to falling ill. For a room to be in balance, it must have a balance of the yin and yang forces in life.

GENERAL FENG SHUI GUIDELINES

The following are some very general guidelines that you can use to improve the energy flow of your home, based on Feng Shui principles.

Front entrance
The area around the front entrance, the objects inside the entrance, and the first room that is seen upon entering your home, are all very important. The main entrance of your home is a major entry point for energy to flow into your dwelling. A tree or telephone pole positioned directly in front of the doorway can impede the flow of energy into your home, and might have the effect of producing obstacles in the path of anything you try to do as a result. It is very important that

IDEAL ENTRANCE

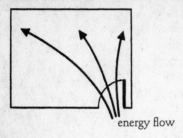

energy flow

RESTRICTED ENTRANCE

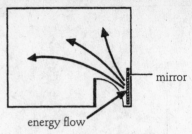

mirror

energy flow

Remedy: place a mirror on wall

FIGURE 1

the approach to the main entrance of your home is not obstructed in any way.

Any door in your house (but especially the front door) that opens into a wall rather than opening into free space will impede energy flow. People who live in homes with many doors hung so that they open this way may find that they are often physically constipated, and may complain that they feel stuck in their lives. It is as though they are met by a brick wall in everything they do. The remedy for this is to rehang the door(s) so as to open the other way. If this is not practical, a mirror can be placed on the wall which the door faces, so as to bring energy into the space more easily (see Figure 1). Make the mirror a large one, as large as the space will allow.

Ideally, a front door should open into a light and bright foyer or a room that feels warm and welcoming. The energy of the entrance influences the energy of the entire house. The more appealing your front entrance is, the more your home will sustain and nurture you. Place strong vibrant plants at the entrance, add pictures which are inspiring and have good lighting and mirrors which can add light and dimension if your hall is small.

In China it is felt that if an entrance door opens directly into the kitchen, then the preoccupation in the home may be with food. This could contribute to household members becoming overweight. If the front door faces a bedroom, the house inhabitants may tend to feel tired and sleepy. A family with an entrance facing a bathroom might find that their fortune flushes away. If your entrance opens into a kitchen, bathroom or bedroom, you can place hanging wind chimes between the entrance and the room in question. Or if there is a door leading from the entrance toward the bedroom, for example, put a mirror on the outside of the bedroom door to deflect the energy.

General theories

- If a room has a column or pillars in it, this interrupts the flow of energy.

    Solution: Wrap the pillar with fabric to soften the effect if the pillar is round. If the column has angled corners, place mirrors around it to diffuse the interruption to the energy flow. If possible place the mirrors edge to edge.

- Any room with a projecting corner (or corners) can create difficulty, as it is a sharp shape and can undercut the energy of the occupants so that, for example, they may receive criticism that they do not deserve.

    Solution: Hang mirrors on either side of the sharp corner, or put a plant in front of the corner. Or you could hang wind chimes or a cut-lead crystal ball in front of it.

- Stairs that have spaces instead of risers keep energy from moving upstairs.

    Solution: Put potted plants underneath the stairs to help the chi to flow upstairs.

- Ceilings that are too low can feel oppressive and constrictive, and can make people prone to depression and headaches.

    Solution: Put mirrors on as many walls as possible to create a more expanded feeling.

- Ceilings that are too high can make one feel too dispersed and not focused.

    Solution: Hang mobiles, crystals or chimes to bring the ceiling down.

- Windows are the eyes of a home. Ideally windows should open outward, or even inward, rather than up and down as this allows more chi to enter the home. In China a broken window can augur eye problems for the occupants.

Solution: Mend broken windows as soon as possible.

• In China bathrooms represent the place where water (which symbolizes money) escapes. Kitchens represent wealth, so a bathroom should not face the kitchen, or else the family's wealth might wash away.

Solution: Put a mirror on the outside of the bathroom door, or put a hanging crystal between the bathroom and the kitchen.

• Exposed joists or beams across beds, a stove, or a work space are thought to obstruct the flow of energy. People are said to feel debilitated or to have physical problems caused by the oppressive beams.

Solution: Either move your bed or work desk, or place something on the beam to disrupt its energy. In China they will place two wooden bamboo flutes angled on either end of the beam with the lower one toward the wall. This is said to release the oppressiveness of the beam.

• A cardinal Feng Shui rule is always to discover the fortunes of the previous tenants of your home. If the previous tenant flourished, then so will you. If their fortunes declined, then so will the fortunes of the occupants who follow. Of course this might seem to be only a superstition, but many ancient traditions are built on the observations of many, many generations.

Solution: Do major space clearing before you move in.

What to do if your toilet is inauspiciously situated
The placement of the toilet is an area of concern in Chinese Feng Shui. Here are a number of solutions for an "inauspicious" toilet. They seem to work best if all are implemented together:

1. Keep the toilet seat down when it is not in use.
2. Keep the door of the room where the toilet is located closed, and put a mirror on the outside of it to deflect energy away.
3. If there is a window, hang a spherical, multifaceted lead crystal so that it brings as much rainbow light into the room as possible.
4. Put plants in the room.

THE BA-GUA SYSTEM

In much the same way that reflexology provides us with a map show-ing which areas of the foot are connected to corresponding areas of the body, so some Feng Shui practitioners use a grid system known as the *ba-gua* to show which areas of your home relate to the corre-sponding spiritual aspects of your life. I personally consider the ba-gua system to be one of the most helpful of the various Feng Shui systems.

Figure 2 is a ba-gua map. It is easy to use. Simply place the center of the grid in the center of a plan of your home, aligning the bottom edge of the ba-gua with the wall in which the entrance to your home or apartment is situated. (You will either be entering through Inner Knowl-edge, Career, or Helpful People.) Every area of your home is related to one of the ba-gua areas. Here is specific information about each area.

Wealth Abundance	Fame Self-expression	Relationships Marriage
Family Ancestors Heritage	Health Chi (Energy)	Offspring Children Projects
Inner Knowledge Self-realization	Career Path in Life	Helpful People Angels

FIGURE 2 Overlay this ba-gua grid over the plan of your home with the entrance of your home opening into Inner Knowledge, Career Path, or Helpful People.

Career area

This area of a building relates to your path in life, your career, your creativity and whatever you spend most of your time doing. If your front door is situated centrally, this will be your front entrance. If your Career area is missing, you may have difficulty making any headway in your profession. To help your career take off put large mirrors, fresh growing plants and hanging crystals in this area.

Helpful people

This is a wonderful place to put an altar in a home, where you can burn incense, offer prayers and leave petitions to the gods and angels. If you are working on a project and need some help from others, put an extra big mirror or a crystal in the Helpful People area. You may be amazed at how many phone calls and offers come pouring in from friends and colleagues. If your Helpful People area is blocked or missing you will feel unsupported and alone.

Offspring

This relates to children, projects or anything which you have created. If you are trying to conceive a child, it is a good idea to put your bed in the Offspring area of your house, or at least in the Offspring area of your bedroom. If you are working on a project which you want to bring to fruition, place blossoming flowers in this position (real ones or paintings of flowers), as well as items connected with the project.

Relationships

The Relationships area concerns marriage, friendships, and also the way we relate to other people in general. It is wonderful to put paired or grouped objects in this area, along with happy photos of you with people you love. It is not advisable to have your television set in this corner. A house with a missing Relationship area can sometimes create relationships which are generally fraught with problems.

Fame

This area represents inspiration, self-expression and what you are known for. If you put a clock here you will have a reputation for being either punctual or late. This spot is often the focal point of a room. It can sometimes happen that if your toilet is in this position in the house, your reputation can go down the drain.

Wealth

This is the area that concerns wealth, prosperity, good fortune, blessings and abundance of all kinds, not just relating to money. It is a good place to put an aquarium, ornaments, or solid objects of good quality. It is a very inauspicious place to have your toilet situated, as you will be symbolically flushing away your wealth.

Family
The Family area concerns parents, ancestors, heritage and influences from the past. It is a good place to put family photos, certificates and trophies of past achievements and so on.

Inner knowledge
This concerns introspection, meditation, inner guidance and studying. It is a good place to situate a meditation room, a library or a study. If you want to improve your intuition and guidance from your higher Self, hang a crystal in the window of this area in the house.

Health
This area concerns health and vitality. If this area of your home has plants that are dying, or is dark and dirty, health problems can ensue.

Missing areas
If your home isn't in the shape of a perfect square or rectangle, or if your home is L-shaped, it is considered to have a missing part. A Chinese person wouldn't build a house with missing areas, but Western architects do not take this into account in their designs. In China, it is felt that a missing part of a house can affect your life. For example, someone missing the wealth area may have financial difficulties. People who experience a dip in finances after a move may find that their new home is missing the wealth area.

Each type of missing area brings its own kind of difficulties. Fortunately, mirrors offer a solution to many of these problems, since placing one mirror on the internal wall of a missing area symbolically draws the energy of that area back into your life. The mirrors need to be as large as the space allows and preferably framed. Raw edges of unframed mirrors and spiky frames can produce distortions of energy, as do mirrors which are leaned against the wall rather than hung.

Another way to compensate for a missing area is to use natural vegetation, plants, garden furniture, etc., to fill the area. The missing area can be filled (if practical) with anything to extend the presence of the occupants into that area. An outdoor light is another common solution for a missing area.

EXAMPLES OF REMEDIES FOR MISSING AREAS

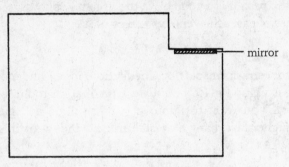

Example of house with missing area and the remedy mirror

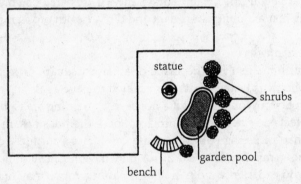

Example of house with missing area and the remedy shrubs and garden furniture

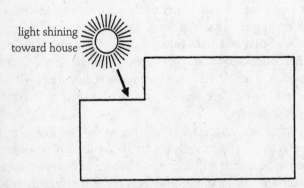

Example of missing area and the remedy light shining toward house

I find that even just cleaning or giving attention to a ba-gua area can produce favorable results. For example, if your career is at a standstill, place an electronic waterfall in the Career area of your home. Having water (symbolizing money, creativity and inspiration) flowing in your Career area will help your career begin to move. Or, if you desire love in your life, put objects which represent love to you in the Relationship area of your home, such as a big bowl of roses, or a photo of two people walking down the beach with intertwined arms.

Karen Kingston, a London Feng Shui consultant, once told me a story about a woman who had not had a love relationship for over four years. This woman was astounded when, within ten minutes of hanging a crystal in the window of the Relationship area of her house, she received a phone call from an admirer inviting her on a date. Within a week she was in the situation of needing to make a choice between two prospective lovers.

People commonly report increases in income, blessings and abundance after hanging a crystal in the window of the Wealth area of their home. Hanging a crystal in the window of the Helpful People area brings in practical help, as well as guidance from angels and unseen helpers. (Crystals are activated by light passing through them, so they will only bring in extra energy if they are hung in windows.)

Each building has a ba-gua, and each room within that building also has a ba-gua. The alignment of the grid is always determined by where the main doorway to the room is situated. Even your desk has a ba-gua, with the front door being where you sit (see Figure 3). So if you want to enhance your prosperity, place a crystal bowl in the top left-hand corner of your desk (which is the area corresponding to wealth) in order to symbolically collect abundance from the universe, and happy family photographs in the top right-hand corner to collect emotional fulfillment. Be sure not to place your trash basket directly under this corner.

Instinctive Feng Shui

The study of any one system of Feng Shui can take many years and can be very confusing to the lay person. However, I believe that deep within us is a vast wellspring of intuitive knowledge about the power

Wealth Blessings Abundance	Fame Self-expression	Relationships Marriage
Family Ancestors Heritage	Health Chi (Energy)	Offspring Children Projects
Inner Knowledge Self-realization	Career Path in Life	Helpful People Angels

chair

FIGURE 3 Example of desk area ba-gua. Place objects of beauty and power in any area of your desk that you want to energize.

of placement. I believe that we can tap into this instinctive wisdom without numerous years of study.

Have you ever moved the furniture around in a room, taken just a moment to "feel" how the room feels in the new arrangement, and then continued to rearrange the furniture until it felt right? Or have you have ever been arranging flowers and suddenly there came a point when you just knew it was right? In both of these cases you have practiced the instinctive art of placement. For me, when the new arrangement is right, I feel I can breathe more deeply.

For example, if there is an area of your home that doesn't feel right, you might try placing the objects in the room in different locations, or try adding new objects or subtracting old ones until it does feel right. Simply by changing the placement of things in your home, you can positively change the energy flow throughout your living space.

Using Instinctive Feng Shui can sometimes yield more remarkable results than just following set Feng Shui rules. A couple from Canada came to see me in Seattle because they were very concerned about their finances. They owned a number of exclusive clothing stores which had done very well, when suddenly they were losing huge amounts of money and were on the verge of going bankrupt. I could not go to their home in Vancouver at that time, so I tuned in and used my "intuition" to see if I had any suggestions for them. I "saw" into their home and noticed a black couch that was creating tremendous difficulty for their energy flow. I asked if they had a black couch.

They answered, "Yes, it's made of black leather. It is the most central object in our living room."

I said, "You must get rid of the black couch."

The husband replied, "We can't. It is very expensive, and besides that it was a gift from my mother-in-law."

I asked them when they had received the couch. They told me that it had been given to them two years previously. I asked them when their money troubles started. They answered that their financial decline had started two years before. They were astounded when they realized that their problems had started at almost the exact same time that they had been given the couch.

I asked the husband how he felt about his mother-in-law. He revealed that he didn't like her and felt dominated by her. The initial start-up money for their company had been given to them by this mother-in-law. Although she had been paid back, she still wanted to be in control of their company. The husband felt subconsciously resentful every time he saw the couch, and he was subconsciously sabotaging the company as a way to retaliate against his mother-in-law. I must emphasize that this was completely subconscious, because consciously he had not felt resentful every time the saw the couch, but this emotion was activated nonetheless.

When this couple returned to Vancouver, they got rid of the couch. When I heard from them a few months later, they were exhilarated. Their finances had turned around completely and they were once again enjoying success.

I don't think it is necessary for every house to have perfect placement. Homes really are like people, and sometimes our greatest growth comes from interrelating with those individuals with whom we have had difficulty. Sometimes living in a home that constricts us allows us to grow spiritually, for we have to reach inside ourselves to overcome our adversity and thereby connect with our greatest strength. I believe that the best Feng Shui is that which is done intuitively, and that we all have this innate ability within us. Trust your intuition. Use your imagination. Be creative. And most of all have fun!

EXAMPLES

Some of the Feng Shui information in this chapter and the following examples came from Karen Kingston, who is a London-based space-clearer and a Feng Shui practitioner. When Karen heard that I was going to have a chapter on Feng Shui in my book, she generously sent me some material and some personal examples from her practice to share.

In one of Karen's Feng Shui consultations, a woman who had been running a large public-relations company from her home was having difficulty financially. After interviewing her, Karen discovered that the woman's doorbell didn't ring. If there is no doorbell, or if it is difficult for the inhabitants to hear when someone is knocking at the door, it can create difficulties, in terms of energy, for opportunities to come. Although this woman's business came from telephone contacts rather than personal callers, the act of installing a doorbell sent out the message on an energy level that she was willing to be more accessible. After doing this, she reported a huge increase in her business.

Another business woman came to Karen for help because, although successful, she felt she had reached a kind of plateau which she could not move beyond. A consultation revealed that a cupboard she had purchased the year before was blocking the energy flow in her Career area. In addition, there were two mirrors hung opposite each other in this area, so that energy was being bounced back and forth between them and going nowhere. Soon after correcting these problems by moving the cupboard and one of the mirrors to more auspicious locations, the woman once again experienced her career as exciting and full of opportunities for further development.

Karen told me about a case of another Feng Shui practitioner who was working with a music teacher. This woman was experiencing financial problems. But after moving her sofa, which was blocking the entrance to her wealth area, she had eleven new students within a week.

Another woman wanted an affair without commitment, having recently divorced. A Feng Shui consultant advised that she put a fish tank in the Relationship area of her house. Shortly afterwards this woman met a lovely man with whom she had a brief but satisfying liaison. Now whenever she wants to end one relationship and begin another she cleans out her fish tank and puts in fresh plants. She says it always works.

A man had been trying to sell his apartment for some time without receiving a single offer. In a consultation with Karen, she advised him to spend $500 on a large mirror and some flowering plants to correct the obstructed energy flow in the space. Within ten days, he had two buyers bidding against each other for the property, and the final sale price was $12,000 higher than his asking price!

Another story, which illustrates the powerful effects of Feng Shui principles, comes from two friends of mine who live in Australia. They live and work from the same building in Melbourne. I had sent them an early draft of this book in order to get their feedback on it. They wrote back that after reading it, they immediately did a major cleaning of their space. Using the information in this chapter, they realized that the wealth area of their home was missing. So they created a beautiful garden in this area, complete with ferns, pebbles and a Buddha. The first week after doing this they had markedly increased sales. But in the week following that one, they had their biggest sales day ever, receiving twice as much as they had during the entire week before—in only one day!

In Feng Shui there are thought to be Nine Basic Cures to uplift energy:

1. BRIGHT LIGHTS AND LIGHT REFRACTING OBJECTS Mirrors, cut-lead crystal balls, and bright lighting activates chi (energy).
2. SOUNDS Music can influence a room's chi. Wind chimes moderate or increase the flow of chi. Often a wind chime will be hung in a long hallway to break up the chi which might be flowing too swiftly. Anything that makes a pleasant sound can increase energy.

3. LIVING OBJECTS Anything alive, such as animals, birds, fish in aquariums, plants, potted flowers, or bonsai trees, increases energy in a house.
4. SOLID OBJECTS The positioning of furniture and the placement of statues can influence a home's energy.
5. MOVING OBJECTS Windmills, wind socks, mobiles, fountains and even hamster wheels can activate chi energy.
6. ELECTRICALLY POWERED OBJECTS Electric fountains or waterfalls, electric chimes or even an electric rainbow can increase chi.
7. SYMBOLS AND SYMBOLIC ORNAMENTS Any symbols, paintings or pictures that are meaningful to you. Bamboo flutes can be played or used for decoration. Flutes symbolize spiritual swords. If you tie red ribbons around them and point them upwards, this helps chi flow.
8. COLOR Choose colors that are meaningful for you. In China, yellow is associated with longevity, red is an auspicious color, and green is the color of new growth and of spring.
9. RIBBONS AND FRINGES Red ribbons can be placed on doors, or fringes can be used to hide wooden beams that obstruct energy flow in a room.

The aim of Feng Shui is to live in harmony with the universe through re-creation of the balance between heaven and earth, yin and yang, man and nature. The study of Feng Shui covers so much more than I have been able briefly to touch on. It is certainly a field of study worth exploring in depth. However, I believe that a Feng Shui master should give you not just a rigid set of rules to which you must unwaveringly adhere, but should encourage you to be the creator of your environment and your own life. He or she should contribute to a gentle and loving transformation for you as a result of expressing yourself through your home. This way you can become more in harmony with the universe through the Art of Placement, and your home can become an expression of equanimity and peace.

14

HOME PROTECTORS
AND ENERGIZERS

*A*lthough sometimes the line between protectors and energizers blur, they are all a part of preservation of energy which is the fourth step in the four-step method for house clearing. Both protectors and energizers help to preserve, protect and enhance the energy field that you have created by house clearing.

Protectors

The inner realms have a multitude of helpers and assistants. In establishing a feeling of safety and protection in your home, an excellent plan is to use a spirit protector. A spirit protector can not only protect your home from outside unwanted intruders but can also create a feeling of safety within your home, so that people are less likely to be injured in home accidents.

Many native cultures all over the world have a tradition of belief in house guardians. House guardians, or protectors, can take many forms, including the form of a spirit animal ally, protecting angels, a house guardian spirit, or even the protecting spirit of a tree. Whatever the form, they are a useful addition to the creation of your home as a safe haven.

I have heard over and over again from people who have had remarkable results using the house-guardian techniques that I teach.

One woman lived in a set of apartments in London. One workday she returned to find that every single apartment had been burgled—except for hers. On the surface there was nothing unusual or different about her apartment that would have caused a robber to ignore it. It was no more or less exposed than the others. Yet her apartment (out of fourteen others which had been burgled) hadn't been broken into. She attributed this phenomenon to the energy field that she had placed around her apartment, and particularly to her house guardians.

Another woman wrote to tell me that she had placed a representation of her animal ally house guardian near the front door as I suggested. She was working with cat energy, so she had a large statue of a cat near the front door. She was gone for a three-day weekend and came home to find that her door had been pried open, yet nothing had been stolen or taken, even though there were many valuable things, some of which were right by the front door. However, another house in her normally quiet neighborhood was broken into the same weekend. These neighbors didn't fare as well, for quite a few things were stolen. The police said that something must have frightened the would-be thief from her home. This woman felt that her house guardian stopped the thief because he didn't go any further than the entrance.

Of course, there could be many reasons why nothing was stolen from her home. I don't think wooden statues actually leap at intruders. What happens is that the energy of the house guardians is such that if someone enters your house with less than honorable intentions, they begin to feel an anxiety that can cause them to retrace their steps. Certainly, you need to take normal precautions to prevent burglary when living in any modern city. However, it could be that the energy in her home, combined with her house guardian, helped protect it.

ANGELS

I believe that the most powerful protective guardian for your home is an angel. Calling upon the angels to be your house guardians for protection and spiritual rejuvenation can bring a wonderful feeling of peace, harmony and safety to your home.

What are angels?

History and mythology are full of references to angels. Beyond the myths, *angels are real.* The veils between the angelic realm and the realm of human beings is thinning, and these messengers from Spirit are making their presence known. They are associated with beauty, peace, joy, fulfillment, laughter and love. They are here to help us lay down our burdens of fear, uncertainty, guilt, pain and worry. They help replace feelings of unworthiness and insecurity with a sense of joy and belonging. Angels assist us in connecting with a powerful yet gentle force, which encourages us to live life to its fullest. They enable us to live with joy instead of fear. Angels help us enter into the world of love.

There are many different kinds of angels and they can each serve a different purpose in your life. There are personal angels, called guardian angels. These are beings who are personally connected with you and your evolution. They can assist you in creative endeavors, protect you, and help you to achieve all of your dreams. There are also nature angels, which are the guardians of particular areas such as mountains or lakes. Places in nature that have a very special feeling are most often under the protective kindness of an angel.

Different forms of angels

Angels can appear in several different forms. The form that most people associate with angels is the traditional church-window angel with wings. Almost every culture throughout the world has had adherents of winged angels. Native Americans called angels the Winged People or the Bird People, alluding to their winged appearance. The winged type of angel is rarely reported, although reports of angels appearing in human form are fairly common. Angels seem to take a form that is comforting and pleasing to the person to whom they appear. In my travels I have heard numerous accounts of the physical appearance of these angelic beings. They appear as both male and female, young and old, all different races, some well dressed and some shabbily attired.

There is another way that the angelic realm affects humanity and this happens when an angelic energy superimposes itself on someone. When this occurs, a person may unwittingly offer assistance and guidance to someone else in need—*and sometimes may not even re-*

member it. It seems that some tremendous force of goodness overtakes them and they offer just the right message to another.

How to recognize angels

Most angels are not seen but felt. There are several different ways you can tell if an angel is present. Often the wonderful smell of flowers accompanies their presence. Sometimes they announce their arrival with a slight breeze, even if the windows are closed. Sometimes you hear the sound of bells, chimes or trumpets. (Yes, trumpets! I believe that the reason for this is that when angels break into our dimension, the sound that most closely resembles that sound in our reality is the sound of trumpets, so this is how we will interpret it.) Sometimes you may see a flash of light which can indicate the arrival of an angel. Or the most usual way is that you feel a wash of love flow over you. If you think you are in the presence of an angel, you most likely are.

Right now angels are bridging our physical reality with their pure spiritual energy. Like a leaf falling softly on the still pool of our consciousness, we recognize their presence. As we trust in them, they will pour their blessings on us. Where intention goes, energy flows. And as you become aware of angels they will be more and more drawn into your life.

Calling a house angel into your home

To call forth an angel for your home, first perform a thorough cleansing of your entire house. Then find the centermost portion of your house. This will be the part of your house that feels like its heart, or center; it may or may not be located in the geographic center of your home. Once you have found this, sit in stillness there. Center your thoughts and ask for a house angel to come forth. Visualize this House Angel beaming a light that completely encompasses your house and the land surrounding it.

You can also call forth angelic energy into a specific room in your house. You might like to bring angel energy into your bedroom, for example, to help you through the night hours, to guide you on your inward travels, or to assist you with the healing of yourself or others in the night.

You also might like to call an angel into the bedroom of your children. Children have a special affinity with angels. Many children have the ability to see angels when adults cannot. When my daughter was three or four years old, she and I used to go to the Theosophical bookstore in Seattle. She would always run to one corner of the store. There were not any children's books or toys in this corner, or anything else that would have particularly held her interest. But she would nonetheless run and stay there while I browsed through the rest of the shop. I happened to mention this to an elderly Theosophical author I knew who also frequented the bookstore. She looked surprised and said, "Oh, my dear, don't you know? There's an angel in that corner!"

Calling for angels of the four directions

Another way to bring protection to your home is to ask that four great tall angels stand around the outside your home. Imagine that their wings are spread, creating a great canopy of light and love over your home. Here is an invocation to call these beautiful Beings of Light:

ANGEL OF THE EAST   I call upon the Angel of the East. I ask that you bring safety, protection and love to this home. May the warm winds of heaven blow gently on this house. I give thanks for your presence.

ANGEL OF THE SOUTH   I call upon the Angel of the South. I ask that you bring safety, protection and love to this home. May the gentle rains of heaven cleanse and heal all within this home. I give thanks for your presence.

ANGEL OF THE WEST   I call upon the Angel of the West. I ask that you bring safety, protection and love to this home. May the warmth of the sun fill all who enter this home with light and love. I give thanks for your presence.

ANGEL OF THE NORTH   I call upon the Angel of the North. I ask that you bring safety, protection and love to this home. May the stability and strength of the earth fill all those who enter this home. I give thanks for your presence.

THE CREATOR   To the Great Spirit that dwells within all things I ask for guidance and love for all who shall enter into this home, that we may grow in peace and love. I give great thanks for your loving presence.

You can either sit in meditation to call these angels or literally go to four areas around the outside of your home and call one angel in each of the four directions. Then leave a gift for that angel, such as a pretty stone, a feather or a flower. It is a native custom that whenever you ask for something you leave a gift. The size of the gift is not as important as the energy with which you give it. If you are fortunate enough to have a garden around your home, you can even plant a plant for each angel in each of the four directions. Do not be concerned if your directions aren't exact. It is truly your Intention that is the most important thing.

To bring the energy of angels more powerfully into your home you might consider putting pictures of angels up on the wall, or having statues of angels or even hanging angels. I can usually find hanging angels for sale at Christmas time. I like to place these on a string and free-float them from the ceiling, leaving them up all year long. Whatever you put your attention on in life will increase in your life. As you put your attention on angels, they will begin increasingly to make their presence known to you. I believe that all prayers are heard and that angels are only a thought away.

ANIMAL SPIRIT ALLIES

Emissaries from Spirit can arrive in many forms. Native cultures' use of allies (also called totems, power animals, animal guides and spirit animals) is well documented. It is believed that each person has an individual animal spirit that gives guidance, strength and protection. Though an individual can have more than one totem, usually there will be one that is predominant at any given time. The Western equivalent of a totem is a spirit guide. Totems can be very powerful home guardians. Although people with native blood tend to have a propensity for working with totems, anyone from any culture can benefit from accessing their totem animal.

Knowing one's totem is a valuable aid to understanding oneself. In many tribes, associations and relationships are based on totem affiliation. One Australian Aboriginal clan with which I have spent time wanted to share sacred Aboriginal information with me. However, they needed to find out what my clan and my totems were first. They needed to make sure that my totems and their totems were harmonious with each other before we shared ceremonies together.

I was taken out into the Australian bush. A pungent mixture of Aboriginal sweat and yellow and red soil was rubbed on me. This was done so the Spirits of the Land would think I was an Aborigine and not a stranger: the Spirits of the Land were said to harm non-Aborigines. I was then instructed to sit with my back to a tree and wait to see what animal approached me. They said whatever animal or bird approached me was my totem. After a very long wait, I was approached by a crow. The Aborigines all sighed in relief, for the crow totem was harmonious with their totem, and I was then allowed to participate in the clan rituals.

How to find your ally

In native traditions, finding one's totem often involves a vision quest or an inner journey. However, as we don't always have the opportunity to go on a vision quest, there are a number of other ways that you can find your ally. Your power animal may be your favorite animal since childhood. Your totem may come repeatedly in your meditations. An animal that appears consistently in your dreams is often your totem. Sometimes you may find your power animal by noticing the animals that you feel irresistibly drawn toward. Perhaps as a child you loved stories about horses best of all, and have always felt an alignment with horses. This might suggest that it is very likely your totem is a horse.

Your animal ally may come in an unusual way. If you are taking a walk and a crow feather drops at your feet, it may be that the crow is one of your totems. Another way to discover your totems is to watch the "signs" or omens in your life. For example, you might receive a card with a deer on it in the mail. And then on posters and billboards you begin seeing deer. You then turn on the television and you see a documentary about deer. There's a song on about deer as you're driving by a field full of deer. Deer begin appearing every night in your dreams. Everywhere you turn, you seem to be seeing deer. You might want to consider this significant. This could be a sign that one of your totems is a deer.

You will tend to share qualities with your totem, so another way to discover your totem is to study the habits and attributes of different animals. Read books about a variety of animals. Find out all about the habits and habitat of the ones with which you feel an especial

kinship. This information is available in nature magazines and ency-
clopedias, as well as books. For example, bears wake up slowly in the
morning and tend to be creatures of habit, traveling the same path
every day. If you leap out of bed in the morning full of energy to start
your day and tend to vary your activities, it is unlikely that the bear is
your totem. If you are always flitting about quickly, eat small meals
all day, never seem to gain weight, and talk quickly, a bird may be
your totem. (This would be a songbird rather than a bird of prey such
as an eagle or a hawk.)

How to discover the meaning of your ally

Each ally has different qualities or abilities. By communing with your
totem you gain access to those qualities. Different cultures assign different meanings to different totems, so I always suggest you trust
your intuition to find the meaning of your totem, for there are no universal meanings for all the totems. A good example is the Owl Spirit
Ally. When I was in Australia discussing totems with Aboriginal el-
ders, I was told by one male elder that men feared the owl, for it is a
woman's totem and represents darkness and the unknown. He said
that as they were afraid of the power of women and of the unknown,
so they feared the owl.

When I was in New Zealand discussing totems with members of
the Terinaki Maori tribe, I asked about the owl. I was told that the
owl was a sacred bird to the Maoris. It is so sacred that its name is
never spoken. In my own Native American culture some tribes re-
vere the owl, saying that it represents deep wisdom. Yet other tribes
see the owl as the bringer of death and darkness. The fact that different cultures often have different meanings for the different animal
allies leads me to suggest that you discover the meaning of your ally
yourself.

There are a number of ways to discover the meaning of your ally.
There are many books that have listings of power animals and what
they represent. It can be interesting and fun to study the traditional
meanings associated with various totem animals. Although these can
be very useful, it is important to remember that you are only reading
one person's interpretation. Different authors have varying ideas
about the meaning of different totems. However, even though a book
interpreting totems shows you only one person's or one tradition's

point of view, this can be a good starting point. You might feel particularly drawn to one totem's characteristics, as described by a particular author. You can read the definition of your totem in the book and see if it "feels" right to you. Your own sense of what a particular totem means to you is unique and is certainly as valid as anyone else's opinion.

A second way to discover the meaning of your totem is to find out about the habits of your totem in nature. For example, if you feel that the leopard is your totem, you might research about leopards. In your research you find that they spend much of their time sleeping but when it is time to hunt they are very focused, direct and swift in their pursuit of their prey. From this research you might gather that one of the qualities of a leopard totem is the ability to rest completely, yet accomplish goals quickly and easily. Your power animal can bring an understanding of what strengths you have, as well as assisting you in times of distress.

Another way to discover the qualities associated with your ally is to go into a meditative state and while in that state imagine that you are talking to your ally. Visualize (or get a feeling if you have difficulty visualizing) the totem clearly to determine its meaning for yourself. Ask your totem what its qualities are and how they can help you.

Totems sometimes change over time. You might find that one totem works well for you at one stage of your life. But then later, as you change and grow, you could feel drawn to another animal's spirit energy. There is something primal and powerful in totem energy and this is excellent for creating a protective energy around your home. Your totem is not only helpful for protection of your home, but aligning with your ally can help bring the qualities of the ally into your home and into your life as well.

How to use your ally in your home
Once you have a sense of what your totem is and what it means, you can invite the energy of the totem into your home. You can offer a prayer to your totem, inviting its presence into your house or office to act as a house guardian. You can also use pictures or statues of it around your house to access further the protective energy of your ally.

For protection in your home, you can either use your personal totem, or you can call forth a totem that is specific to your house.

You might want to use different totems for different areas of your house. For instance, if you want to promote a feeling of healing energy throughout your house, a bear totem would be a good choice, since the bear is traditionally associated with healing. Or perhaps there is one specific room in your house where you do healing. You could call forth the bear totem for that room only.

If you want to feel a lot of strength and freedom in your home or office, then you could call forth a horse totem. The horse is often associated with grace, strength, freedom and movement. If you think you would really like to see into the realms of the unknown, you might want to use an owl. If you live in a large family or have a lot of people living in your house, and if you want to promote a real sense of community and communion, you might want to work with the wolf. Wolves are very family-oriented. Bird energy could be an excellent choice for your kitchen, as they are very active and energetic and cheerful.

A good way to bring totem energy into your home is to have a statue, a photo or a painting of your totems. These objects have their own energy and can assist in calling forth the energy of the totem into your home.

Totems for your home's entrance

In the entrance to your home, put a representation of a totem that feels strong and powerful. The totem that you have represented in your entrance sets the tone for the energy of the entire house, so this in many respects is the most important totem placement.

In my own home, I have a lizard totem near the front door. The lizard is one of the keepers of the dreamtime to the Aborigines, and one of the keepers of the inner mysteries. It is a very female totem. When you open the door to my home, you are greeted by lizards. I have a couple of large carved wooden lizards from Bali and a picture of a lizard near the door. They serve as protectors of my space, and also help to establish the energy that I want to be present throughout my home. Their presence provides a sense that one is entering sacred space.

At one time we lived in neighborhood where there were a number of tramps. Although almost all of the tramps were kind people who were just down on their luck, there was one rather sinister-looking tramp who used to come into our garden and up to the door to look in the house. Our daughter Meadow was young then and I felt a concern for her safety. One day when my concern had reached a peak I carefully took my large wooden lizards outside on the front steps and asked them to make sure that only good-hearted people would approach our home. I happened to be glancing out of the window when the tramp approached again. He looked from one lizard to the other, quickly turned around and left. I never saw him again after that.

Bedroom totems

Bear is often a good choice for the bedroom. The bear hibernates and pulls energy in for healing. Intuitively, people buy teddy bears to put on their beds. It seems that this could be an unconscious primal way of inviting bear energy into the bedroom.

Fish can also be equally effective totems for the bedroom since they live in the water, which is representative of the dream state and the emotions. Another excellent choice for the bedroom is the turtle. Turtle represents Mother Earth. It is also associated with a protective state, going into the womb, the darkness, and the comfort of the darkness. Using turtle energy in your bedroom would promote deep rest, regeneration and a strong sense of safety.

Eagle energy is a very powerful energy to work with and many people feel drawn to it. However, in the bedroom, sometimes the eagle can be a bit too powerful for sleep. If you want to work with a bird there, try a bird of the night, such as an owl. The eagle would be better for living areas, or perhaps a meditation area if you want to pull in very powerful, intense energy there.

Two totems that are very powerful symbols of the transformation that's occurring on the planet now are the dolphin and the whale. These are excellent totems to put in a child's bedroom. They are also good for any place where there is a lot of communication. Dolphins are a powerful symbol of joy, communication and interconnectedness. Whether you use a picture, a carving, or a little photograph, these will all create and generate the energy of the totem you have called.

Sometimes snake totems can be used in the bedroom. Though many people have negative feelings about snakes, the snake is a very powerful totem to use. Throughout history it has represented such things as healing, personal transformation and basic life force. Two intertwined serpents form the symbol of caduceus, the symbol of physicians. In ancient Greece there were hundreds of dream temples (temples of Asclepius, who was the god of sleep as well as the god of healing) which one could enter for healing. Undulating over the floors of these temples were snakes because they were thought to represent healing. To gain healing one would sleep overnight in the temple with the snakes. Snakes also represent transformation since they shed their skins. To the Hindus, snakes represent the kundalini energy, the life-force energy which lies coiled like a snake at the base of the spine.

Snake energy is a powerful totem to use anywhere in your house. It is a very potent form of energy that you might want to use only occasionally, as you need it. If you are in a time of great change or are going through a period of initiation where you really need to let go of the old and move on into the new, snake energy is an excellent energy to place around you. Normally, it can be too intense for use in the bedroom, however during periods in your life of great transformation it can be excellent. Then it could be useful to completely surround yourself with the energy of this reptilian spirit helper.

Living room totems

The best totems to use in the living room are communal animals like the wolf or dolphin. Any animal that brings forth the energy of community and interrelatedness is excellent. Animals that are playful, such as the sea otter, are good as well. Herd animals, such as elephants, are also good because they represent and hold the energy of community and friendship.

Bathroom totems

Frogs and turtles, dolphins, whales, fish and seals are all totems that work well in bathrooms. They bring a sense of the spirit of water and they contribute to a feeling of life and nature in your bathroom.

Kitchen totems

As the kitchen is the source of nourishment for the entire family, the totems used in a kitchen are important. Although our diet is mostly vegetarian, I like having the cow (which I feel is an underrated animal) as a totem in the kitchen. The cow, to me, represents peace. It also has the energy of service, for every part of the cow is given in service. I know one woman who thinks the best totem for the kitchen is the fox because they are clever. She feels that you need to be clever to be a good cook!

Office totems

The totem for a home office or study depends on the type of work done there. If your study is a place for relaxation and intellectual pursuit, you might consider a deer totem. Deer energy is associated with gentleness, softness and love. If you are in a place where you are very outgoing in your life, very projecting, you might want to bring deer energy into your home. If you feel you have too much yang energy, the use of deer totems in your house or office can help counteract this.

If you spent enough time in the woods to get to know the tracks of various animals, you would notice that the tracks of deer go very delicately around the vegetation growing there. Elk, on the other hand, usually make a straight line between where they are and where they want to go. Nothing gets in the way of elk; they just crash on through! They are very large and powerful animals with antlers that can reach five feet in spread. They have tremendous stamina and strength.

If you are working on projects in your office where you need a feeling of power and stamina, where you need to let nothing get in the way of your goal, despite whatever obstacles you encounter, then you might consider putting elk totems in your office. There is almost a kind of warrior energy inherent in elk spirit. This energy can also be a useful antidote to feelings of victimization in your life.

Another good totem animal for the office is the crow. Crows are extremely intelligent birds who are known for their persistence and curiosity. A crow never leaves well enough alone, but will continue to investigate whatever catches its interest until it is completely satisfied that it has figured it out. The crow is cunning and able to command its environment to get what it needs and wants from it. Crow qualities can be useful for running a successful business.

Totems as house guardians

Totems can be very useful house guardians. If you take the time to connect with your totems and then place physical representatives of these totems throughout your home, you'll have silent protectors throughout the day and night. To continue to have the power of the totem in a consistent and steady way, it is valuable to periodically acknowledge the totem. You can do this by occasionally saying hello (either aloud or silently). Cleaning the representation of your totem when it gets dusty is another way of acknowledging and honoring it. Taking care of and honoring your totems will keep them energized.

Anything that you give attention to will respond by becoming more energized. It is not the physical object itself that is creating the protection; is the meaning that you assign to it and the energy that you radiate to it that will make the difference. Remember that totems are very individual and the best totem for any room is the totem that you feel an affinity with.

Also, I suggest that you include totems from the geographical area that you live in. For example, if you live in Australia, you might want to work with the dingo or the kangaroo or the wombat. Whereas if you live in North America, you might choose an animal indigenous to that area, such as coyote, wolf or elk. In Great Britain perhaps you might work with the deer or the fox. You will probably feel a much stronger connection to animals native to your area, although occasionally people do experience an undeniable and inexplicable affinity with an animal from a place they have never even visited.

HOUSE GUARDIAN SPIRITS

Another house protector can be called the spirit of your home. Everything has spirit, and everything has *a* spirit within it. In native tradition it is always important to honor the spirit of things: the spirit of your home, the spirit of the mountain, the spirit of the river that offers irrigation for the plants, the spirit of the plants and animals that give sustenance, the spirit of the earth beneath your feet. The more you honor and respect the world around you, the more you are supported and protected by that world.

An interesting story about house guardians comes from Bali. The Bali Beach Hotel in Sanur was destroyed by fire in January 1993. A fascinating feature of this fire was that one room on the third floor, room number 327, had no fire damage whatsoever. Adjacent rooms were completely gutted, but the furnishings in this room were not even singed.

Room 327 had a very interesting history. Prior to the fire, staff at the hotel were used to receiving frequent complaints from guests who stayed in this expensive hotel room. Often they would not stay long because they said their sleep was disturbed by strange noises in the night. Also, the air-conditioning system, the electrical apparatus, the plumbing and telephone service in that room would frequently and mysteriously break down. But when the repair staff would come up to inspect the problems that had been reported, they couldn't find anything wrong.

After the fire, as is often the practice in Bali, a native trance medium was called in to discover the reason for the fire. This medium communicated with the spirit of the building, who in Bali is referred to as Lord of the Premises. This spirit was named Ane Meduwa Karang, and he said that he had wanted Room 327 as a Holy Room dedicated to his worship. He also said that he had given many signs which had not been heeded, such as the disturbances in the room, before he finally resorted to burning the hotel down.

Local tradespeople agreed that there had been other omens as well, such as the fact that the hotel had been constructed on the site of a cemetery (unprecedented in Bali). Also some members of the hotel staff had been afflicted with seizures, which in Bali is always considered to be a sign that something is wrong in the spirit world.

Because of these ill omens, offerings had been made to placate the spirits before the fire, but as the *Bali Post* expressed it in an article published on 26 January 1993:

> It might not have been sufficient. One of the reasons advanced [for the fire] is that many of the higher-ups in the hotel hierarchy did not understand much about Balinese offerings. How can a German Food and Beverage Manager understand that he has to feed "souls" in addition to his regular guests? His budget does not allow for this, and it is not in his job description anyway.

After a fire in Bali, they will either rebuild on a different site or give the building a new name. The final outcome of this story was that the hotel was rebuilt, bigger and better than before. The Bali Beach

Hotel was renamed the Grand Bali Beach Hotel, and Room 327 was set aside for use exclusively as a Holy Room.

To "call" the spirit of your house:

- Sit very still in the area that feels most central in your home.
- Take seven deep full breaths and with each breath let yourself relax.
- Close your eyes and begin to feel the energy of the room around you.
- Expand your awareness to feel the overall energy of your entire home. (This is similar to listening to the overall melody played by an orchestra. Even though the orchestra is made up of many separate instruments, all together the sounds they make create one symphony. Although there are many different energy fields in your home, they culminate in one overall energy field.)
- Once you have connected with the feeling of your home, ask your home its name and see if you become aware of a visual image that goes along with the feeling and the name. (We can better relate with objects if we personalize them.) If you are unsure how to do this, ask yourself questions, such as: does this home seem male or female, tall or short, young or old? Questions such as these can help you become aware of the overall personality of your home.
- After receiving a name, you can then ask your house if it has any particular needs. You might be surprised when you find out what your house spirit has to say. For example, he or she might say that it needs a clean filter on the heating unit, or the chimney needs cleaning, or it would like the windows open more often. Or even, as in the case of the Balinese hotel guardian, that your home would like an altar or a place set aside as a holy place.
- Then you can ask this house guardian to keep your home safe and protected. Make sure to give thanks in advance.

I knew some people who named their house Summerfield House. They said that they had named their house after their house guardian spirit whom they had named Sara Summerfields. They said she was a warm, happy, loving, almost mothering guardian. When they leave their home they say, "Good-bye, Sara. Thank you for keeping our home safe." When they return they say, "Hi, Sara. Good to be home again." And when they walk back into their home they say that they feel a warm rush of welcome energy envelop them.

RITUAL FOR THE PROTECTION OF A HOUSE

Rituals have been used since primordial time. A ritual is a symbolic act done in an altered state of consciousness, in order to cause a desired change. Basically, you are projecting energy through the form of the ritual. The ritual in and of itself has no power, but it is a focusing device for your intention. It can distill the energy that you project through it, as well as symbolically embody your intention. A ritual's main value is the way that it allows you to focus energy toward a desired result.

The power of your ritual is dependent on your Intention, but also you must take into account the rising and changing currents of energy around you. Everything from the phase of the moon to the positioning of the stars and the seasons can affect your ritual. Sometimes the currents of energy are running with you and sometimes you may be sailing upstream. Some people make a study of just when the time is exactly right to do a ritual. However, I prefer to use intuition to determine when to do a ritual. I usually choose a time when it just feels right.

You can use the following ritual to bind an energy of safety and protection around your house. However, I believe that the most powerful rituals are created spontaneously, using your intuition and the materials at hand.

- Start by standing at the front door.
- Take a moment to relax and center yourself.
- Hold a candle (either a taper or a glass-enclosed votive candle).
- Peer into the center of the candle and imagine that the light of the candle is expanding to envelop you in a glowing, shimmering orb of light.

- Hold the candle near the center of your chest, infusing the candle with the energy of love. Slowly move the candle out from your heart center and upwards. Then in a straight line bring the candle down, saying over and over "Safe . . . Protected and Well." As you bring the candle down have the feeling of calling down the light into your home. Then return the candle to near the center of your chest. Slowly take the candle to your left and move it across to the right, saying, "Safe . . . Protected and Well." You are making the sign of the cross, which is protecting and strengthening.
- Continue throughout your home, bottom to top in a clockwise direction, doing this at every outside door and window as you say, "Safe . . . Protected and Well," and making the sign of the cross.
- Return to your starting point and repeat the cross once again, thus completing your ritual. Then blow out your candle.

You have now made a sign of the cross in every door and window of your home. The cross is a holy sign that goes back even before Christ. It is a powerful symbol of peace and protection. It is not a coincidence that if we want to avert something bad from us we make the sign of the cross. Even if it is done as a joke, it still betrays a deep psychological symbolic association within our collective consciousness.

PRAYER

Of all things that you can do to protect and preserve the energy of your home, I find that prayer is the most effective and the most powerful. A simple prayer to Spirit can bring immediate and positive results. You can say, "Great Spirit (or God or whatever you acknowledge as the source of all life), I ask for your blessings and protection for this home." Sometimes you will immediately feel the rustle of angel wings and a gentle surge of Spirit fill your home.

Another way to use prayer is with a Tibetan prayer wheel. This unique object consists of thousands of Buddhists prayers that have been handwritten on very thin paper. These papers, in turn, have been very tightly wrapped inside a silver cylinder which swings around a stick. The person holding the prayer wheel twirls it to disperse the prayers out into the world. I love my Tibetan prayer wheel. When I use it I can see the energy of prayers swirling out into the universe. These are available at many New Age bookstores.

Energizers

Energizers are those things that can increase the energy in your home. Here is a brief list of some home energizers that you can use to increase the life force of your home.

HAPPY PHOTOS

The photos you have around your home are very important. A photo of someone who is unhappy, especially if it is one of the household members, can create a very difficult energy in a home. It is important that the photos that are out on display portray happiness, and peace.

A family called me in for a consultation because they were having great difficulty with their teenage son. The teenage years are very important and formative years where a certain amount of rebellion is an important part of our evolution into adulthood. But the parents were concerned because their son was taking drugs, and was often gone for two days without letting anyone know where he was. And when he was home, he stayed in his room and wouldn't communicate with anyone. I wasn't convinced that house clearing was all that was needed in the situation. It seemed to me that psychological counseling for the entire family was in order. However, I went to the home to see if there was anything that could help ease their difficulty.

I was astonished when I entered the front door because the first thing I noticed was a photo of their son looking very unhappy. The parents were artistically inclined and the photograph of their son was a black and white photograph done by a well-known photographer. However, in the photo he looked very sad, as if he was about to cry. Aesthetically speaking, it was a good photo. But for the energy of the house and family it was a very damaging one.

The photo had hung in the same location for several years—it was taken when their son was eleven, and he was now sixteen years old. Hence, for five years, every time someone entered the house, they saw the photo of the boy as an unhappy person. Subconsciously, other people may have been projecting this negative view on to him. Also, the negative image portrayed by the photo was being embedded into his subconscious every time he entered the home. It was a continual affirmation of his unhappiness.

When I suggested to the parents that they change the photo to a color photo of their son in a happier time, they weren't enthusiastic. They said that the photograph was very artistic and the photographer was famous. They didn't want the first thing that people saw when they entered their house to be an ordinary family snapshot. However, I suggested that they try it for a while, and I then went through the rest of the house. In addition to cleansing the somewhat stagnant energies in the home, the biggest changes I suggested were to make the home more homey.

The house was a showcase for prized art and sculptures, but it had a "don't touch" feeling to it. It didn't feel like a place you could be comfortable in. I felt that making the home feel more like a home, instead of a museum, would contribute to their son feeling happier in himself, and perhaps would make him like being at home more. I also suggested they seek family counseling.

A few weeks later I received a phone call. The parents had implemented the changes I had suggested and were astonished by the difference in their son. Even before they started family counseling, he seemed to be changed. He was more approachable and more willing to talk with them. I feel that the shift in their son came from two sources. First, it helped enormously to alter the energy in the home. Their house began to feel comfortable and warm. Secondly, the parents had begun to take some responsibility for the situation themselves, and not blame only the son. The young man perhaps sensed this and thus felt less alienated.

SPECIAL OBJECTS

The objects that you have in your home, especially the objects that you have on display, are very important for the overall energy of your home. If you strongly dislike an object in your home, every time you see it your energy will fall. This will happen because subconsciously you feel dislike whenever you are in the same room with the object in question.

If you don't love or use the objects in your home, get rid of them. Even if it was a special wedding gift from your great aunt, if you hate it, get rid of it. Having an object in your home that you dislike lowers the energy field of your entire home. Conversely, having objects in your home that you love increases the energy in your home. Objects that can uplift the energy in a home are:

SACRED OBJECTS   Things that belonged to Spiritual Masters or belonged to people that you admire or love will energize your home. Every object carries the emanations of whoever has owned it. If you have something that was given to you by a Spiritual Master or a revered teacher, it will continue to emanate the master's energy field into your home. An object that once belonged to someone you admired will also increase the life force in your home. Any sacred objects such as a rock from the Himalayan mountains or an eagle feather will also bring energy into your home.

HANDMADE OBJECTS   A handmade object can bring a wonderful life energy into a home, especially if you know the person who made it. Hand-painted pictures, hand-woven rugs, handmade furniture, handmade sculptures, a child's drawings—all of these things can increase the energy in your home. For example, if you purchase a pot personally from the potter who made it, or if you watched the creation process of the pot, then it will energize your home much more than one that was made in a factory. The more handmade objects that you have in your home, the more life force will be in your home. This is especially true if the creators of the objects were feeling happy or content when they were creating them. Drum makers in native cultures will not make a drum during unhappy times because they say that the unhappy energy stays in the drum.

I have many birdhouses that were made by the most wonderful old man who lives down the road. He loves birds and he loves making birdhouses. His enthusiasm spills over into every house he creates. My birdhouses have the energy of his kindness and love emanating from them, so every time I look at them I'm subconsciously reminded of these qualities. The more objects in and around your home that are filled with love and caring and pleasant associations, the more energized your home will be.

If you are unsure about whether an object is uplifting the energy of your home or depressing it, take a moment to look at the object and hold it. What emotion does it elicit in you? What do you feel like when you are touching it? Do you feel your energy level rise, decrease, or stay the same? If you feel your energy level drop, then find another home for the object. We are in constant relationship with all the things in our lives. There are so many things in our environment outside the home which lower our personal energy fields, that it is very important that everything in our homes contributes to uplifting our energy.

NATURAL OBJECTS Natural objects are great energizers. A throw for the sofa that is made of wool or cotton has more energy than a throw made of synthetic fibers. The closer an object is to its source origins, the more energy it has. Just as honey is a more vital food than refined sugar, because it is closer to its natural source, so natural fibers and natural products in your home will carry a stronger life-force energy field than objects that have been processed. Although everything has energy, a wooden chair will have more life-force energy than a plastic chair.

ANIMALS Animals can contribute greatly to the life force in a home. Although each individual animal will affect the overall energy fields in your home in a different way, the most essential component that will uplift your home's energy is the love that you have for your animal. This love will fill your home with a beautiful light.

PYRAMIDS Pyramids can bring an exhilarating energy into your home. Each pyramid acts as a vortex to attract cosmic energies. These gifts from the ancient Egyptians contain secrets of energy not fully understood. Just having them in your home will increase the energy fields there. They are excellent to have as we approach the millennium.

CUT-LEAD CRYSTALS Cut-lead crystals can bring rainbow energies into your home. They elicit magic and joy and vibrant color. The energy field in your home absorbs and retains the color vibrations long after the sun has set. You can feel the difference in the energy of a room that has crystals in the windows, even at night. The room will sing with energy.

MIRRORS Mirrors have been called the aspirin of Feng Shui because they can fix unbalanced energy flows. Mirrors can expand a room. They can make *you* feel more expanded just by being in a room with them. They can bring the outdoors indoors, as, for example, when a mirror reflects trees, a lake or river into your home. Reflected water views are excellent as they promote serenity, healing, intuition and in some cases even wealth. If there is a place in your house where you feel cramped or confined, try putting up several large mirrors. Usually you will immediately feel more expanded. If a door opens to face a wall, or if a hall ends in a wall, this can create a blocked feeling. Putting a mirror up in these situations can increase feelings of flow and expansion.

Mirrors can also be a way of deflecting unwanted influences. A client of mine was having a difficult time with her neighbor. If leaves from her tree fell in her neighbor's yard, the neighbor would take the leaves and put them in a heap on my client's porch. Almost every day the neighbor did something that was disturbing, to the point where my client constantly felt overwhelmed with negative thoughts regarding the situation. I suggested that she put mirrors on the wall that faced toward her neighbor as a way of deflecting her neighbor's unruly energy. She was uncertain that anything could make a difference in the situation, but did as I suggested. She was astonished when her neighbor came over a few days later with a fresh-baked loaf of bread as a peace offering.

GODS AND GODDESSES Pictures or statues of gods and goddesses can have an inspiring effect on a room. If you want to increase romantic love in your home, you might consider placing a statue of Venus in a prominent place. If you are feeling the need for a strong and powerful home energy, you might consider having a photo or statue of Thor. Gods and goddesses have been venerated for so many generations that a photo or statue connects you to the collective-consciousness vibration that is attached to each deity, thus bringing that energy into your home.

15

GHOSTBUSTING

$\mathcal{I}$n my early apprenticeship years, I trained with several Hawaiian kahunas. My training included releasing earthbound spirits (ghosts) from homes. After my training I was asked by a distraught schoolmaster to clear a school building that was reported to have ghosts. The schoolmaster explained to me that at night lights would go on and off, doors would open and close, and the students were frightened.

Since most of the activity happened at night, none of the students actually saw anything while they were at the school during the day. But even second-hand reports of it were enough to frighten some of them, and the head of the school wanted the ghosts removed. At that time I didn't feel confident enough to clear the school myself, so I asked one of my kahuna teachers if he would accompany me. As we stood outside the school in the lovely soft Hawaiian moonlight, we prepared the salt, water and ti leaves (a Hawaiian herb) that we would use for the ritual. The schoolmaster was waiting for us and opened the front door to the school.

As we entered the ground floor I was only aware of the happy residual emanations of the students. The energy felt alive and positive. Just to be on the safe side, however, we did minimal clearing with salt and water on the ground floor. We then went up to the first floor and again the energy felt fine, although we continued doing minimal clearing. I began to think that the reports of ghosts were in fact merely student pranks, and was regretting that I had asked the kahuna to accompany me. We completed the first floor and began to ascend to the second floor. Suddenly the warm night air was replaced with chilling cold air. I felt a heaviness weighing on my body and the last steps seemed an effort to climb. I felt as if it was difficult to breathe.

I looked at my teacher. He was evidently experiencing the same heaviness as he labored up the stairs. Suddenly we heard a door slam just down the hall. I asked the schoolmaster if there was anyone on the second floor. He said that to his knowledge, there was not. As we walked down the hall we heard another door slam. My logical mind is never far from the surface, especially in scary situations, and I remember repeating to myself over and over, "It's a draft. It's a draft. It's a draft."

I began sprinkling the salt while my teacher was flicking water and chanting expulsion prayers in Hawaiian. As I continued to cast salt about each room, I walked near an open window, which abruptly slammed shut. My logical mind began to shout louder, "It's just a draft! It's just a draft!"

I didn't want to look scared to my teacher, so I acted as if this kind of thing happened all the time, while repeating inside myself, "I'm cool. I'm cool."

As I went into one room by myself, I remembered a South American Indian banishing technique I had learned. The technique had seemed so gross that I was certain at the time that I would never use it. But somehow the circumstances seemed to warrant using something drastic. So I took some of the water from the sink in the room and blessed it, and then took a large amount into my mouth. I swished it around and spit-sprayed it into the different corners of the room. Looking back I suppose I was so distracted by the grossness and humor of what I was doing that my fear was temporarily suspended.

We completed the clearing and went outside. My teacher thought it was important to wait a while for the spirits to leave. Remarkably, as we waited, several lights in the unoccupied second floor went on, then off. Then it felt as if a subtle shudder rumbled through the earth, followed by a soft sigh. I knew at that moment that it was complete. There were no more reports of the school being haunted after that.

Afterwards my teacher very lovingly chided me, reminding me

that it does a disservice to the earthbound spirits to be afraid of them. They are in a difficult situation and they need understanding, comfort and support. This was a very important lesson for me because, in my fear of unusual circumstances, I had forgotten essentially what an earthbound spirit was, which is another human being (albeit without a body). I had forgotten the natural compassion that one would feel for someone in a hard situation. And I had forgotten that basically, "ghostbusting" is a gentle reminder to a spirit that they no longer have a body—it is an encouragement to them to seek the Light. Like attracts like, and if you approach a ghost with fear, you will create a fearful situation. If you approach a ghost with a gentle but firm understanding of the situation, most often they will seek the Light.

In the "ghostbusting" that I did on my own after that, I never encountered such dramatic phenomena. I can't help but wonder if my fear didn't intensify the phenomena. If I hadn't been afraid, perhaps we wouldn't have had doors opening and closing and lights going on and off.

I believe that what you fill your consciousness with is what will fill your life. At the time when I was learning how to release earthbound spirits, almost every house in which I did a Space Clearing Ceremony had ghosts to be freed, so I became convinced that almost every home had an earthbound spirit. Later, I recognized that my focus on ghosts was pulling them into my life. I changed my focus, and immediately after doing that I was no longer called into homes that were having ghost problems.

The universe around you is always a reflection of your inner beliefs and thoughts. I haven't encountered a ghost in many years. I believe that changing my subconscious focus changed the experiences that I was pulling into my life. I also believe that the fastest way to pull ghosts into your life is to be afraid of them.

Occasionally houses, particularly older homes, will have a ghost. However, there is nothing to fear from ghosts. Ghosts cannot hurt you if you are not afraid of them. Nevertheless, I believe it is to one's advantage to live in a house without any ghosts in it. And even the happiest of ghosts would be much happier if they were in the spirit realm instead of being trapped in this plane.

Often, earthbound spirits can be cleared out of your home without having to call in a specialist. To help you do this, I've included information on what ghosts are, how to recognize them and techniques for clearing them out of your home.

What Are Ghosts?

GHOSTS

A ghost is basically someone who lived on the earth, but when their body died their spirit remained or was bound to the earth, hence the term earthbound spirit. Ghosts usually reappear again and again and are seen by numerous people. They may appear as wispy mists seen only out of the corner of your eye, or as various solid-looking figures that will mysteriously disappear in front of you. They do not follow people from house to house; they are associated with a particular location rather than a particular person.

The most traditional belief about ghosts is that when someone dies they are either too attached to the earth (didn't want to leave their treasure, want revenge on a wife's lover, etc.), or that they die a sudden death and are in a state of confusion, not having realized that they are dead. Researchers of the paranormal have offered many explanations for ghost phenomena. Italian psychical researcher Ernesto Bozzano believes that ghosts are not the souls of the dead but rather are telepathic messages from their lingering bodiless minds.[1]

Another theory is that ghosts are not dead people's souls, but are instead projections from objects that have absorbed psychic impressions. These impressions are then broadcast back to people who enter the vicinity. The clarity of the resulting image is said to depend on the emotional force of the original psychic imprint as well as the psychic sensitivity of the recipient.[2]

An Oxford University professor, Henry Price, thinks that images are created by mental activity that more or less hovers in a multitude of planes. He suggests that these psychic impressions play back over and over again like a psychic tape loop. Some researchers even postulate that ghosts are a psychic projection of a sensitive person's mind when they respond to telepathic residue left in an area. The theory contends that these percipients will unconsciously create a ghost to satisfy their own emotional needs.[3]

Although all of the theories about ghosts sound possible, personally I am inclined to take the traditional view that a ghost is someone's soul that has become earthbound for any number of reasons.

POLTERGEISTS

Poltergeists are very different from ghosts. The term poltergeist comes from the German words *poltern*, meaning noisy and mischievous, and *Geist*, which means spirit. Poltergeists' activity often includes loud sounds, such as wall rapping, thumps, taps and bangs, often accompanied by displacing of objects. Some objects are lifted, temporarily float and then crash. Some are merely moved or displaced.

Whereas ghostly appearances often occur only at night, poltergeist activity happens at all hours. Poltergeists are usually centered around a person rather than a place and the poltergeist's activity will often follow a person from location to location. It usually begins suddenly and lasts anywhere from a few days to a few years and then abruptly stops.

Although there are opinions to the contrary, I believe that a poltergeist is not a ghost or even a restless spirit. I believe that it is an uncontrollable type of psycho-kinetic energy that emanates from people with unresolved issues in their life, or from deeply suppressed emotions such as the repressed sexual desires of a teenager. I have a friend who experienced harrowing poltergeist activity as a teenager. In later years I asked him about it and he said he had discovered the source. He said it was some deep unresolved emotions regarding one of his family members. Poltergeist activity occurs when emotions build up and then flash out in an uncontrolled flare from the auric field.

Usually I suggest therapy, in addition to house clearing, for poltergeist activity. I feel the therapist working with someone who is experiencing poltergeist activity needs to be qualified in psychology as well as having an understanding of the world of the occult. Most people who are plagued by poltergeists will experience a release from the phenomena once they discover and relive the inner unresolved issues that are the psychological source of the difficulty.

CRISIS APPARITIONS

These apparitions look like ghosts but are very different. As their name suggests, they appear at times of crisis. For example, a mother will "see" her son at the exact moment that he is wounded in battle. Or a wife will "see" her husband at the moment that he dies of a heart attack, even if he is miles away. These crisis apparitions are seen only once and they are usually seen by a relative or a very close friend. They result from a powerful psychic projection in a traumatic moment. A house does not need to be cleansed after the appearance of one of these apparitions unless the person who saw it experienced fearful emotions. The cleansing would address any residue from fear emanations rather than the apparition itself.

BI-LOCATION

A bi-location is actually a spirit of a living person who appears (usually unbeknown to themselves) at a location many miles away. Although highly unusual, there are many cases of apparitions of someone who is living appearing to another, even though their physical body is far removed. Usually, there is some kind of emotional link between the person who is "seen" and the percipient. And usually the person who is seen is either sleeping or in meditation when it occurs. I have a friend whose grandfather was a teacher of "higher thought" in England. He was asked to give a lecture in the north of England but was unable to because of illness. Thinking that the organizers of the lecture had been contacted, he was sound asleep during the time that he was to have given the lecture.

The next week he received letters of praise for his lecture. He was astounded, because he had been ill in bed in the south of England during that time. When he checked with the organizers, who knew him well, they assured him that he had indeed given a lecture during the time he was safely asleep in his own bed! This is an example of a bi-location. This gentleman, perhaps subconsciously, so desired to keep his word and give the lecture that during his sleep his spirit projected to the lecture location.

Recognizing Ghosts

Usually, the best way to tell if your home has a ghost (if you don't actually see it), is to trust your feelings. If there is an area of your home that always feels cool or damp, and there is no physical source of the coldness, this could be evidence of the presence of a ghost. If there is a location in your home where you feel physically heavy and where it is more difficult to breathe, this can also indicate an earthbound spirit.

Often you will feel cold or depressed as a result of ghosts being present but this is not always the case. There are some quite happy ghosts, but even with one of these the atmosphere will seem dense or heavy. All of these sensations of coldness, heaviness, depression and shortness of breath could be attributed to impeded chi flow in the room. (See Chapter 13.) However, if you adjust the flow of chi throughout the house and you still have a location or room where you feel these symptoms, a ghost could be the cause.

Clearing Ghosts

All the methods described in this book can be of benefit when freeing earthbound entities. However, it is valuable to learn specific techniques aimed specifically at releasing ghosts from your home.

First of all, it is important to remember that *ghosts cannot hurt you unless you act primarily out of your fear of them*. If you are afraid of ghosts it becomes much more difficult to free them from your home. What you resist persists, and the more you fear ghosts, the more they will cleave to you. Your fear can harm you more than a ghost will.

The second principle to recognize is that your house ghost needs your support. Ghosts are basically stuck here on the earth plane without bodies. They are playing an old tape loop over and over again. Ultimately, they are just as unhappy about being here as you are unhappy about having them. When you realize that your ghost once had a body and had feelings—both triumphs and disappointments—then compassion begins to unfold within you. This puts you in an excellent position to clear the ghost from your home.

Not all ghost clearing is easy. Some ghosts are stubborn, and you will have to use a little persuasion to reassure them that it is all right to leave. Sometimes, clearing a ghost is like telling a child that it is time for bed. They may resist, but ultimately they will be happier if they go. If you have a resistant ghost, you must be kind but firm in letting them know, in no uncertain terms, that they have lost their body and that they need to go to Spirit, or the Light.

Talk to the spirit attached to your house just like you would talk to a friend. Talk straight from your heart and without fear. Say, "Forgive me for telling you, but you're dead. You don't have a body. You need to go to the Light. There are friends on the other side who are waiting for you, so it's okay to go." That kind of sincere, straight talk works very well. Usually a no-nonsense approach is sufficient. If you have a very obstinate ghost you may need to call in a professional who specializes in clearing ghosts out of homes. However, most of the time you can clear the ghost yourself with compassion and love.

GHOST-CLEARING TECHNIQUE

1. Totally clean the room in which you believe the ghost resides.
   * Clean the room thoroughly, including the floor, windows and carpets. Pick up clutter, dust, etc.
   * Burn a mixture of sea salt or Epsom salts and alcohol in the room (see Chapter 4).
   * Take salt and sprinkle an entire circle around the room, leaving a small opening in your salt circle by a window or a door to the outside for the spirit to exit through.
   * Leave the window or door open while you do this salt ceremony. If it is very cold outside you can just leave it open a crack.

2. Dedicate an energy to the release of the ghost.
   * Obtain a seven-day candle specifically for the release of the ghost.
   * Place the candle close to the location where you perceive the ghost (making sure that it is not a fire hazard).
   * As you light the candle, focus your attention on the ghost and say three times, "You are now free to go to the Light!" Say these words with confidence and certainty.
   * Strike a gong or ring a bell (the deeper the sound the better), and with power and love say, "Go to the light *now*." Do this three times.

- Before you leave the room, call forth spirits from the other side to help with the journey of the earthbound spirit, saying, "I ask that the spirits and guides who assist the transition of the soul from earth to heaven help this being in the transition. I give thanks for your guidance and love."
- I usually add, "Journey well, fellow traveler. May peace be with you on your journey."
- Leave the candle constantly burning for the seven days as this fire-light energy creates a focus point for the helpers from the other side to come and continue to offer assistance if it is needed.

In almost all cases the above technique is enough to release the earthbound spirit. It is most important to remember that there is nothing to be afraid of, and to be firm yet loving in your communications.

16
CIRCLE-OF-LIFE
METHOD

One method I use for space clearing is based on the Sacred Circle of Life. This is a complete system that you can use to cleanse and clear the energies in your home. Many native cultures have symbols and legends which are based on the concept of the circle as a metaphor for life. My Native American ancestors called the Sacred Circle of Life the Medicine Wheel. I use this method not only to honor my ancestors, but also because I believe the philosophy of the Medicine Wheel expresses a powerful understanding of the energy forces around us. I also believe that it is essential that the energy of the Medicine Wheel be activated for the years ahead.

To understand the philosophy of the Native American Medicine Wheel you must know that Native philosophy is built around the ideas of good medicine and the Medicine Wheel. To comprehend the concept of medicine in the Native American way, it is necessary to redefine *medicine*. The medicine referred to in this book is not traditional allopathic medicine; it is anything which helps you to achieve a greater connection and alignment with Spirit and the world around you. When this occurs, your body as well as your emotions, mind and spirit are healed. Medicine is anything that allows you to step into your personal strength and power—anything that assists you in becoming more self-actualized. Native American medicine encompasses all of the visible and invisible realms and teaches you how to become more in harmony with nature. It declares that there is only one holy book and that is the sacred manuscript of nature.

The Medicine Wheel is the understanding of the cyclical nature of life. It is the pulsating circle that infuses all of life. It spins into being and spins out again. It is birth, death and rebirth. It is a mandala of the greater Medicine Wheel of the universe in which everything created has its appropriate place. It is our bodies and our mind, our spirit and our heart. It is the zodiac, the Wheel of Life, the serpent swallowing its tail, Ezekiel's vision, the calendars of the Aztecs, Navajo sand-paintings showing the creation of the world, the Four Winds, the Four Elements and the Four Directions. Jakob Böhme, a sixteenth-century mystic, wrote, "The Being of God is like a wheel, wherein many wheels are made one in another, upwards, downwards, crossways and yet continually turn all of them together. At which indeed, when a man beholds the Wheel, he highly marvels."

The Medicine Wheel is the magic circle that encompasses all of life. Native people knew about this magic circle. They respected what it represented and used it in their everyday lives. Many of their homes were made in the form of a circle. As the circle was so important, it played a central theme in Indian ceremonies and rituals. They purified their bodies in the Sacred Circle of the Sweat Lodge, a cleansing ritual that represented returning to the womb. They came together in council in a circle so that all were included, each having an equal say. Music was made with the circular drum. Dancing was done in a circle.

A circle has no beginning and no end. Life, to my ancestors, was seen as a circle from birth to death to rebirth. They understood that they, like the four seasons, passed through several stages of life. Stepping out of the cyclical rhythm of life caused disharmony and even illness. The circle was thought to be an outer manifestation of an inner understanding of life. Different quadrants of the wheel represented the Four Directions and the Four Elements, and every quadrant had different qualities assigned to it. In psychological terms, each quadrant of the Medicine Wheel represented a different aspect of an individual's personality. This is not a new idea. Noteworthy pioneers in the field of human psychology, such as Jung, have advocated the idea that there are four aspects of the personality.

The elements of Air, Water, Fire and Earth, as well as various colors, plants and animals, are assigned to the cardinal points of the

Medicine Wheel. Although the specific details vary from tribe to tribe, all agree on the importance of the Sacred Circle of Life. Some tribes extend the wheel to twelve points, which align to the twelve months of the year and a type of earth astrology.

How each of the various elements (animals, birds, plants, minerals, etc.) are assigned to each of the Four Directions varies from one tribe to another, and from one culture to another. So do not be too concerned about trying to figure out which is the most appropriate or "authentic" interpretation. The important thing is to understand that each direction has its own power and represents a different aspect of yourself. It is what works best for you personally that matters. When the parts of yourself and your home, as represented by the Medicine Wheel, are in harmony, it will not matter what element you assigned to which direction. You will be much more balanced in your life, and that *is* what matters. Use your intuition for determining what feels right to you, in much the same way that you used your intuition for discovering your totem animal (see Chapter 14). The Four Directions and Elements that I present here are based on my personal experience. Feel free to improvise in order to find the meanings and combinations that work best in your life.

East—Air

The power of the East is the power of Air. Air is lofty ideals. When a baby is born it takes its first breath of air. Air is new beginnings. It is allowing your spirit to soar. Light breezes, cyclones, dust devils, jet streams, tornadoes, whirling winds, warm winds and cold winds are part of the element of air in nature. In nature, Air circulates high above the land and has an overview of life. The part of you that is Air has the ability to see afar. It is that part of you that is universal. It is illumination and integration, freedom and movement. Air uplifts, exhilarates and expands. Air is your thoughts. *Air is power of the mind.*

South—Water

The medicine power of South is Water. Water represents feelings and emotions. It is your intuition. It is your deep connection to spirituality. It is your sacred dreams, psychic impressions and your inner knowing. It is the female part of your being. Waterfalls, the great fierce ocean, gentle seas, mountain streams, soft spring rains, torrential rains, the fog and mists, snow and ice are all Water in nature. Water is fluid and soothing. Water is healing. *Water is power of emotions.*

West—Fire

Fire is the medicine power of transformation. It represents the alchemy that occurs when you release the old and embrace the new. When wood burns, it changes form. Fire is changing old patterns and old habits. Fire is purification and renewing. The sun is the greatest embodiment in nature of the element of Fire. Forests fires, candlelight, campfires and even rust, which is a slow form of Fire, are all Fire as it occurs in nature. Fire is radiance and vibrant energy. Fire is light and transmutation. *Fire is power of spirit.*

North—Earth

Earth is wisdom. It is grounding. It is completing. It is the powerful inner knowing that comes from being connected to nature, to the earth. It allows you to stand your ground in times of adversity. It is your health and the food that you eat. In nature, Earth is the ground that you see, as well as the rocks and the deeply embedded stones and boulders, some of which you cannot see. Earth encompasses all those things that have their roots firmly within it, such as the trees and plants. Earth is fertility and abundance and stability. *Earth is physical power.*

The Four-Directions House-Clearing Method

The use of the philosophy of the Medicine Wheel, the Four Directions and the Four Elements is not new. Most Earth-based cultures around the world honor the Four Directions and utilize the Four Directions in their clearing rituals. Below is a method I have developed which utilizes the Four Sacred Directions and Elements. There are seven parts to this method. The first two are preparation steps and can be done at any time. They do not need to be done before each house clearing.

1. HONOR AND BECOME THE FOUR DIRECTIONS

The Medicine Wheel is based on natural forces, such as the earth's magnetic forces. Each direction has its own energy and affects us in a different way. Scientists have found that humans possess sub-atomic magnetic particles within the brain. It has been hypothesized that these brain particles have the capacity to perceive and respond to the magnetic fields of the earth. Though researchers don't agree on how these magnetic fields affect us, some believe that our bodies do react to magnetic fields. It could be that the ancient cultures' honoring of the Four Directions has its roots in the fact that our brain reacts to the magnetic flows of the earth. There *is* a difference in the individual energies of the Four Directions. Each direction has a specific energy and power. To become aware of the different energies of each direction it is valuable to sit in meditation facing each of the directions until you can feel the separate energy of each direction.

Steps to honor the Four Directions

- Ascertain which direction is East. Do this either by observing the rising sun (the sun rises in the east in the morning), or by obtaining a compass.
- Sit in meditation and stillness facing the East.
- Take a few deep breaths to calm your mind.
- Allow yourself to be open to the Spirit of the East.
- Silently observe your thoughts, body sensations, and emotions while facing East.
- Imagine that you are shifting your shape and becoming the essence of the East. (To do this you might personify the Spirit of the East and imagine yourself as that personage. Or

you might just expand the feeling that you have as you face East and allow that feeling to completely envelop you.)

- When you feel complete, then give thanks to the Spirit of the East.
- Face the three remaining directions, and repeat the above steps.

Honoring the directions should not just be giving lip service to them. It is important that you understand in the depth of your being the power of the directions, the power of what some cultures called the Four Sacred Winds. Continue to do the above exercise until you truly feel and know the power of the directions.

2. HONOR AND BECOME THE FOUR ELEMENTS

Every part of this great and beautiful universe is a part of you. The wind is your breath, the rivers are your blood, the sun rises in your heart and the mountains rise in your soul. To clear a home using the elements it is important to be able to realize that the elements—Air, Water, Fire and Earth—dwell inside you. They are not separate from you. To "become the elements," spend time in nature feeling a unity with each of the elements individually. For example, to connect with the element of Earth, lay down on the Mother Earth. Imagine that you can feel her heart beat beneath you. Then imagine that your awareness keeps expanding and expanding until you feel that you are one with the entire earth. Feel the heat at your core. Feel the cold at your poles, the heat at your equator. Feel the great mountains that soar out of you as you feel the vibrant life of your rain forests and the arid dryness of your vast deserts. Just putting your hands and feet into the earth can assist in connecting you with the energy of Earth.

Here is a simple meditation that you can do to connect with the Four Elements. You can record this on a tape and play it back to yourself or have someone read it to you while you are in a very relaxed state.

Four-element meditation
Take a moment to place yourself in a comfortable position. Make sure that your spine is straight and your body is relaxed. Begin breathing natu-

rally, slowly and easily. With every breath allow yourself to relax and let go. Now travel in your imagination to a beautiful place in nature. It might be somewhere you've been or it can be a place that dwells in your imagination.

Imagine you are strolling around your place in nature. Find a location that is quiet and still in which to sit. Imagine that you are sitting down and closing your eyes. Focus your attention on your breath and allow the mind to still. When you feel comfortable and relaxed, focus your attention on the air around you. Begin to feel the air. Feel the whispers of the wind stroking your skin. Listen to the sigh of the breeze in the trees. Let every movement in the air around you become part of your consciousness. Begin to connect with the air so that you feel every part of it. Feel the wind become your friend and even become an extension of yourself. Use all of your senses to perceive the air.

Hear the sound of your own breath, imagine opening your eyes and imagine that you can watch the movements of the air patterns. Imagine becoming the Air. Notice how you feel being Air. Notice your emotions and your thoughts. Allow yourself to imagine that you are soaring through the treetops, that you are whistling down rocky canyons, that you are dancing over wide fields of grasses—become Air. Now take a breath and bring your awareness back within yourself sitting in nature.

Allow yourself to sink even deeper into a very relaxed state and bring your attention and thoughts to the element of Water. Imagine that your place in nature is close to a waterfall, stream, river or ocean. Let the sound of the flowing water flow through you. Imagine a gentle mist fills your place in nature. Sense the caressing touch of fine droplets of water on your skin. Imagine all the forms that make up the element of Water. Imagine the soothing blue ocean waters of the Mediterranean. Imagine your body being immersed in a warm fragrant bubble bath or plunging beneath a cascading, clear, cool, spring waterfall. Remember that water comes in different disguises, soft and gentle or wild and ferocious. Smell, feel, touch, taste and sense the water. Let it irrigate your soul. Journey within the element of Water. Become a cloud—visualize yourself as a torrential downpour, then become a mysterious swirling mist. Visualize yourself at one with Water. Allow yourself to experience total fluidity. Then take a deep breath and bring your attention back to your breathing.

Now allow the element of Fire to surge into your consciousness. Imagine the heat of the golden sun dancing across your body; feel the warmth of the *sun penetrating into every pore of your skin. Visualize the Spirit of the Fire approaching you and feel yourself being purified through ceremony. As the shaman becomes one with the Fire, so too imagine yourself becoming the flames. Feel the energy and the power surge through you. Connect with the sensation of a warm friendly fire. Feel the camaraderie experienced around a campfire. Incorporate each expression of the element of Fire into your being. Fire is change and transformation. Imagine yourself changing into each aspect of Fire, from a single candle in a mountaintop temple to a raging forest fire. Be Fire, feel the power and strength, the warmth and the healing that Fire exudes. Be the companionship that it can represent. Let Fire become you. The element of Fire gives light and life. Merge with the liquid-gold rays of the sun.*

Now begin to introduce the element of Earth into your being. Imagine that you are looking about your place in nature and seeing the beauty that is displayed within the mineral and plant kingdom that is all a part of the element of Earth. See the grandeur of trees—the complex and intricate forms of these stately beings. Feel the Earth beneath you. Feel her constantly refurbishing and nourishing strength and support. Be aware of the mountains and their towering strength: they have witnessed many changes over the millennia. Feel their wisdom. Close your eyes and begin to sense the web of power and alliance between Self and Earth. Concentrate and allow yourself to become truly connected to the element of Earth. Feel the grounded, stable and serene energy of Earth.

Gradually allow yourself to come out of this meditation and be aware of the alignment you feel toward all the elements. Do this meditation again and again until the elements do not seem to be something outside yourself.

All the elements have their source in the spirit world. Each element has a special store of wisdom that may be garnered by forming a relationship with it. In ancient times shamans acknowledged and honored the elements to gain wisdom, power and mastery. They understood how to form a relationship with an element. Just as personal relationships are vital for successful living, so a relationship with the elements is important in the quest for gaining an understanding of yourself. When you open yourself for communication with the elements you become more integrated; you become part of nature, not an antagonist to or victim of it.

In order to effectively use the Medicine Wheel Method to cleanse a house, you must feel and understand the Four Elements and Four Directions, not just with your mind but in your soul.

3. "DRUM THE CIRCLE"

The drum is used to break up any stagnant energy and circulate energy throughout the home. Begin by standing outside the front entrance of your home with your drum held close to your heart (see pages 129–31). If you are unable to stand outside the front entrance, you may stand just inside the front door facing in toward the home. Say a prayer asking for the assistance of Great Spirit, the Spirits of the Four Directions and the Four Elements to assist you in cleaning the energy of your home. Prayers are best said in your own words, but here is a sample prayer you could say:

> *May the Great Spirit that dwells in all things come forward at this time, bringing blessings and peace.*

To the Spirit of Air:

> *I ask that your sweet cleansing winds fill this home and I give thanks for your guidance and assistance.*

To the Spirit of Water:

> *I ask that your essence of purifying and healing fill this home and I give thanks for your guidance and assistance.*

To the Spirit of Fire:

> *I ask that your transforming warmth fill this home and I give thanks for your guidance and assistance.*

To the Spirit of Earth:

> *I ask that your grounded strength fill this home and I give thanks for your guidance and assistance.*

To the Spirit of the Four Directions and the Four Sacred Winds:

> *Coming through time and space from the Four Quadrants of the*
> *Universe, I ask that you help cleanse and balance the energies in*
> *this home. Ho!*
> ("Ho" roughly translates as "so be it.")

Then slowly and solemnly make a clockwise circle with your drum around the door, striking the drum once in each quadrant. If you imagine that you are facing a large clock, you strike the drum at three o'clock, six o'clock, nine o'clock and twelve o'clock. Focus your Intention on the results that you desire within the home while drumming at the entrance. Complete the circle four times.

Open the door and enter the home. If there is more than one level in the home, start at the lowest level and work up. If possible, also begin in the room facing east on the lowest level and work clockwise. In every room, start in the easternmost corner and work your way around the room clockwise.

Face toward the easternmost corner of the first room to be cleared and hold the drum to your chest. After taking just a moment to still your mind, hold the drum near the floor and begin to drum. Move the drum upwards toward the ceiling. I find that a medium-steady beat is good. (Using a beat in which the moving drumstick looks like a fan is a good rhythm. This is about three beats per second.) One sweep up the corner might be sufficient. However, if the sound in the corner is dull and thudding then continue until you hear a crisp sharp sound with each strike of the drum. When each beat of the drum sounds crisp, this will indicate that the energy is clear.

Continue your steady drum beat as you circle the periphery of the room. Every time you come to a corner, or anywhere that the energy feels sticky, then sweep your drum up from floor to ceiling. When you have completed circling the room, you should end up in the corner you started in. To complete the circle of energy that you have placed around the room, move your drum in a clockwise circle, striking once in each of the Four Directions (right side, down, left side and up).

Now go to the center of the circle. Facing East strike the drum four times. Then face South striking the drum four times, and continue for the West and the North. Next, hold the drum with the head of the drum facing down and beat the drum four times and then hold the drum overhead and beat it four times. Then hold it at chest level and one last time strike the drum four times. You have now "drummed the circle" in one room. Continue this way for the remainder of the house. Remember as you drum to hold the clear Intention in your mind of what results you desire. The drumming is breaking up any stagnant energy, getting the energy moving, and calling for the help of Spirit.

4. *"SMUDGE THE CIRCLE"*

Drumming gets energy moving and smudging purifies the energy. (To learn about smudging, see Chapter 6.) Begin at the front entrance and, using a feather or wing and your smoking herbs in a fireproof pot, repeat the circles around the front entrance the same way you did with your drum. (You do not need to repeat the prayers.) Using your feather, whisk the smoke into a circle as if you were facing a clock—first whisk the smoke to three o'clock, then six o'clock, then nine o'clock and then twelve o'clock. Be very careful to whisk smoke and not small embers from your smudge stick. You are creating a circle so that anyone who enters the home steps through this circle of energy.

Repeat the same steps as with the drum, but this time using your smudge stick and a feather. Start from the lowest floor in the easternmost corner of the easternmost room, and work clockwise around the room and from room to room. Use crisp clean movements as you circle each room, keeping the Intention of the smoke cleansing and purifying the energy in the home.

5. *"CHANT THE CIRCLE"*

Drumming moves energy, smudging cleanses the energy, and chanting calls in Spirit. Starting at the lowest level in the easternmost room, stand in the center of the room and chant "Hey Ya." This is the Native American way of calling in Spirit. I usually repeat:

Hey Ya. Hey Ya. Hey Ya. Ho.

Another chant that you could use is:

> The Air, the Water, the Fire, the Earth. Return. Return. Return.
> Return.

Chant for two or three minutes or until it feels right to stop. Then be still for a moment, holding the thought of Great Spirit filling the room. Go from room to room in this manner.

6. ASK FOR BLESSINGS OF GREAT SPIRIT
AND THE SACRED FOUR

Go to a room that feels central to the energy of the occupants (in many cases this is the living room). Ask the occupants to join you in a circle as you ask for the blessings of Great Spirit. Call upon the Spirits of Air, Water, Fire and Earth to fill the home with peace. You can add special requests at this time as well. Here is a sample prayer:

> May the Great Spirit be here with us now, bringing blessings and peace. We ask that this home be a sanctuary for all who shall enter here and that those within this home prosper and find peace in their hearts. May this be a home of joy and excellent health and love.
>
> May the Spirit of Air fill this home . . . may our thoughts be pure.
> May the Spirit of Water fill this home . . . may our emotions be balanced.
>
> May the Spirit of Fire fill this home . . . may Spirit be with us always.
> May the Spirit of Earth fill this home . . . may our bodies be strong.
>
> May this home be a way station for the weary and a transmitting station for the Light.
> We give many thanks for blessings received.

A variation to ask for the blessing of Great Spirit is to use a rattle (see pages 131–32). Stand in the center of a central room in the home. Hold the rattle in the right hand and breathe in a relaxed easy manner. Unfocus your eyes and place your awareness in your abdomen.

Allow your wrist to be loose and easy. Shake the rattle into the direction of the East, stop and say:

> *Spirit of the East, realm of the winds of time,*
> *Gateway to the Element of Air and the realm of mind,*
> *Come into my Circle and teach me,*
> *Come into my Circle so that we can be free.*

Turn to the South, rattling as you do. Then continue to rattle until you can feel the energy of the South fill you. Stop rattling and say:

> *Spirit of the South, realm of rivers of feeling,*
> *Gateway to the Element of Water, holy and healing,*
> *Come into my Circle and open me,*
> *Come into my Circle that we can be free.*

Turn to the West, rattling as you do. Then continue to rattle until you can feel the energy of the West fill you. Stop rattling and say:

> *Spirit of the West, realm of the radiant Light,*
> *Gateway to the Element of Fire, transforming and bright,*
> *Come into my Circle and transform me,*
> *Come into my Circle that we can be free.*

Turn to the North, rattling as you do. Then continue to rattle until you can feel the energy of the North fill you. Stop rattling and say:

> *Spirit of North, realm of ancient and wise Mother Earth,*
> *Gateway to the Element of Earth, death and rebirth,*
> *Come into my Circle and strengthen me.*
> *Come into my Circle that we can be free.*

Turn again to the East, rattling as you do. Then continue to rattle until you can feel the Energy of the Above Beings fill you. Stop rattling and say:

Spirit of Above Beings
Come into our Circle and inspire us.

Then continue to rattle until you can feel the energy of the Below Beings fill you. Stop rattling and say:

Spirit of Below Beings
Come into our Circle and ground us.

Then continue to rattle until you can feel the energy of Great Spirit fill you. Stop rattling and say:

Great Spirit within all things,
Come into our Circle and fill us,
We ask that you fill this home with grace, beauty and peace.

You have now cleansed and purified the energy of the home. You have called Great Spirit to bless the home. Before you leave, create a Medicine Wheel to be a point for gathering and transmitting energy.

7. CREATE A MEDICINE WHEEL FOR YOUR HOME

An excellent way to bring the energy of the Four Directions, the Four Elements and Great Spirit into your home is to construct a Medicine Wheel. It can be made outside if the home has land around it, or it can be created inside where it will function as a living mandala, constantly focusing and drawing cosmic energy into your living space. A Medicine Wheel can be made large enough to sit and meditate within, or it can be as small as just a few inches in diameter. Size is not important—a small Medicine Wheel can serve your purposes just as well as a large one. No matter what its size or how elaborate the Sacred Circle that you create is, it will bring a constant supply of energy and the spirit of nature into your home.

Creating a Medicine Wheel outdoors
The first stage in setting up a Medicine Wheel is to collect stones that feel significant or special to you. Ideally, they should be indige-

nous to the area. You will need to have four cardinal stones to represent the Four Elements. These will be laid out to form the perimeter of the circle. I suggest going on a power walk to obtain these stones, as described below. Go to an area where you are likely to find stones—it's fine if this is twenty or even fifty miles away. Go on your power walk and collect the stones before you start your house clearing, so that you can have them on hand when you are ready to create the Medicine Wheel. You can collect a number of stones on your power walk, if you like—enough to make a number of Medicine Wheels.

To power walk, begin by closing your eyes. Feel the element of Air. Allow your eyes to open slightly and begin to walk *toe to heel*. Breathe deeply and slowly as you walk, knowing that you are being pulled toward a perfect stone for the East section of your Medicine Wheel. You may feel a tug or a feeling of warmth in the area of your solar plexus as you do this. With your eyes unfocused, the Air stone will look or feel different from the other stones around it. Do this power walk until you have collected stones for each of the Four Directions, and also stones to form the pathways that will complete the perimeter of the circle between the cardinal stones.

Select a place on the land around your home where you want to create the circle. Once you have decided on an exact center for your circle, ask permission of Mother Earth to plant a stake there. Attach a string to the stake and create an exact circle by moving the string around the stake. Allow sufficient space in the circle for you to step inside it (a diameter of at least three feet). Mark the circle you've created. With reverence, place the four cardinal stones around the circle in each of the Four Directions, allowing equal space between each stone. (If at some point you wish to create a Medicine Wheel for someone else's house, I suggest you have the occupants of the house participate in the creation of the circle, as this weaves their energy into the circle.) Then place four smaller stones between each of the four cardinal stones all along the perimeter of the circle. These smaller stones create the pathway from one element to the other. Now you have a circle made of twenty stones (four stones for the Four Directions and sixteen connecting stones). Place four more stones in the center of the circle, one for each direction, thus forming a small central circle within the larger circle. This inner circle is the most sacred part of the wheel. It is the part dedicated to Great Spirit.

Take time setting up your wheel. Let each step be done with love and care, not rushed or hurried. This is a sacred tool, treat the circle with reverence.

TO MEDITATE IN YOUR MEDICINE WHEEL   The beginning of the Wheel is East. Always enter and leave the Wheel through the East. If you use the circle to sit in for meditation, you might consider smudging before you enter it. Leave the circle in nature to be nourished by the rains and replenished by the winds. Periodically renew the circle by cleaning or re-energizing the stones. Your circle will continue to function as a living mandala, drawing energy from the universe into your home and the surrounding lands. The Wheel is a never-ending process of renewal, like nature itself. The Medicine Wheel is a healing tool we can build for ourselves to soothe our spirit and to realign with the elements. It can be an interface between the outer worlds and the inner realms of life.

Creating a Medicine Wheel indoors
You will need the following items:

- Small circular tray with an edge on it.
- Red sand. (If no red sand is available, any sand is suitable.)
- Small smooth pebbles. (These can also be gathered on a power walk, as described on page 259.)

To create this small Medicine Wheel, first place the sand in the tray, almost up to the top of the rim. Leave the sand-filled tray outdoors for at least twenty-four hours to imbue it with the elements and with nature.

Bring the tray inside your home. Pick a first stone (the stone of the East). Hold it in your right hand for a moment to bless it.

Hold smouldering smudge in your left hand and pass your right hand, holding the stone, through the smoke while saying, "I dedicate you to the Spirit of Air. I ask the Spirit of Air and the Spirit of the East to fill this home."

Carefully assemble the stones in a clockwise manner starting with the easternmost quadrant. (At every quadrant hold the stone for that direction, pass it through the smoking herbs and dedicate it to connect with its direction and element before placing it in the circle.)

Another option is to use precious or semiprecious stones in the Sacred Circle. I use citrine in the East, amethyst in the South, clear quartz in the West and smoky quartz in the North. A round table can be used to create a Medicine Wheel in a corner of a room, or at the end of a hall or entrance way. Or you could set up your Medicine Wheel on a round coffee table in the center of your room. Feathers, moss, shells and other things from nature can be used instead of stones to create a Medicine Wheel, which is a living creative expression of the Four Elements and of nature. I know many people who have created these tabletop Medicine Wheels. Not only are these wheels beautiful to look at, they also serve as a focal point to draw energy into the home.

Filling Your Home with the Four Elements

PURIFICATION BY AIR   Use clapping, rattles, drums.

PURIFICATION BY WATER   Flick energized water throughout the room. Spray the room with aromatherapy essential oils.

PURIFICATION BY FIRE   Burn Epsom salts and alcohol. Burn candles. Smudge.

PURIFICATION BY EARTH   Toss salt in the corners and throw it upwards and downwards.

INVOKING THE AIR   Burn incense. Use wind chimes or bells.

INVOKING THE WATER   Use fountains, waterfalls, and fish tanks.

INVOKING THE FIRE   Burn seven-day candles.

INVOKING THE EARTH   Use crystals, stones and plants.

Place things on your altar to represent the Four Elements. For example:

AIR   A bowl of Air

WATER   A bowl of Water

FIRE   A burning candle

EARTH   A bowl of pebbles

The Medicine Wheel takes us back to the simplest forms of living. It returns us to living in the present, without the complexity of ego or social norms. It tells us what we need in order to be full and complete. It is already gained, in wholeness, within the context of the circle. The Medicine Wheel can be used as a symbolic tool for obtaining knowledge and making connections with different realms of reality. The Sacred Circle is also a place for receiving all the energy of nature into your home, a place where the Elements, the Directions and Spirit are acknowledged and blessed. And so the home is blessed.

17

INTERIOR
REALIGNMENT SYSTEMS

*I*n this chapter I have provided information about space-clearing practices from different cultures around the world. I use the words *Interior Realignment* to describe the field of study which encompasses all of these traditions and practices. The earlier portions of this book are concerned mainly with specific techniques for use in clearing your own home. I have included the information here in order to give you an overview of how these techniques can fit together to form a whole system for cleansing and rejuvenating the spaces we inhabit.

Not all of the techniques mentioned here are described in enough detail for you to be able to follow them exactly. (That would have meant writing another whole book!) Nonetheless, I hope that seeing how these techniques fit together within the context of a culture will increase your understanding of space clearing, and thus be helpful in the work you do. At the end of the chapter there is a troubleshooting section that answers additional questions you may have about space clearing.

Zulu Space Clearing

On a recent trip to Bophuthatswana in Africa, I spent time in a Zulu village with a remarkable Zulu holy man, Credo Mutwa. I asked this revered medicine man how space clearing was done in his tradition. He told me that all over Africa, "they sanctify everything . . . graves, places where people gather, ceremonies, moving into a new house— after a fight, everything." If lightning strikes a homestead, it is sanctified. When a new path is made from one village to another, the path is sanctified so that no evil walks along it. If a goat is stolen, it is sanctified after its recapture to release the thief's energy from it and to remove ancestral spirits that attached themselves to the goat in its absence.

The Zulus use herbs to make medicine for sanctification. They either light the herbs and then blow out the fire so that purifying smoke is produced, or mix the herbs in water to spray about a room. Three different types of herbs are used: one which protects from outside influences, a second kind for strength, and a third that makes everyone happy.

An example of the use of smoke would be the practice of blowing a sagelike smoke throughout the campsite when they are camping for the night. (It was interesting to me to see that the herb the Zulus use for smoke purification is a gray-green herb that smells and looks very similar to the sage that the American Indians use extensively for their smudging ceremonies.)

When herbs are mixed with water they are placed in a vessel. A utensil or branch is dipped into the mixture and then flicked to form spray around the area that needs purifying.

Because of the great political and social difficulties in South Africa until very recently, many sanctifying rituals have been created to purify after violence and jail sentences. For example, when a husband and wife return from jail they must bathe in a bath of sacred herbs. Then they need to sleep on either side of the bed on the floor until one or the other dreams that it is all right to get in the bed. This way they are not bringing the energy of the jail into their bed.

When someone has returned from the hospital, has been sexually assaulted, or if there has been child molestation, the Zulu sangomas (medicine men and women) grind herbal medicine and blow it on the individual, so that they are not bringing residues of their trauma into their home. When a person goes to prison or to the hospital, the old clothes are burned and new clothes are worn upon their return home.

This way the old clothes do not bring the energy of the jail or hospital into the home.

When there have been diseases or ailments, or when someone has been having bad dreams, the whole house is sanctified with the whole family participating in a steam ritual using salt and water, or sea water. Salt is placed in the water, and the water is boiled to make steam. All the family members sit under a blanket close to the steam to purify themselves. Since African tribal houses tend to be small, the steam from this one source also penetrates the entire home and sanctifies all the space within.

When a man dies, the relatives mourn for one year. After the year of mourning, a ceremony of purification takes place. The shovels that were used for digging the grave are placed in the earth for twenty-one days, so that the Earth Mother can purify them. Everything in the home is purified. This is a sign of rebirth.

When moving into a new home, the whole family sits on the floor in the center of their old house. Then they make a sacred fire for the spirits of the house, and ask the spirits to follow them to the new house. When they move into the new house, they sweep the house clean with a branch with green leaves. This purifies their new home.

A green leafy branch is also used for other ceremonies. When Credo's son was murdered as a result of intense intertribal violence, Credo explained that he swept the spot where his son had fallen with a branch with green leaves to purify the area.

Credo also explained that if a sangoma doesn't have time or medicine to sanctify an area, then he or she chants a song and says: "So this place is blessed." If there is no sangoma to sanctify a space for you, you should first look to see if anyone is watching, and then urinate all around the area that you wish to purify.

To the Zulus salt is one of the great purifiers, and water and salt are often mixed together and sprayed nine times ("one time for every moon that the baby is in the womb") into the area being cleared. If no salt or sea water is available, plants are burned and the ashes (which have some salt residue) are used.

In Zulu purification rituals, all of the Four Directions, as well as above and below, are acknowledged. Zulus, like Native Americans, feel that it is essential to honor the Elements and the Directions. Like most native cultures, the Zulus don't like corners in homes or in structures. They say that this is where evil dwells. The Zulus call corners the "ugly hiding places." Native Americans also say that "evil dwells in the corner." This is why in most native traditions homes are made in circles.

Estonian Space Clearing

Astrid Neeme is a highly regarded Estonian healer and space clearer, and one of my teachers. Her work extends into the Scandinavian countries and has been acknowledged by the World Health Organization. I have been honored to have her clear energy before my seminars in Finland. She kindly shared information with me about her traditions for clearing a house of stagnant energies.

Astrid talks about evil energies in a way similar to Credo Mutwa. Although my personal philosophy doesn't include evil energies, every native culture that I have spent time in refers to the energies that are being cleared as evil. I tend to think of energy as stagnant, rather than evil. When I ask a space clearer from another tradition to describe the evil energies, they use these same words I use for stagnant energies: heavy, dark and unmoving. Perhaps we are only using different words to describe the same experience.

I asked Astrid what she did when called to clear a house before someone moves in. She first spends time talking to the people and visiting the house because the activities and tools that she uses "very much depend on the person and the spirits that are in the house. The items that I use the most for house clearing are water, salt, prayers, smoke and fire. I prepare myself before the clearing by asking permission from my inner teacher and spirit guides if the day is suitable and if it is the right time for the house clearing."

I asked Astrid if someone needed extensive training to practice house clearing. She said, "The most important thing is concentration." (Astrid calls it concentration and I call it intention of purpose.) "When I first started house clearing I lost a lot of energy and power. Now, however, I have learned how to concentrate so I don't lose power to such an extent," she continued.

Astrid relies on astrology and the phases of the moon. "I never do any house clearing on the new moon. There isn't enough energy at that time to be successful in my clearing. I find that my best house clearings are at night during the full moon, particularly on a Thursday night. Each day of the week has its own energy and Thursday is the best day for a house clearing."

Astrid uses smoke from classical church incense as well as native plants, such as juniper, to clear out bad energy from the lower astral planes in many of her house cleansings. She said: "When I work with incense I start in one corner and then I walk anticlockwise around the room. [This is one area where we differ in technique, as I always work clockwise.] When working with incense I use prayers that have been used in the church in Estonia for centuries. These prayers have already created a cosmic energy from so many people praying the exact same prayers.

"Prayers are very powerful. They can create harmony. Prayers become very potent when I say them with smoke and with great concentration. Some of the techniques I use have been passed down from my great-grandmothers and my great-great-grandmothers and even further back."

SALT CLEARING

"This is a powerful space-clearing method using salt that may come from Egypt. Place the sea salt in a frying pan and heat the salt over a fire or on the stove. The person who is heating the salt should say the Lord's Prayer and ask that bad forces go away and good forces fill the home while heating it. The cleaner should not be afraid if the salt starts jumping around and he or she hears strange voices or sees strange things. This is just the bad forces leaving. The cleaner should not pay attention to these things, and it's very important that he or she doesn't turn in the direction of the voices or strange goings-on.

"The salt should continue to be heated until it doesn't jump around and there aren't voices or strange sights. When the cleaning is complete, the salt should be poured down the toilet and flushed several times. At the same time as the salt is being flushed, the cleaner should say prayers that the spirits go back to where they have come from.

"Here is another salt-clearing technique that I have used. This isn't an ancient technique but one I learned from someone visiting my country. I begin by asking the home residents to write down on a piece of paper a request that their living space be cleared. Then I open all the doors and windows and drawers and I throw salt everywhere, even inside the drawers and cupboards. While doing this I ask all unwanted energies to leave. I then light a candle and burn the request.

"Everyone is asked to leave for ten minutes. Before everyone returns, they take a little amount of salt into their mouth so that the evil that is leaving the home will not go inside them when they go back into the house. I then ask each person to imagine or visualize that the palms of their hands are like fire. When they return into the house they use their hands to drive the bad energy out of the space.

"Once all the bad energy has been driven out, the doors and windows are closed. An important condition is that it should be dark outside by this time. The people next leave the house for five more minutes. The remaining salt is then put in small vessels and put into the corners of the rooms, and the salt should stay there overnight. No one should sleep in the house for that night for the salt to complete the house clearing.

"The next morning the house is completely cleansed. The salt can be removed by pouring the salt down the toilet and flushing several times. And for completion, a prayer or mantra is said. The very last thing, a pentagram is made with my hand while I am saying a mantra. Sometimes I use Sanskrit mantras. I find these to be excellent in any space clearing. Repeating the Sanskrit mantra over and over again, as you clear each room, calls into the home the ancient wisdom of the mantra."

Scottish Space Clearer

Vicky Patterson clears homes in Scotland. She is a down-to-earth woman who radiates a powerful, loving acceptance of all whom she meets. She said that her method combines a variety of techniques, with a strong emphasis on her pagan work. She also encourages the person whose home it is to develop their own rituals, so that they can continue to make their own space safe without having to rely on her. I have been fortunate to have experienced her space-clearing techniques in Scotland first hand, and they are excellent.

Vicky said, "When working in someone's home, I will first visit and talk with them about why they want to clear their space. This gives me a chance to experience the space. Sometimes the problem has nothing to do with the house, but it has to do with the person, not the space. Sometimes it is just the space that needs work. That's often easiest. Sometimes it is both."

When Vicky enters a home to see if it needs clearing, she uses her hands to experience a room's energy. She said that sometimes she experiences stagnant house energy—a cold feeling or as if there is a weight on top of her head and shoulders, or sometimes there is a place in the room that feels like a curtain that is difficult to pass through. She also checks the plants in a room as an indicator of energy. A corner where plants die for no apparent reason often has blocked energy.

Vicky will also use Tibetan Prayer Bells to determine if a room is clear. She said: "The bells' sound is so pure that it reverberates for a long while if the space is clear. If the space is not clear then the sound is dull and clipped. On my first visit, I talk to the resident, experiencing the energy with my hands and with my bells. Basically, I'm establishing what needs to be done.

"For clearing a house's energy I use salt, water, and smoke by smudging. When I'm smudging, I use herbs that have grown in this country, and I burn them in special containers on top of a charcoal circle. I also use clapping and Tibetan bells to shift energy flows in a room. In addition, I also burn different-colored candles for different effects. I also have special incense that I use for protection.

"At the onset of a clearing I will draw a circle in the room with salt, big enough for myself and the person whose home it is. We stand in the center of the circle with all the tools that will be used during the ceremony. I usually will have a candle of the color that is appropriate, a bowl of moon water (made by leaving spring water in a black container outside overnight, so that the full moon's reflection could be caught in the water).

"We smudge each other using herbs, like rosemary, mint, thyme, or if these aren't available, then I will use a purchased smudge stick. I pay homage to the Mother Goddess, I ask for her blessing on the space clearing. Sometimes the person whose home it is wishes to join in and add prayers at this point. We then leave the circle and sprinkle salt around the door frame, the window ledge and the area in the room which I feel most needs clearing. I make sure that I have put salt in the corners of the room. If there is an open fireplace, I put salt there too.

"After the salt, I smudge the entire room, paying particular attention to the vulnerable energy areas of the room. I then use my hands to test the feel of the energy. Then I clap in each corner and up and down the walls, along the windows, and around the door frame to shift and change energy. I often move things around in the room and this has remarkable results.

"If I am in a room with a lot of nooks and crannies, I use my drum and/or my rattles and my other percussion instruments to reach into the farthest corners. When I have completed this stage I take the candle and walk through the room to see how the flame flickers. I use Tibetan bells again to check and see how the sound is. Once the room's energy has shifted I sprinkle moon water around as a final purification, remembering to sprinkle ourselves as well.

"I then move into the next room. If I am doing an entire house I leave the entrance hall to the very end. When I am complete with the house, then I open the door and allow the negative energy to leave through the open door. If I am only doing one room, I keep the door closed and open a window and let the negative energy out through the open window.

"When the clearing is complete we celebrate with songs, food and drink, and welcoming prayers to the new energies that have entered into the home."

Troubleshooting

I wanted to include a section in my book to address some questions you might have about space clearing. These are questions I'm often asked.

WHAT IF YOU CAN'T
FEEL ENERGY WHEN YOU ARE ROOM CLEARING?

I've seen excellent clearing done by people who said they couldn't feel or sense anything. This is why Intention is so important. If you have your Intention focused on clearing the energies in a room, that Intention is felt in the room very strongly, even if you can't consciously feel energies. Your subconscious mind and your higher self direct your movements, even when your conscious mind is feeling unsure.

WHAT IF THE HOUSE IS ON TOP OF A BURIAL SITE?

If your home is on top of an old graveyard or a battlefield where soldiers died, or anyplace where there was great suffering, it is very important to honor and communicate with any souls that may be lingering (see Chapter 15). Remember, ghosts are nothing to be afraid of, but they need your compassion. It may be that you were led to live in that location to be of service to them, so that they could move on. This will help your evolution as well.

WHAT IF YOU DON'T HAVE ANY TOOLS BUT YOU WANT TO CLEAR A SPACE?

To break up stagnant energy, use your hands and clap. Clap an area until your clapping sounds crisp and clear. When you have completed clapping, you can "tone" a room or chant into the corners and into every part of the room. Then to complete, use your breath to invoke or blow energy into the space.

WHEN DO YOU NEED TO SPACE-CLEAR YOUR HOME?

At least once a year, cleanse and clean your entire home. The two weeks preceding the spring equinox is the best time for this. Wash all the windows inside and out (if possible), take everything out of the drawers and cupboards and clean inside them. Mop under the rugs. Take rugs outside for an airing, or take them to the cleaners. Dust under tables and chairs. Dust the vases on top of cupboards. Get rid of things that you don't need. If you don't love something or use it, then get rid of it. Anything in your home that you don't love or use pulls down the energy of the whole house. If possible, touch or acknowledge every single object that is in your home. Fix things that need to be fixed. Get rid of things that don't work. This spring cleaning sets the energy for the rest of the year. Once every month, preferably around the time of the full moon, it's good to do a moderate cleansing, just to refurbish your home's energy. And once a week, do light clearing as needed.

Other good times to clear your home are:

When you need a change in your life

If you feel stuck in your life or your job and need a change in direction, change the energy in your home. If you are in a relationship that is going nowhere and you need a change, this is also a good time to clear your home. Or if you are bored, change the template of your home to change your life.

After sickness or an injury in the home

After illness or an accident it is important to reinstate a strong healthy energy into the home.

After difficult guests or negative experiences in the home

Negative experiences and visitors can leave energy residues in the home. This is a good time to clear your home energies.

If you are feeling tired and drained all the time

It could be that there are psychological or physical reasons, but if you change the energy in your house, this often helps get the other areas of your life into motion as well.

After a robbery

It is essential after a robbery or a break-in to do a complete and thorough cleansing of your home. Otherwise the residual energy from the thief, as well as your own emotions of dismay, will permeate the home and affect everyone within it.

Remember when you are cleaning your home that not only are you removing debris and dirt from the surface of your home but also, by giving it loving attention, you are re-energizing and spiritually empowering your home. And this in turn recharges your own spiritual batteries. The job of cleaning a Zen Buddhist monastery is considered an honor by the disciples. They are all eager to be assigned tasks because they know that cleaning is considered to be one of the sure paths to Enlightenment.

Say affirmations to yourself and your house as you clean it. Say, "As I clean these windows, so am I clearing the way for the light to enter my home, and the souls of all who live here." When you are cleaning the basement, connect with the feeling of groundedness and solidity that a basement represents for the whole house. Feel the spirit of Mother Earth as it comes up through the floor, up through the soles of your feet, filling your whole self with a sense of peace and calm joy.

DOES ONE'S HOUSE ALWAYS HAVE TO BE CLEAN?

Sometimes having a perfectly clean house can be a reflection of dysfunction and not necessarily indicative of a home with cleared energy. A fastidiously clean house can sometimes signal deep emotional difficulties. For example, people who are survivors of abuse from a difficult childhood will often have a compulsion to have everything in their home in its place. They may need to control their surroundings because they don't have a sense of control in their inner emotional base.

Sometimes mess is creative and comfortable. A clean house is not always a cleared house or a happy house. When a house is clean it should feel good and natural, not confined and artificial. If a house is messy it should feel comfortable and happy, and not feel dirty and unconscious.

Life goes in cycles—nothing ever stays the same. Homes become messy and clean—it's part of the living cycle of creation and life. If you are naturally messy accept that part of yourself. However, if you are in a stagnant or blocked place in your life, consider cleaning your home. Often this will assist you in releasing the blockage and getting on with your life.

WHAT IF YOU HAVE TEENAGERS WHO ALWAYS HAVE MESSY ROOMS? DOES THIS HAVE A NEGATIVE EFFECT ON THE ENTIRE HOUSE?

I believe that it is important for a child to have a space that feels like their own domain. Bless the door to the child's room and bless the child, and their room won't negatively affect the energy of the whole house.

WHAT WOULD BE A GOOD STARTER KIT FOR CLEARING ONE'S HOME?

I suggest having something from each of the Four Elements. Here are several good sample starter kits:

Starter kit for clearing etheric and subtle energy fields

Air: Large bell and small bell
Water: Crystal-charged water
Fire: Lavender candle
Earth: Mortar-pulverized salt

Order of use:

1. Light candle with prayer.
2. Toss finely ground salt throughout the room.
3. Use the bells, largest to smallest.
4. Complete by sprinkling charged water.

Starter kit for jump-starting energy fields and invoking nature spirits

Air: Feather, drum or rattles
Water: Spring water with pine sprig for flicking
Fire: Sage or cedar smudging
Earth: Rock salt

Order of use:

1. Take rock salt and place in each corner with prayer.
2. Smudge the entire room with sage and feather.
3. Drum the room.
4. Flick water with pine sprig throughout room.

Starter kit for creating temple of light

Air: Pure white feather
Water: Full-moon water in atomizer
Fire: White candle
Earth: Four quartz crystals

Order of use:

1. Light candle.
2. Cleanse room with feather.
3. Place four crystals in four corners of room to create etheric pyramid—leave in room after clearing.
4. Spray moon water throughout room.

I'VE HEARD YOU MENTION "HOUSE READING." WHAT IS THAT?

A person's home is as individual as their fingerprint. Each person's home is as readable as the lines on their hands or their handwriting or their astrology. Each room tells a story. You can find a person's past lives and even future lives by "reading" the energy fields and the positioning of objects in their home. You can tell about their past, present and future relationships, and, in particular, you can tell the way that people in the home relate to each other. You can tell their present health and things they will need to watch out for in the future regarding their health. The exciting thing is that you can avert potential future disaster by changing the flow of energy through the home and by changing the house's template.

WHAT DO YOU MEAN WHEN YOU TALK ABOUT THE POWER OF "NAMING" THE THINGS IN ONE'S HOME?

Anything that you name and relate to in a personalized manner will emanate more life-force energy than an unnamed object. This is not uncommon in native cultures where weapons were named, cooking utensils were named and sacred tools were named. Cars that are named run better than unnamed cars. If you name objects such as your vacuum cleaner and your refrigerator (especially if they are older models and need a little babying), they will run better.

WHAT IF THE PEOPLE IN A HOUSE
DON'T AGREE ABOUT HOUSE CLEARING?

If there are some things in the home that aren't to your liking that you can't change or cleanse because you live with people that have a different agenda from you, then at least have one area in the home that is your domain. It might be your bedroom, or if your bedroom is shared and you aren't able to change it, then somewhere in your home, have a place that is yours. Even one small corner that you have cleansed can vibrate a powerful energy that can affect the entire home in a positive, loving way.

WHAT CAN YOU DO IMMEDIATELY
TO UPLIFT THE ENERGY IN YOUR HOME?

- Give your home a surface cleaning.
- Toss salt in all the corners of every room.
- Briefly open all the doors and windows.
- Take down any negative photos and paintings.
- Get rid of any dead or dying plants.
- Put out fresh flowers.
- Light a candle.
- Burn incense or essential oils.
- Put inspiring music on.
- Say a prayer and ask that Divine Light fill your home.

18

CREATING SACRED SPACE
IN YOUR OFFICE

*J*ust as your emotions and energy are affected by your home, so
too can they be influenced by your office space. An office can
provide aesthetic nourishment where the colors and textures of the
interior space touch your soul, where you can breath in beauty . . . or
it can leave you feeling exhausted and unfocused. We need only to
step into different offices to see how they affect us.

Imagine this scene. You walk into an office. You are enveloped in
fresh air from an open window. The sound of leaves quivering in the
breeze can be heard outside. Your steps are muffled by natural wool
carpets laid over wooden floors. You move your hand across a hand-
some wooden desk. It feels warm and comforting to the touch. A corner lamp softly infuses a pleasant glow throughout the room. Your
eyes are drawn to a painting of a pastoral scene filled with green
rolling hills, contented cows grazing on green pastures, and a sky dot-
ted with delicate fluffy clouds. Several large healthy, vibrant plants
are scattered throughout the room and a fragrant profusion of daf-
fodils in a blue ginger pot sits on a corner table. The wonderful smell
of oranges wafts from a bowl of orange-peel potpourri on the office
desk. A cut crystal in the window scatters rainbow light throughout
the room.

Even imagining such an office scene can be uplifting. However,
very few people have the luxury of an office that is truly nourishing

and uplifting. For many, an office is a place where they feel trapped and oppressed. Too often "office" is filled with hard-edged shapes and forms. It is an overheated, depersonalized square box with harsh fluorescent lighting, sterile air, debilitating electrical fields, irritating noise, synthetic carpeting and cold, shiny, lacquered imitation-wood furniture. It is an environment that feels uncaring and insensitive, a brutal vandalism of the human spirit.

Plants and animals respond negatively to depleting environments. Many humans, however, have suppressed this natural response. We conform to office environments that impose their presence on us and do not sustain life. We have become numb adapting ourselves to limitations imposed by most offices, rather than molding our work spaces to adapt to our needs. The more immune we become to the negative forces in our environment, the more we are damaged and the less humanity we have. Modern offices that disregard the human spirit can make us dull and listless, *and this is reflected in our work and even in our entire life.*

An office environment can nourish and support the human spirit as much as it can deny and suppress it. If our offices are humane, loving and sacred, then what is produced in those offices will have a sense of humanity and integrity; that in turn will affect us all. The challenge is not to change yourself to fit the space but to seek a way to occupy your office space in a way that harmonizes with your personality and energy.

Purpose of Your Livelihood

Environments dictate consciousness. We cannot separate the purpose of our livelihood from the space that we occupy while fulfilling that purpose. Your quest concerning how to occupy your office is actually a powerful process of self-discovery, one that asks such questions as "What is the value of my work in the world at large?" and "What do I hope to gain personally from this work?" When questioning the worth of your work, you should feel you are involved in "right livelihood." "Right livelihood" means that your work is valuable and makes a positive difference in the lives of others. It isn't the specific type of work that you do that makes it right livelihood, but the context in which you hold what you do. *Any* job can be right livelihood if that is the way you view it and if you operate within that context.

A man once told me he hated his job as a designer of specialized frames for a large company and wanted to quit. As I talked with him it emerged that he felt that his job didn't matter and that it was inconsequential. Accordingly, he felt *he* didn't matter and was inconsequential. But after exploring the deeper nature of his job, he realized that a photo of a loved family member, a cherished painting, or a prized child's drawing would go in the frames that he designed. He realized that he was creating beautiful frames that would enhance objects which added enjoyment to people's lives. He decided to bless his frames, imbuing them with beauty and strength. His frames would then not be merely pieces of joined wood, but would exude a warm and loving energy beneficial to all.

When he changed the context within which he held his job, he also implemented changes in his office (at my suggestion) to reflect the esteem with which he now held himself and his job. A few weeks later, he said that he felt entirely different about his job because he knew he was making a contribution to other people. He sounded vibrant and truly happy.

It is important to see *your* job in the greater context of the world at large. Just as the frame designer gained satisfaction from the knowledge that his frames would bring enhanced beauty to the lives of people, you must find value within your job. If you are unhappy in your job but feel that you have no alternative, find some value in what you do so you are not poisoning your spirit. You must know that your job can make a contribution to the world and that your office space can reflect this intention. Before you begin to implement any physical changes in your office, take a moment to still your mind and ask yourself these questions:

What is the value of my work in the world at large?
What do I hope to gain personally from this work?
What am I gaining spiritually by being in this job?
Why am I working in this job?
What work would I do if I didn't need a paycheck?
What is my long-term intention for myself in this job?

Answering these questions can help you understand the purpose of your job in your life. This understanding can then assist you in deciding what changes you want to implement in your office environment.

Creating an Office Template

Once you understand the purpose and value of your job, the next step is to define the template that you desire to create within your office environment (see Chapter 11). To create a new template, you must determine your present one first. What is the message that your office or work space currently communicates to you and others? Is your office door squeaky and hard to open? This can subliminally communicate that you want to keep people out. Are you seated with your back to the door, giving out a message that says you're not interested in talking to anyone? Are the shelves so high you can't reach them without effort? The message to yourself might be "Whenever I want to attain something I must work hard for it."

Here is an exercise to find your present template. Stand outside your office building and notice how you feel. Step inside and compare how you feel before and after entering the building. Notice the response of your senses—sight, sound, smell, hearing, touch—as well as your emotions. Now repeat the same exercise, but do this going into and out of your individual office.

Ask yourself the following questions when doing the above exercise:

When you enter your office, do you feel stronger or weaker, more or less focused, lighter or heavier?

What is the primary message that the energy in your office presently communicates?

What does the "spirit of the place" seem to be?

What judgments about you might a stranger make if he or she walked into your office?

How do you feel emotionally when you are at your office?

How do you feel about your workplace when you are not there?

Does your office say, "I care about myself and others," or does it say, "I just do this job because I have to, but I don't like it"?

If you are unhappy with the current template of your office, ask yourself if there is another message that you would like to convey. What do you want your office energy to convey to your co-workers? What message do you want your office to communicate to your inner being? Creating a new template will help you do that. Perhaps you don't like people dropping into your office unannounced and hanging out. If that is the case, then your office template needs to project a message that says, "I'm here to get the job done with intensity and passion and focus . . . and individually." Perhaps in your position in the company you must be freely accessible to others. Your office template then needs to say, "You are welcome to come in and visit. This is a friendly, inviting place." Difficulties arise when you desire one thing while your office template projects another. For example, if you want to gain abundant expansion from your livelihood, yet your office space looks austere and constricted, this will lessen your ability to create what you desire.

Once you are clear about the message you wish to project, the suggestions below can help you incorporate a new template, as well as enhance and clear the energy in your office.

Placement of Objects Within Your Office

We are dramatically affected by the forms, shapes, spaces, and lines of all the objects in our homes and offices, and the relationships between them. This interplay of dynamic forces can create harmony or disruption in our lives. The way the objects in your office are arranged can influence your health, well-being, creativity and abundance, as well as your office morale.

DESK POSITIONING

The placement of your desk is essential. Its position is the most important of all the furniture in the room. Often a simple repositioning of your desk can alter your fortune and your emotional well-being. As a general rule, the most powerful spot for a desk is catercorner to the door. In this position you will usually have a commanding view of the entire room. This position conveys power, maximum strength and authority. It can increase your concentration and the feeling of control.

Don't position your desk so that your back is to the door; for most people this can create a subconscious feeling of apprehension and can be symbolic of turning your back on opportunities. Try to sit facing the door but not directly in its path. If you are unable to turn your desk so that you can see the door, place a mirror so you can see it as well as the space behind you. Even a small mirror can be useful psychologically.

Also consider the positioning of your desk in relation to light sources. If your back is against a large bright window, people entering your office will have trouble seeing your face clearly because of the bright light around you. When they are unable to see your eyes or facial features clearly, communication diminishes. It is comparable to talking to someone with sunglasses on. I've noticed that when I give a presentation with a window or a bright light source behind me, people are less attentive and don't seem to connect as well to me or to the material presented.

Avoid having your back to an interior window, especially where people can pass and "view over your shoulder." Not only can this be disconcerting, it can weaken your position in the company. If this is unavoidable, place a mirror on your desk or on the far wall so that you can see the people passing by the interior window.

If possible, have your back against a solid, unadorned wall. Do this so that visitors will be able to focus on you and what you are saying without becoming distracted by the view or the artwork behind you.

If there is a window in your office with a pleasant scene, position your desk so that the energy and beauty from the scene can flow into you. Alternatively place a mirror so that you can see the scene from where you sit. (Avoid having a mirror directly behind your back, as this can be distracting for those who meet you.) Facing directly toward a window can sometimes shift your focus from your work to the outside world, so position your desk so that you can see out the window without directly facing outside.

If your desk faces anything unpleasant (a person you dislike, a long, dark hallway, an unattractive computer terminal, etc.), place a plant, crystal or beautiful bowl on your desk between you and the object. These objects can help protect you from those disturbing sources of energy. If your desk faces the desk of a colleague, place objects of beauty and harmony between the two of you so as to strengthen the feeling of rapport between you.

If you want to make more money, then place your desk in the wealth corner of your office. (See the information on the ba-gua system of object placement in Chapter 13 to determine where this would be in your office.) Wherever you place your desk in the room will be affected by the corresponding ba-gua.

The position of your desk in relation to other desks in the same office can also affect your energy at work. One woman consulted me regarding the difficulty she was experiencing with her administrative assistant. She explained that her assistant (with whom she shared an office) did a good job, but that they were in a continual power struggle. Her assistant tried to take control of every situation and often undermined her boss's authority. In addition, whenever anyone entered the room, the assistant was the first to greet the visitor and inevitably tried to control the ensuing situation.

When I asked about the position of their desks, I was told that the assistant was in a corner desk facing the door (the power position), while the executive's desk faced a wall with her back to the door (one of the worst possible positions for a desk). In other words, the assistant's desk was placed in a far superior position in the room. Subliminally, this had communicated to the assistant that she was the one in control. The position of the desks affected the relationship between this executive and her assistant as if a private and a general wore each other's uniforms.

The executive exchanged desks with her assistant and later reported that the corresponding change in their relationship was extraordinary. They now have a much more harmonious connection.

Since each office is affected by myriad energy fields, use your intuition for positioning your desk, rather than relying on hard-and-fast rules. After taking your intuition into account, use the above information to guide you in making your decisions.

THE OFFICE POWER POINT

Every room has a power point. If possible, place your desk over the power spot. Even if this is not possible, it is still valuable to be aware of the location of the most powerful spot in the room.

The Office Power Point is individual. Your power center in a room may strengthen you and yet weaken someone else. To understand this phenomenon, picture people arrived at a beach. Some will want the security of putting their towels near the sheer rock face surrounding the beach, some will choose an open flat area, and others will choose to be right near the ebb and flow of the water. Each location offers its own beauty and power. The rocky cliff provides protection, shade, and the comfort of containment. The open sand gives a feeling of expansion, openness, and freedom, while the surging surf offers excitement, energy, and movement.

EXERCISE FOR FINDING
YOUR OFFICE POWER POINT

1. Find a time when you can be in your office undisturbed. Also clear debris and unneeded accessories out of the way before you do this.
2. Take a moment to quiet your mind and take a few deep, relaxing breaths. Partially close your eyes so you can still see but are not relying solely on your eyesight to get around the room.
3. Go to the area of the room that seems to be the most powerful area of the room.
4. Sit in the area that you have chosen. Close your eyes and notice how you feel emotionally and physically.
5. Face different directions while you are in that one spot and notice how each direction feels to you.
6. Move to different spots within the room and repeat this process again and again. Continue to do this until you just know the best place for you. If it is convenient or possible, place the chair to your desk directly over that location so that you will face the direction that felt the best to you.

You may not be able to move your desk to your power point. However, even if you can't move your desk there, at least spend some time in your power center. For example, during a coffee break, stand in your power spot or move a chair over to sit in that area.

If you have a table in your office, consider these things. A round table will contribute to a feeling of community and the feeling that "we are all in this together." In offices geared toward creative ventures, round tables are best, as the spiraling energy that a round table inspires will stimulate creativity. Square or rectangular tables are best when you want to get the job done quickly and efficiently. Use them if your work is involved with details or money management.

When conducting a meeting at your office table, keep in mind that the most powerful position is facing the door. Another position of power, though more subtle, is the northernmost spot at the table. This is a power position because we are all subliminally influenced by magnetic forces of the earth, which flow (in the Northern Hemisphere) to the north. In a meeting the energy will naturally flow to the person who sits to the north.

When positioning the office equipment in your office, try to place yourself as far away as you can get from electrical fields (see Chapter 12). Wherever possible make sure that clocks, radios, air conditioners, and so forth are at least three feet away from you. Locate yourself as far back from your computer as you can. Don't work with your head close to fluorescent or halogen lights. Check electric fields in your office with a gauss meter and position yourself as much as possible so that you are not in the strongest fields for continuous periods of time.

Cleansing Office Energy

The fastest way to uplift the energy in your office is to clean it. It's essential to clean an office thoroughly when you first move in; then at least once a year do a complete Spring Cleaning. This annual cleaning is a time of energy renewal. Clean and organize everything. Don't just clean the surface of your desk, but empty the drawers and get rid of anything that you don't need, use, or love. Clean windows and closets and every outer and inner surface. As you are cleaning, affirm your intention (either mentally or aloud) for your job; for example, *"The work that I do makes a contribution to my family, my community, and my planet, and I am uplifted and strong while I make this contribution."*

In addition to physically cleaning your office, use this time to organize everything in your office—every piece of paper, every memo, even the pens and pencils. Every item in your office has energy, and it's important to honor and acknowledge it all. Give everything attention during your Office Spring Cleaning. For example, if you have a fountain pen that doesn't work, either fix it or throw it away. If your typewriter needs a new ribbon, replace it. Everything that you don't use or love combines to lower the energy in your office. If during your cleaning, you discover letters or memos that need attention, either answer them or create a plan for answering them. Give attention to folders, files, memos, your personal working library and the equipment in your office. Organize, complete or fix absolutely everything. In addition to your annual cleaning, a periodic surface cleaning can make an immediate difference. Cleaning and giving attention to all aspects of your office can make it shimmer with light and energy and joy.

AIR QUALITY

Another way to cleanse energy in an office is to improve the air quality. Too often office air is stale, recycled, and not health-enhancing. Not everyone can afford or obtain an air purification system, but one simple remedy is simply placing plants in your office. Former NASA environmental scientist Bill Wolverton suggests that plants in the office may be one of the easiest ways to rid the air of benzene fumes, formaldehyde and the other airborne pollutants that often fill office air.

"We've always known that plants fight pollution," Wolverton says. "We just didn't know how." When Wolverton was doing NASA research on how human colonies could survive on the moon or Mars, he found that plant leaves will actually absorb airborne pollutants, funneling the contaminants to the roots, where microbes literally absorb them (*OMNI* Magazine, August 1993). Several well-placed plants in an office can instantly give a feeling of healthful vibrancy. A caution, however: if the plant has dead leaves, remove them. If it begins to look spindly and unhealthy, get rid of it. A sickly plant not only negatively affects the overall office energy but will also affect the ba-gua position in the room where the plant resides.

Another way to improve air quality in your office is to place a small ionizer next to your desk. Almost instantly you will notice a difference in the room. When people are around your desk they will perk up and be more energetic. If the air is very dry, as most office air is, you might consider a humidifier. Not only is this good for the plants that you have in your office, but the energy of water from the humidity can be soothing to the spirit.

Aromatherapy is an excellent way to create a wonderful ambiance instantly. In most offices you would have a hard time getting away with using sandalwood or frankincense. However, most office managers would not be displeased with a subtle lemon, orange, tangerine or rose scent in your oil burner. If you can't have a candlelit burner, just a few drops of essential oil with water in an atomizer can be sprayed periodically in the room. You might also consider a bowl of potpourri (naturally scented, not artificial, which can cause allergic reactions in some people). This can shift the entire energy of your office. People will walk by and comment, "Great smell!"

Enhancing Energy in Your Office

In some professional environments beauty and utility are thought of as separate. Some might even consider beauty a liability or even an indulgence. However, the more aesthetic and pleasing you can make your environment, the more you will flourish, both professionally and personally, and the more the energy in the office will be enhanced.

COLOR

One area to consider when creating a beautiful office environment is color. There are four things to consider in the colors you choose for your office.

1. COLORS TO ACHIEVE DESIRED EFFECTS Blue is a soothing, tranquil color that has the effect of encouraging peaceful feelings. Yellow is uplifting and encourages communication. Red is a stimulating color that encourages action. Some colors will strengthen you, and some will weaken you. For example, the color pink has been used to calm prisoners. It's important that the colors you are surrounded by all day make you feel strong and balanced, so pick col-

ors that are in alignment with your needs and goals for your job. (For more in-depth discussion of the effects of individual colors, please refer to Chapter 12.)

2. COLORS YOU LOVE   You will feel better if you surround yourself with colors you love. For example, if you adore the color sky blue and you are able to have this in your office (either paint the walls in that hue, or if that is not possible, then place objects colored sky blue around the room), this will create a beneficial emotional response within you. When you are surrounded all day by a color that you really don't like, this will numb your senses and have a detrimental effect on your productivity. For example, if as a small child you were always punished in a green room, green will be an aggravating color for you, a color to avoid having around you on a daily basis.

3. COLORS THAT MAKE YOU LOOK STRONG, ENERGIZED AND HEALTHY   In recent years there has been a trend by corporate executives to wear the colors that enhance their best physical features. For example, one person might look vibrant and alive in navy clothes and yet wear a pale yellow and look wan and sickly. Someone else might look perky and animated in pale yellow, yet look ineffective and weak in navy blue. Executives are purchasing clothes in colors that will put their best foot forward in the business world; however, they are not realizing that it is also advantageous to surround themselves in their office environments in those same colors. If you look best in clear, bright colors, it's best to surround yourself with clear, bright colors at work. If you look best in soft pastel colors, have those colors as your backdrop at work. Office colors (whether wall color or room accessories) can have a dramatic effect on the way you feel and the way that others view you.

4. LIGHTING'S EFFECT ON COLOR   An important component of a room's color energy is the lighting, both the amount of lighting and the type, whether artificial or natural. Daylight color varies depending on geographic location and the orientation of the windows. Southern light is warmer than northern light. In parts of the country such as the Northwest where the foliage is dense, the

quality of the light often has a muted green hue to it. In desert environments, the warm-colored light is often bright and sharp.

Consider the type of artificial light you use when you are contemplating office room colors. Incandescent light is yellowish and can cast a yellow hue. Fluorescent light (even color-corrected fluorescents) emit a cool, bluish light. Halogens come in both warm and cool light. Full-spectrum lights are said to be closest to sunlight. But as most of us are used to the yellowish tone of incandescent lights, full-spectrum lighting sometimes seems cool colored. (For more information about full-spectrum lighting, please see Chapter 12.) While the light sources in your office affect the office colors, you can use those colors to balance the warmth and coolness of artificial and natural lighting.

If you aren't happy with the light sources in your office, bring a lamp to work. Even if you can't turn off the fluorescent lights, bringing in a small lamp with a pink shade for your desk can help to create a color balance for you.

Janet was doing fine in her career, but she sometimes felt that she wasn't completely appreciated for her contribution to her company. In addition to working with the placement of the things in her office, I also suggested that she change the colors in her office. She was in the fortunate position of being able to have her office repainted. The room had been a dull gray-beige and she changed it to a bright golden color. She also put a lamp in her office with a tangerine-colored shade. She reported that not only did she feel stronger and more energetic in her office because these were colors that she really liked, but when people came into her office they commented on how good she looked (Janet's complexion was complemented by the new color). Senior executives who hadn't noticed her before began dropping into her office to chat.

Janet picked colors that fit all four criteria. The colors (1) achieved the desired effect of uplifting the energy in the room and stimulating communication, thereby encouraging a warm social atmosphere; (2) were colors she loved; (3) complemented her hair and skin tone perfectly; and (4) were enhanced by the lighting. Janet felt that the change of color in her office had made a significant difference in her professional life.

PHOTOS

Photos of your family and of people you love can bring a wonderful sense of community into an otherwise sterile environment. It is also valuable to place photos of people you admire in your work space. In my office, over the area where I sit at my computer, I have a large photo of my Cherokee grandmother in full regalia and crowned by a headdress of feathers blowing in the wind. (Although Indian women didn't usually wear headdresses, I'd like to think that my grandmother was declaring her strength by wearing one.) My grandmother was stoic, but she exuded a quiet dignity and deep sense of integrity. Even though I do not sit and stare at her photo, in a powerful subconscious way I feel her looking over my shoulder. I like to think that the work I do is influenced by her presence.

Moving into a New Office

If you are just moving into an office it is essential to get off to a good start. The energy of the previous occupant and the placement of the objects within the office can dramatically affect the way you feel and perform within the office.

1. *Define the purpose of your job*
As you understand the value of your job, both materially and spiritually, you will be able to form an intention about why you have that job and what that job can give you. This is essential because form will coalesce around your intention.

2. *Define the office template*
What do you want your office to communicate to others and to your subconscious mind?

3. *Clean absolutely everything*
Clean the inside and outside of the desk. Even if the inside of the drawers look spotless, wipe them down with a lemon-water solution. (To make this, you can either squeeze a whole lemon into a gal-

lon of water or you can add lemon rinds from three lemons into a gallon of water.) Check the inside of all closets and storage areas. Make sure that the windows are clean and get any curtains or blinds cleaned. Be scrupulous as you cleanse every part of your office.

If the fortunes of the previous occupant were not good, consider doing extra cleaning and wiping down the walls and the door and window frames with the lemon-water solution. You want to get off to a clean start in your new office, and a thorough cleaning is the best way to do this.

As you are cleaning, hold this affirmation in your mind or say it out loud if circumstances permit: *This is my space. The energy is clear and clean.*

4. *Fix it or get rid of it*

Go through everything and make sure it all works. Check for burned-out lightbulbs, pencil sharpeners that jam, paper cutters that are rusty, and so forth. Every electrical and mechanical device in your office has consciousness and is conveying a message. If the phone in your office has a faulty connection and the voice quality isn't clear, chances are that people will perceive *you* as unclear and unfocused. If the buttons on the telephone stick and are hard to push, this can be a subliminal message to your subconscious saying that it's hard to communicate with others. If the clock keeps losing time, you may find yourself losing time. If the clock gains time, you may find yourself always ahead of yourself. If there is something in the office that doesn't work and serves no function, get rid of it.

5. *Perform an office blessing*

If possible, use the four steps of Preparation, Purification, Invocation, and Preservation using the methods described in this book. However, in many modern offices you can't walk around holding a burning smudge stick in one hand and a feather in the other while casting smoke to the four directions. If this is the case, you might consider surreptitiously sprinkling salt in the corners and around the perimeter of the office. (Perhaps you could come in on a weekend or some other day off.) Then clearly (either aloud or in your mind) ask that your office be blessed. You can say the following:

*May this office be blessed by the powers of goodness and love.
May all who enter and dwell here be happy healthy, creative and
prosperous.*

or

*May this office be a refuge of peace, manifesting a peace for the
larger world. May angels guard its corners and gifts fall upon all
who dwell here.*

To Create Good Fortune in Your Office

1. For insight, place books in your office so they are visible when you first enter.
2, For clarity, place wind chimes inside the door.
3. For peace of mind, place the desk so you can see the door. (Traditional Feng Shui advocates avoiding being in a direct line with the door, but your own intuition is best.)
4. To increase prosperity, pay attention to the wealth corner of your desk and office (see the information on the ba-gua in Chapter 13).
5. To bring more love into your office, place a round mirror on the wall.
6. To increase good luck, have a bowl of flowers on your desk.
7. To clear work blockages, unblock the doorway and move objects that are stored behind doors.
8. To invite opportunity in, oil squeaky or sticky doors and doorknobs. Clean your entrance door until it sparkles.
9. To expand your vistas and open your creativity, clear your desk.

Our offices can become humane and sacred places. They can become sacred by the way that we care for them. Simply placing a bowl of flowers or a photo of a loved one on your desk or changing your desk position can make all the difference. I believe that those who create offices should imbue them with humanity. Creating offices as sacred spaces will ultimately increase productivity, financial gain, creativity, and interpersonal office harmony. The act of turning the places where we work into places that we love can transform our own lives, and will in turn positively affect the lives of everyone around us.

19

TRANSMITTING
THE LIGHT

One person can make a difference. Instilling an oasis of peace into your home, in a small corner of the universe, can make all the difference in the world.

I met an angel once. I mean a real angel that I could see and talk to. He was an elderly black gentleman on roller skates in a park near our home. Never mind how I knew he was a real angel. I just knew. He said only a few words to me. (I wonder, are angels ever garrulous?) He said there are only two things that are really important in life: love of other human beings and love of God. I think of his words often. When I'm thinking about the meaning of my life, and weighing the value of any given activity, I try to base my priorities on his two statements.

When you are clearing your home, you might want to ask yourself: Does this activity contribute to my love for myself and my love for others? If your answer is yes, then do it. If you are changing your home because your house is not okay the way it is, then don't do it for a while. Hold off for a bit until you can come closer to gentle loving acceptance. Houses are beings, no less than your friends or family. They need love and acceptance, just as human beings need love and acceptance. If you have a friend who is overweight, as a compassionate being, you would not say, "You are not okay the way you are. You've got some problems that need to be fixed." You might say, "You are my friend. I love you exactly as you are, whatever shape you are in. I am here to support you in your personal process, and I want you to know that you are special to me exactly as you are." This same compassionate, loving approach works wonders with houses, too. A bouquet of wild flowers, a fresh baked pie, a pot of coffee, and a happy tune on the radio can transform a house into a joyous and healing home.

In the end it must be our hearts and our souls that decide how we want to inhabit our homes. An open heart and an open mind will envelop and embrace with love all of our living spaces, from the privacy of our own house or apartment to the global village that is our planetary home. A rigid belief system of what is right and wrong in our home will lessen the positive-energy field radiating around our home much more than would a pile of dirty clothes in the middle of the room, dishes not washed or an uncleared room. It is your Intention, your love and your compassion that allow the living spaces around you to glimmer and radiate with life and spirit.

Holding your home sacred within yourself, at the beginning and end of every day, is not about what you do—it is about who you are. Accepting yourself with love and gentleness, exactly the way you are, creates one of the greatest forces in the universe. It reaches beyond all form. Who you are is enough. There is nothing more that you need in order to be all right. You are all right exactly as you are right now. Your home is all right, too, just as it is. To accept yourself and the extension of yourself that your home represents is the first step toward Spirit.

It is your vision for your home that matters. It does not matter if you do not have the money or time or physical energy to create all that exists in your heart all at once. Your Intention is holy and will bring all that you love and hope for into being when the time is right. It is your Intention and prayers that will bring the energy of light and joy flooding in through your doors and shining back out through your windows into the darkness. The love that you put into your home as you physically clear it, the affirmations that you say as you spiritually cleanse its space, all form a kind of spiral to Spirit, which in turn funnels the loving energy of Spirit back to you.

A happy home is a distilling point for the surging explosion of the new and vital energies available at this time in the evolution of our planet. Your home can be a sanctuary in the changing times ahead, it can function as a lightning rod to disseminate and transmit energies, through you and out into the universe. Your home can act like a magnet, attracting positive energy which will be distilled and transmitted outwards in all directions. This has a positive, powerful affect on the area surrounding your home, radiating goodness in ever-expanding circles throughout the planet.

Your home can resonate, sing and pulse with vibrant Light energy that can touch the lives of everyone around you. Your home can become Sacred Space. When you are enveloped in its Sacred Space, you reconnect with your own energy sources, with the love and the angelic forces around you. You open new channels for energy to flow in and radiate outwards. And then, as if by magic, love, health and abundance seem newly created everywhere around you. Do not doubt the power of who you are and the power of the energy field you can create within your home. You and your home can make a difference in the times ahead. May your living spaces bring you comfort and health and joy as we open our hearts to a new millennium.

APPENDIX

SOURCE FOR MAIL-ORDER SPACE-CLEARING PRODUCTS
To receive a catalogue of space-clearing and other holistic products for the home, write to: Denise Linn, PO Box 75657, Seattle, WA 98125-0657, USA.

SOURCES FOR FLOWER ESSENCES
For **Bach Flower Remedies,** contact The Dr. Edward Bach Healing Centre, Mount Vernon, Sotwell, Wallingford, Oxon, England. Also available from most major health food stores.

SOURCES FOR ESSENTIALS OILS
In the Northern Hemisphere the Tisserand Company is excellent: **Tisserand Aromatherapy Products,** Brighton, England BN3 ZRS. Also available from most major health food stores.

SOURCE FOR OZONE AIR PURIFIER
Panda Ozone Air Purification System, Quantum Electronics Corporation, 110 Jefferson Blvd., Warwick, RI 02888 USA, telephone (401) 732-6770, fax (401) 732-6772.

FOR MORE IN-DEPTH STUDY OF STONES
Soozi Holbeche, **The Power of Gems and Crystals,** Judy Piatkus (Publishers) Limited, London, 1989.

FOR FURTHER READING ABOUT THE CONSCIOUSNESS OF PLANTS
Peter Thompkins and Christopher Bird, **The Secret Life of Plants,** Avon Books, New York, 1973.

SOURCE FOR HANDMADE DRUMS
David and Denise Linn personally create handmade drums in the Native American tradition. Each drum is made to correspond to the individual vibrations of the person who orders it. The fifteen-inch drums are individually named and blessed and come with a certificate of authenticity. For information on how to order, contact: **Denise and David Linn,** PO Box 75657, Seattle, WA 98125-0657, USA.

TO EXPLORE FURTHER THE POWER OF COLOR:

Lilian Verner Bonds, **Discover the Magic of Colour,** Optima, A Division of Little, Brown and Company (UK) Limited, London, 1993. In this book, Lilian gives in-depth information of all the shades and hues of the different colors (rather than just the traditional rainbow palette).

Vicky Wall, **The Miracle of Colour Healing,** The Aquarian Press, An Imprint of HarperCollins Publishers, London, 1990.

FOR COLORED WATER AND OIL PRODUCTS

The Aura-Soma and Aura Light companies have a beautiful array of bottles filled with colored water and oil (with scents added). They have carefully researched the power of color for their products, which can be used on your body or simply placed where you can enjoy the beauty of the pure colors.

Aura-Soma Products, Dev Aura, Tetford, Lincs., LN9 6QL England.

Aura Light, Tony Cooper, "Unicornis," Obi Obi Road, Mail Service, 956, Mapleton, Queensland, Australia 4560.

SOURCE FOR FULL-SPECTRUM LIGHTS

Light Energy Company, 1056 NW 179th Place, Seattle, WA 98177 USA; telephone (206) 542-7612; toll-free number (for calls made within North America only) 1 (800) 544-4826.

FOR FURTHER READING ABOUT THE POWER OF LIGHT AND EMFs

Jacob Liberman, **Light: Medicine of the Future,** Bear & Company Publishing, Santa Fe, New Mexico, 1991.

Ellen Sugarman, **Warning: The Electricity Around You May Be Hazardous to Your Health,** Simon & Schuster, New York, 1992.

Laurie Tarkan, **Electromagnetic Fields: What You Need to Know to Protect Your Health,** Bantam Books, New York, 1994.

SOURCE FOR GAUSSMETER

Safe Technologies, 1950 NE 208 Terrace, North Miami Beach, FL 33179 USA; telephone (305) 933-2026; toll-free number (for calls made within the USA only) 1 (800) 638-9121.

INTERIOR REALIGNMENT SPECIALISTS

Denise Linn, who teaches professional certification courses for Instinctive Feng Shui and Interior Realignment, PO Box 75657, Seattle, Washington, USA 98125-0657.

Astrid Neeme, Alakartanontie 6 B33, 02360 Espoo, Finland.

Vicky Patternson, 27 Queen Mary Avenue, Glasgow G42 8DS, Scotland, U.K.

Karen Kingston, c/o 24 Creswick Walk, London NW11 6AN England, U.K.

NOTES

CHAPTER 6: ALCHEMY OF AIR

1. Robert Massy, *You Are What You Breathe,* Boulder Creek, California: University of the Trees Press, 1980, p. 1.
2. Fred Soyka with Edmonds, Alan, *The Ion Effect,* New York: Bantam Books, 1977, p. 20.
3. Massy, pp. 25–8 (Appendix).
4. Ibid., p. 28 (Appendix).
5. Ibid., p. 25 (Appendix).
6. Ibid.
7. Soyka with Edmonds, pp. 64–8.
8. Massy, p. 28 (Appendix).
9. Ibid., p. 4.
10. Ibid., p. 5.

CHAPTER 7: HEALING EARTH

1. Pamela Louise Chase and Pawlik, Jonathan, *Trees for Healing: Harmonizing with Nature for Personal Growth and Planetary Balance,* North Hollywood, California: Newcastle Publishing Co., 1991, pp. 25–6.
2. Ibid., pp. 26–7.

CHAPTER 12: INTO THE LIGHT

1. Jacob Liberman, *Light: Medicine of the Future*, Santa Fe, New Mexico: Bear & Company Publishing, 1991, p. 9.
2. Ibid.

3. Ibid., p. 41.
4. Ibid., pp. 45–6.
5. Ibid., pp. 46–7.
6. Ibid., pp. 58–9.
7. Ibid., pp. 59.
8. Ibid., p. 10.
9. Ibid., pp. 121–7.
10. Time-Life Books, Ed., *Mysteries of the Unknown: Earth Energies,* Alexandria, Virginia: Time-Life Books, 1991, p. 61.
11. Rodney Girdlestone, "Electromagnetic Fields," *Mind Body Soul: The Alternative Lifestyle Magazine,* Sept./Oct. 1994, p. 21.
12. Ibid., pp. 22–3.

CHAPTER 15: GHOSTBUSTING
1. Time-Life Books, Ed., *Mysteries of the Unknown: Hauntings,* Alexandria, Virginia: Time-Life Books, 1989, p. 22.
2. Ibid., p. 23.
3. Ibid.

INDEX

For information about Denise's professional certification courses write:

Interior Re-Alignment Practitioners International
P.O. Box 75657
Seattle, Washington 98125-0657

For information about where to obtain Denise's audio tapes contact:

QED Recording Services
Lancaster Road
New Barnet
Hertfordshire, England
EN48AS
telephone 44-181-441-7722

ABOUT THE AUTHOR

Denise Linn's personal journey began as a result of a near-death experience at age seventeen. Her life-changing experiences and remarkable recovery set her on a spiritual quest that led her to study the healing traditions of many cultures, including those of her own Cherokee ancestors. She trained with a Hawaiian kahuna (shaman), Reiki Master Hawayo Takata, the Aborigines in the Australian bush, and the Zulus in Bhophutaswana. She was also adopted into a New Zealand Maori tribe. In addition, Denise lived in a Zen Buddist monastery for over two years.

Denise is an international lecturer, healer and practitioner of Interior Re-Alignment, and she holds regular seminars on six continents. She is the author of PAST LIVES, PRESENT DREAMS and POCKETFUL OF DREAMS (Piatkus UK) and appears extensively on television and radio programs throughout the world.